# PECONIC BAY

# PECONIC BAY

Four Centuries of History on Long
Island's North and South Forks

Marilyn E. Weigold

Foreword by John Cronin

*Syracuse University Press*

Copyright © 2015 by Syracuse University Press
Syracuse, New York 13244-5290

*All Rights Reserved*

First Paperback Edition 2019

19  20  21  22  23  24      6  5  4  3  2  1

∞ The paper used in this publication meets the minimum requirements
of the American National Standard for Information Sciences—Permanence
of Paper for Printed Library Materials, ANSI Z39.48-1992.

For a listing of books published and distributed by Syracuse University Press,
visit www.SyracuseUniversityPress.syr.edu.

ISBN: 978-0-8156-0942-1 (paperback)      978-0-8156-1045-8 (cloth)
978-0-8156-5309-7 (e-book)

Library of Congress has cataloged the hardcover as follows:
Weigold, Marilyn E.
   Peconic Bay : four centuries of history on Long Island's North and South Forks /
Marilyn E. Weigold ; foreword by John Cronin. — First edition.
      pages cm
   Includes bibliographical references and index.
   ISBN 978-0-8156-1045-8 (cloth : alkaline paper) — ISBN 978-0-8156-5309-7 (e-book)
1. Long Island (N.Y.) —History, Local.   2. North Fork (N.Y. : Peninsula) —History.
3. South Fork (N.Y. : Peninsula) —History.   4. Peconic Estuary Region (N.Y.) —History.
I. Title.
   F127.L8W44 2015
   974.7'21—dc23                                              2014049371

*Manufactured in the United States of America*

*For*
*Charlie*
*a lifelong conservationist*

Marilyn E. Weigold, Ph.D., is Professor of History, University Historian, and Assistant Chair of the Department of Economics, History, and Political Science at Pace University. She is the author of five books, including *The Long Island Sound: Its People, Places and Environment* (New York University Press, 2004) and articles for scholarly and popular publications, including the *New York Times*.

# Contents

List of Illustrations  ·  *ix*

Foreword, John Cronin  ·  *xi*

Preface  ·  *xiii*


1. At Home  ·  *1*

2. At Work  ·  *58*

3. At Play  ·  *116*

4. At War  ·  *159*

5. At Peace  ·  *204*


Notes  ·  *253*

Bibliographic Note  ·  *273*

Bibliography  ·  *283*

Index  ·  *293*

# Illustrations

1. Map of Suffolk County, Pub. 1858  ·  *xvii*

2. Cedar Island Lighthouse, Sag Harbor  ·  *51*

3. Long Beach Bar Light (Bug Light), Orient  ·  *52*

4. Bug Light rebuilt  ·  *53*

5. Eagle's Nest Farm, Orient  ·  *65*

6. Beebe and Latham, Orient, 1890  ·  *67*

7. Fahy's Watch Case Manufactory, Sag Harbor  ·  *86*

8. Bay House postcard, Orient  ·  *139*

9. Mt. Pleasant House, Orient  ·  *140*

10. Montauk Steamboat at Long Wharf, Sag Harbor, L.I.  ·  *181*

11. West Main Street, Riverhead, 1936  ·  *239*

# Foreword

I remember the day I hauled my first net, though I better recall day's end. My back hurt. My hands were cut. I smelled like fish. I felt suffocated by my foul weather gear. I was queasy from the unfamiliar roiling and rolling of a windy tide . . . and I wanted more.

I had grown up a city boy more fascinated by baseball and cars than the estuary next door. But for the first time I felt part of something larger than myself. Water can do that.

In 1981, I quit my job as an environmental legislative assistant in Albany and moved into the back of a pickup truck. "You sure about this? There are easier ways to go broke than fishing," said a surprised Bob Gabrielson when I reported for work at his commercial shad and crab fishing operation on Burd Street dock in Nyack, New York. For the next three seasons I worked the lower Hudson River estuary, an arm of the Atlantic Ocean and cousin to the Peconic Bay estuary. I would later go on to serve as Hudson Riverkeeper for seventeen years, a position that spawned the Peconic Baykeeper.

There is no simile that applies to life on the water. It is not *like* anything. To be understood, it is a life that must be lived or a story that must be told. With these pages in hand you are the beneficiary of Marilyn Weigold as Peconic Bay historian and storyteller.

During my fishing days, I had the good luck to meet Arnold Leo of the East Hampton Town Baymen's Association, who first introduced me to the unique culture of Long Island's East End and Peconic Bay, and the connection we shared through the kinship between lives and waters. In addition to an ecological and cultural bond, the Hudson and Peconic were connected by the twin crises of PCB contamination and a crashing striped bass population, issues in which Arnold figured prominently and that are well told by Marilyn in chapter 2. Defining environmental controversies of their time, they remind us that the age-old struggle between power and rights is not limited to world affairs. It also lives in the legacy of the world we create around us.

Peconic Bay has a rich sense of place built over the course of centuries. There is surprising depth to its history and Marilyn's telling of it—but so little space in this introduction. So, imagine a place where farmers and fishermen, sailing vessels and submarines, Native Americans and the wealthy elite are all jostling for their rightful place in history; where the dictum of a long-dead English colonial governor could trump contemporary state and federal statutes; and where a people have struggled, and continue to struggle, over the quality of their community, their estuarine connection to the planet, and their place in world affairs. Then you will have a small taste of what Marilyn has in store in the pages ahead.

Through the lens of Peconic Bay history she reveals the role of one locale in the destiny of our nation while also performing the historian's duty to link that history to the present day. She sees an America imprinted by its past and challenged by its future, and a people still wondering "whether humans can live in peace and harmony with the natural environment and . . . with our fellow human beings on a global level."

America is a great story and its waters are on every page, to paraphrase the inestimable Charles Kuralt. But great stories call for great storytellers. We are fortunate for Marilyn Weigold's voice and her reminder that even on our own home waters we are each part of something larger than ourselves.

John Cronin

Director and CEO, Beacon Institute for Rivers & Estuaries

Managing Editor, EarthDesk.org

Senior Fellow for Environmental Affairs, Pace University and

Clarkson University

# Preface

The idea for a book about the Peconic Bay region of Eastern Long Island originated a decade before a significant part of the area—the North Fork, then a sleepy agrarian area with an emerging wine industry—was "discovered." In time, largely because of the expansion of the acreage devoted to the cultivation of wine grapes, the awards won by selected vintages, and increased press coverage of the burgeoning wine industry, the North Fork became well known. Gone were the days when few people living only a hundred miles to the west in the great metropolis of New York City had heard of the North Fork. At the very time the north side of Peconic Bay, the beautiful waterway separating the North Fork from its glitzy cousin, the South Fork, home to the various communities comprising the Hamptons, was becoming better known, the bay was being recognized for its environmental and economic significance. Long overshadowed to a certain extent by the mighty Atlantic Ocean bordering the south shore of the South Fork and the Long Island Sound bordering the north shore of the North Fork, Peconic Bay was designated a national estuary in 1992. A year later it was recognized as an Estuary of National Significance. The story of the waterway and contiguous land masses on both forks of Long Island's East End, however, began centuries earlier and that is the tale that is recounted in this work, which utilizes a combined topical and chronological approach to such aspects of the region's development as lifestyles, from the seventeenth century to the present; economic activities, both on land and sea; tourism; conflicts from the Revolutionary War to the War on Terrorism; and the struggle to find solutions to the challenges facing the area in the twenty-first century. (See fig. 1.)

Uncovering the material needed to recount the history of the Twin Forks and the islands in the Peconic Bay Estuary entailed research at numerous archival repositories on the North and South Forks and Shelter Island. The bibliographic note included in this volume provides information about the collections of libraries and historical societies. At these repositories this author had the good fortune to encounter knowledgeable and extremely helpful archivists and librarians. At the inception of the project, considerable time was spent in the Long Island Collection of the East Hampton Library, where longtime librarian Dorothy King was most generous in sharing her knowledge of the collections and East End history. Her successor, Diana Dayton, was also very helpful. In recent years Gina Piastuck, department head of the Long Island Collection, has provided invaluable assistance in rounding out the research, reexamining certain materials, particularly the East Hampton Baymen's Association Collection, and providing overall guidance. Elsewhere the following individuals not only have made their collections available to this researcher but also have patiently answered questions and provided exemplary guidance: Julie Greene of the Bridgehampton Historical Society and Hampton Library, Bridgehampton; Judith Wolfe of the Amagansett Free Library and the late Carlton Kelsey, who assisted the author at the Amagansett Free Library during the early phase of this project; Robin Strong of the Montauk Library Archives; Beth Gates of the Rogers Memorial Library in Southampton; Mary Cummings of the Southampton Historical Society; Dorothy Zaykowsi of the Sag Harbor Historical Society; Jessica Frankel formerly of the John Jermain Library, Sag Harbor, and subsequently of the Southold Free Library; Phyllis Wallace of the Shelter Island Historical Society; Ann Arnold of the Floyd Memorial Library, Greenport; Daniel McCarthy of the Southold Historical Society and Whitaker Collection, Southold Free Library; Antonia Booth, Southold Town Historian; Ellen Barcel of the Southold Indian Museum; Mariella Ostroski of the Cutchogue-New Suffolk Library; Jeffrey Walden of the Mattituck-Laurel Library; Herb Strobel of the Hallockville Museum Farm; and Edward H. L. Smith III and Wendy Annibell of the Suffolk County Historical Society. Without the help of these knowledgeable and generous professionals, this book could not have been completed.

In addition to all of the outstanding East End archivists and librarians who guided and assisted the author in obtaining relevant primary and secondary sources, there are several other individuals who deserve thanks: Dr. Natalie Naylor, professor emeritus, Hofstra University, and president of the Long Island Studies Council, and Dr. Gaynell Stone, museum director, Suffolk County Archaeological Association, both of whom read the manuscript and offered helpful suggestions for enhancing it; and Steve Feyl, Daniel Sabol, and Madeline Philbert of the Edward and Doris Mortola Library, Pace University, Pleasantville, New York, whose assistance in obtaining digitized material was invaluable.

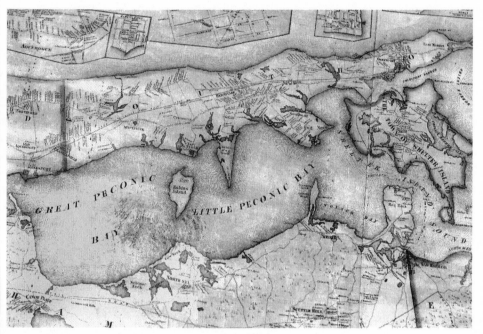

1. Map of Suffolk County, L.I., N.Y.: Peconic Bay area, John Douglass, Pub. 1858. Courtesy of Suffolk County Historical Society, Riverhead, N.Y.

# PECONIC BAY

# 1

# At Home

## A Little Place in the Country

Gazing at the sparkling waters of Peconic Bay, a 120,000-acre estuary separating the North and South Forks of Long Island's East End, one could have scarcely imagined, at the dawn of the new millennium, what was in store for this strikingly beautiful area, which the Nature Conservancy called "one of the last great places."[1] Terrorist bombings toppling iconic skyscrapers a hundred miles to the west and fallout from a global financial meltdown would pose immense challenges for this quasi-remote region during the first decade of the new century. In the aftermath of the 2001 attacks on the World Trade Center, some New Yorkers retreated to Long Island's East End, where they found comfort in the illusion of safety despite the presence of potential terrorist targets: the U.S. government's Animal Disease Laboratory on Plum Island, a short distance offshore, and the Millstone nuclear power plant in nearby coastal Connecticut. As the first decade of the new millennium neared its end, the federal government decided to relocate the laboratory to the Midwest. Almost immediately environmentalists were lobbying for public access to this prime piece of real estate while developers envisioned a residential enclave with homes rivaling those in the Hamptons. Would-be developers were thinking beyond the Great Recession that had wreaked havoc with the global economy during the last three years of the decade. With visions of dollar signs dancing in their heads, they longed for a return to the good old prerecession days of skyrocketing real estate prices.

For practically every year from 2002 through 2006, the median price of a single-family residence in each of the five East End towns increased by over 10 percent annually. Increases between 23 and 29 percent were the norm. Before the bottom fell out of the real estate market, the tiniest cottage was a hot property, especially if it was located on the water, because so many people were eager to own a piece of paradise on either side of the waterway that both separates and unites the two regions of the East End. As buyers scooped up homes, whether to occupy year-round or seasonally, there seemed to be no end in sight as far as prices were concerned. Then, suddenly, the real estate bubble burst and prices began plummeting. Even magnificent homes on the south side of Peconic Bay were sold for considerably less than what they would have fetched a few years earlier. Their owners, some of whom had been Wall Street wizards prior to the 2008 financial meltdown, saw their net worth decline, making them feel poorer even if they still had multiple millions left. What a difference a few years can make! Not long before, money had been plentiful and financing, including jumbo mortgages, flowed like the bay area's famous wine.

Prerecession, on the North Fork, where the majority of vineyards are located, grapes weren't the only thing keeping the open space open. Golf courses were serving the same purpose. On a beautiful August day in 2004, the recently completed Laurel Links Golf Club hosted an open house for prospective members. The club is the focal point of an exclusive residential community located a stone's throw from the hamlet of Mattituck. That summer, with New York City bracing for the Republican National Convention, the fear of another terrorist strike, whether related or unrelated to the convention, was palpable and many people decided to stay close to home. If home happened to be a McMansion at Laurel Links, staying put was not exactly a hardship. Quite aside from the fact that the homes were spacious and comfortable, all of life's necessities were conveniently nearby. Right outside the entrance to the private golf course community is the North Fork's only car wash, while just down the road is a shopping center with a multiplex theater and a large supermarket. If

Laurel Links residents were not in the mood for cooking or barbecu-
ing during the summer of 2004, they could head over to the area's
only McDonald's, which is practically within walking distance.

The lucky folks who had moved into the upscale abodes at Laurel
Links worked up an appetite playing golf on their private eighteen-
hole course or swimming at nearby beaches on Peconic Bay. The
Olympic-sized swimming pool at Laurel Links had been completed
but not yet filled by the day of the open house, when developer David
Saland welcomed visitors inquiring about the few remaining golf and
house memberships. These memberships included use of the pool,
tennis courts, and dining rooms in the resplendent clubhouse near-
ing completion. More South Fork than North Fork, the new building
was reminiscent of the Shinnecock Hills Golf Club, which had hosted
the U.S. Open just a few months earlier. Shinnecock Hills is not that
far distant from Laurel Links, and both clubs are near Peconic Bay,
a waterway that formed the scenic backdrop of the U.S. Open's RV
colony, populated by well-to-do professional golfers who journey from
one tournament to another in luxurious motor homes. Accompanied
by their families, they spent a week "roughing it" on the south shore
of Peconic Bay.

Meanwhile, on the north shore of the estuary, restoration work
was proceeding on a log cabin mansion that had figured prominently
in local news stories in the summer of 1998. Back then it was rumored
that actress Whoopi Goldberg was about to buy the place. According
to local gossip, Whoopi wanted to avoid the South Fork, which, in
the 1990s, had become such a mecca for celebrities that at least one of
the fabled Hamptons, East Hampton, was dubbed "Hollywood East."
Rather than seeking a Hamptons dream house overlooking the mighty
Atlantic, Whoopi was said to be searching for a place on Peconic Bay.
Forsaking the ocean for the bay is, well, downright unusual, especially
when money is no object, but even more amazing is that Whoopi was
looking on the *other* side of the bay. In the end Whoopi decided to
pass up the log house, which, when the light is just right, looks like a
gigantic topaz flanked by the sapphire waters of the bay, on one side,
and an emerald green lawn on the other, but her periodic visits to the

North Fork that summer focused attention on a place that hardly anyone had heard of until the end of the twentieth century.

Even today, if one gives a Southold, New York, address when ordering something from a catalogue, it is not unusual to be peppered with questions such as "Where is that, upstate New York?" or "How do you spell it? Is it two words?" or "Oh, it's one word but with two H's, right?" In all fairness, one has to admit that North Fork natives refer to everything west of Riverhead as "upisland" and anyplace north of the Bronx on the mainland as "upstate." Yet by the early twenty-first century, many Hamptons types were flocking to the North Fork and going native by embracing the region's low-key lifestyle. Not since the Revolutionary War, when the "refugees of 1776," as historian Frederic G. Mather called them, fled north, had so many South Fork people pulled up stakes and headed for greener pastures. Of course in 1776 the refugees' destination was Connecticut, across Long Island Sound from British-controlled Long Island, but two-and-a-quarter centuries later, well-heeled refugees moved no farther than the north side of Peconic Bay. Interestingly, at the very time ex-Hamptonites were migrating across the bay, an ad appeared for a unique residential compound on the South Fork side of the bay. Set safely back from the water, both the main house and the guest house/office overlooked a wide expanse of Peconic Bay and charming Squires Pond. Some years before, the homeowner, who had redesigned and rebuilt the structures on the property, conducted an archaeological dig in his backyard that turned up items left behind by Native Peoples who had once frequented this area.

## The Shinnecock

The Indians who dwelled in this part of the East End were the Shinnecock, whose descendants still reside in the general vicinity on a reservation in nearby Southampton. On Labor Day weekend each year the Shinnecock hold an annual pow-wow that attracts tens of thousands of people. Begun in the mid-1940s, this festive three-day gathering is a reaffirmation of Indian culture and a source of funding for various tribal projects. As welcoming as the Shinnecock are on Labor Day weekend and on days when their museum, which was established in 2001, is open to the public, the rest of the time they tend to keep to themselves. Past interaction with the outside world has made them wary because those encounters resulted in the forfeiture of valuable land, including all of the property between Southampton village and Eastport, including the area where the Shinnecock Canal, linking Peconic Bay and Shinnecock Bay, is located.

Built in 1892, the canal was originally envisioned as a segment of an intracoastal waterway along the South Shore of Long Island linking New York Harbor with Peconic Bay. As interesting as this may be, what is really important, however, is that in 1703 the Shinnecock obtained a thousand-year lease for valuable property in the surrounding area. A century and a half later, when the Long Island Rail Road needed some of this land for a new South Fork line, the Indians were induced to exchange this property, exceeding 3,000 acres, for 600 acres made up of two noncontiguous parcels. Some members of the tribe objected to the deal, but to no avail because the New York State legislature authorized it. An appeal to the federal government was futile because Indians in the Eastern United States were not covered by a 1790 act giving Congress the final say on Indian land transfers.

Dr. John A. Strong is the author of two books, *The Algonquian Peoples of Long Island from Earliest Times to 1700* and *"We Are Still Here!" The Algonquian Peoples of Long Island Today*, which provide a comprehensive overview of the history of East End Native Peoples. Strong has questioned the authenticity of signatures on the document affirming the Indians' consent to the land deal. If the Shinnecock were able to mount a successful legal case to recover this land, they would end up owning a swath of Southampton that includes the former campus of Southampton College and the world-famous Shinnecock Hills Golf Club. In an effort to stake their claim to the prestigious golf course, young Shinnecock activists risked arrest by staging sit-ins on the eighteenth hole. They also threw themselves in front of bulldozers attempting to enter the site of a thirty-eight-lot subdivision on St. Andrew's Road. Claiming that the property had cultural significance, as evidenced by archaeological artifacts unearthed there, the Indians sued the developer, the Southampton Town Board, and the Town Planning Board. In February 2000 a state supreme court justice issued a stop-work order, but two months later a state supreme court judge dismissed the Shinnecock lawsuit. In 2006 a federal judge dismissed a Shinnecock suit that sought compensatory damages for 3,600 acres they claimed had been taken from them illegally in the nineteenth century.

In 1997 it was a different story. Back then the Shinnecock scored a minor victory when a Suffolk County judge ruled that most of the half-acre lot on which a new home was to be erected was not *contiguous* with the reservation, as the purchaser claimed, but rather *part* of the Shinnecock property. Four decades earlier, in the 1950s, the Shinnecock successfully battled the Cove Realty Company, which was in the process of erecting homes on the border of the reservation. The Shinnecock enlisted the aid of the Suffolk County district attorney, thanks to a provision in New York State Indian law requiring a district attorney to remove trespassers from reservations. They then proceeded to convince a Suffolk County court that the land in question was actually part of the reservation.

## The Quest for Federal Recognition

Persuading the federal government to grant official recognition of their tribal status proved considerably more difficult for the Shinnecock, however. They began this process in the 1970s and two decades later, when the goal seemed within reach, there was considerable speculation about whether they would open a gambling casino. Southamptonites immediately envisioned traffic jams even more monumental than the usual Memorial Day to Labor Day tie-ups as the masses invaded their beautiful area to try their luck at the casino. In reality they had little to worry about because securing federal recognition was an agonizingly slow process. Without it, Shinnecock property was not about to become "Foxwoods South" (referring to the Connecticut casino), especially in light of a 2003 judicial ruling barring the tribe from any additional land clearing in preparation for building a casino on a beautiful stretch of waterfront it owns at Westwoods on Peconic Bay in the northern part of Hampton Bays. Citing potential water pollution and "irreparable harm to nearby areas because of incredible traffic congestion," the judge granted an injunction prohibiting any development for a minimum period of eighteen months.[2] A permanent injunction was voided on appeal in 2012 but by then the Shinnecock, who three years earlier had finally received federal recognition, decided not to erect a casino on their reservation.

In the years between the original ruling on the Westwoods casino proposal and the securing of federal recognition, the Shinnecock had to temporarily abandon their dream of accumulating wealth through gambling and were compelled to rely instead on revenue generated by tax-free cigarette sales and tourist dollars spent at their museum and cultural center, which was erected with some funding from the Mashantucket Pequots of Foxwoods. The proceeds from these sources paled in comparison to the revenues gambling would generate. But for the next six years, as the Shinnecock awaited a ruling from the U.S. Bureau of Indian Affairs on their petition for federal recognition, they could only dream of the millions gambling would pour into the tribe's coffers. The long-sought goal was finally attained in December 2009 when the tribe was notified that the United States would acknowledge the Shinnecock Indian Nation as a federally recognized tribe. This determination was based upon the Shinnecock having met specific requirements, namely continuous identification "as an American Indian entity" going back to the turn of the twentieth century; "being a distinct community since historical times, maintaining political influence over its members"; possessing a document detailing its governance and membership requirements; and submitting "a list of current members who descend from an historical Indian tribe and are not members of another federally recognized tribe."[3]

The formal announcement by the Bureau of Indian Affairs was made in June 2010. For the Shinnecock the successful culmination of their thirty-year quest was bittersweet. According to Gordell Wright, a tribal trustee, it had been "a long time and . . . tribal members who started the process . . . have since died."[4] In 2010 the Shinnecock Nation had 1,292 members and the Bureau of Indian Affairs of the U.S. Department of the Interior acknowledged that 97 percent of them had descended "from the historical 1789 Shinnecock tribe as determined by their descent from the 1865 reservation residents listed in the New York State census."[5]

Almost before the ink had dried on the formal announcement of long-awaited Shinnecock recognition, one branch of the Montaukett Indians and the Connecticut Coalition for Gambling Jobs filed objections with the Bureau of Indian Affairs. The Montauketts asserted that they should have been included in the bureau's determination of the status of the Shinnecock, but their claim was dismissed because they failed to prove that they would be harmed by the stand-alone recognition of the Shinnecock. The Connecticut claim was also dismissed because the coalition did not enumerate who would be impacted by job losses in the state's gambling industry if casinos opened on Long Island. With the dismissal of these challenges, the Shinnecock became eligible for health, education, and residential finance grants available to federally recognized tribes. According to Randy King, the chairman of the Shinnecock Indian Nation, this "opens a bright future that will include new opportunities."[6] The biggest opportunity of all is a gambling casino. But before the Shinnecock can move ahead with plans for a mega gaming resort, they must work out the details of a compact with New York State. Should an off-reservation site, perhaps in Calverton, Brookhaven, Nassau, or Queens, be chosen for their new enterprise, the federal government will have to take the property in trust for the tribe. In the meantime, the Shinnecock were permitted to open a modest gambling installation featuring video lottery terminals on their land in Southampton. Something more grandiose will most likely have to wait.

Declining revenues at Foxwoods and other Indian casinos due to the economic downturn of 2008 and subsequent years did not bode well for the establishment of new casinos. Nevertheless, with access to federal money for medical and educational grants, the Shinnecock hoped to weather the lingering downturn better than some of their wealthy neighbors in the Town of Southampton. Two months into the economic crisis, the *East Hampton Star* declared, "The South Fork's Feeling the Pain."[7] By Thanksgiving 2008 the paper ran a front-page story bearing the headline "Foreclosures on South Fork Are Rising."[8] Even if they were not forced to sell, for some wealthy Hamptonites the global financial meltdown of 2008 symbolized a world turned upside-down. The world of the Shinnecock, on the other hand, was finally turned right-side-up with federal recognition.

One can only wonder what the ancestors of the present-day Shinnecock would think of this reversal of fortunes. If only Mary Rebecca Kellis, better known as "Aunt Becky," could see her people now! In the 1930s when this elderly woman, whose father was a Shinnecock and mother a Montaukett, was living in a cottage on the Shinnecock reservation, a newspaper reporter trekked from New York City to Southampton to interview her. He began his lengthy story by painting a verbal portrait of early evening when "cocktail glasses tinkle in many a palatial villa in Southampton" as exquisitely dressed people chatted and laughed; yet, the Shinnecock, who had previously owned the land occupied by the great villas, lived "in bare, paintless, kerosene lamp–lighted shacks."[9]

The reporter went on to say that the Shinnecock, who had once manufactured large quantities of shell currency or wampum, now worked "for the great wampum-makers of today" who spent their summers on the South Fork.[10] In her younger years Aunt Becky, who lived to the ripe old age of 102, dying in 1936, had worked for big "wampum-makers," the Roosevelt family, when future president Theodore Roosevelt was but a young, asthmatic child. Becky recounted details of Theodore's first wedding, to Alice Lee, which she witnessed, but the reporter seemed more intrigued by her tales about life on the Shinnecock reservation in the mid-1800s when Becky herself was a child. At that time, some of her relatives dwelled in sea grass wigwams. Becky recollected that the sea grass was woven using long wooden needles and that a relative's two-room wigwam was "quite nice."[11]

## The Montauketts

Nice or not, the dwellings of the Native Peoples were generally sec-
ond-rate in comparison with the abodes of non-Indian residents of the
East End. That was surely the case in Freetown, an area of East Hampton where freed slaves and Montauketts resided. Like the Shinnecock,
the Montauketts had intermarried with African Americans despite a
ruling by the Town of East Hampton that Montaukett women were
debarred from Montauk if they married a man of African ancestry. The
Montauketts were also prohibited from marrying members of other
tribes. As with the Shinnecock, the Montauketts were persuaded to
part with their land, starting in 1648 when they sold 30,000 acres
between Napeague and Southampton to the English. Following the
death of Chief Wyandanch (ca. 1660), Montauk Point itself was sold
to the English by the deceased sachem's young successor, Wiancam-
bone. Although the latter's guardian claimed that this had taken place
without his consent, it was a done deal and the only concession the
Montauketts obtained was the right to reside on the property. The
Indians' residency rights were reaffirmed by the Town of East Hampton in the early eighteenth century, but in the late 1700s there was a
migration of Montauketts and Shinnecock to upstate Brothertown, a
haven for Indians who had embraced Christianity.

For Montauketts remaining on the East End, the next hundred
years was a time of sporadic encounters with non-Native East Hamptonites who encroached upon their land, helping themselves to wood
and cattle. Since the 1600s Montauk had been the summer pasture
for settlers' cattle. The cattle drives sometimes caused as much congestion as twenty-first-century summer traffic on Montauk Highway;
at the very least, they probably elicited the kind of stares that greet
the bison herd that real estate broker Ed Tuccio keeps on a Riverhead
farm. In the olden days, once the animals had crossed the Napeague
strip and had scrambled onto Montauk itself, they found themselves
in a veritable summer camp. For the Indians it was a different story.

An eighteenth-century visitor to "the Indian Village of Montauk"
observed that it had "about 100 souls" and that the cornfields were

"overgrown with weeds."[12] Describing the houses, which "made a curious appearance," he said: "They were principally of a conical form, and made of flags and rushes, without windows, except an opening on the peek or top, to let out the smoke and admit light."[13] A century later the Montauketts were dwelling in unpainted cabins. Even David Pharaoh, who was known as the king of the Montauketts, lived in a cottage, both unadorned and unpretentious, at Ford Pond. This well-regarded man, who was described by a non-Native contemporary as "impressive, standing full six feet in height and very erect," had features that "were of Roman mode especially as to profile. . . . In his movements he was agile, . . . and as he moved along the thoroughfares [*sic*] with head tipped slightly back and eyes cast straight forward, he was surely the appearance of a king."[14]

Upon his death, from tuberculosis, in 1878, David Pharaoh was succeeded by Stephen Talkhouse Pharaoh, a marathon hiker who had once won a walking contest between Boston and Chicago. The year before he died, Stephen Talkhouse Pharaoh, age fifty-nine, walked from Brooklyn to Montauk in a twenty-four-hour period! At the time of his death, in 1879, only a year after succeeding David Pharaoh, the widowed Stephen Talkhouse was engaged to a fortysomething half-Indian from Moriches. She was late for the funeral at the African American church in Freetown and missed the sermon delivered by the Reverend John Stokes, pastor of East Hampton's First Presbyterian Church. After praising the deceased, Stokes held out the hope of a better life in which Montauketts would be the equals of those who had oppressed them in this life. Although late for the service, the almost bride accompanied the body on the long ride through the mosquito-infested Napeague strip to Montauk, where her fiancé was laid to rest in Indian Field on the east side of Lake Montauk.

Among the people who gathered at the gravesite was William Fowler, patriarch of a Montaukett family whose members had vied with the Pharaohs for leadership of the tribe. Debilitated by alcohol and opium, Fowler paid scant attention to his home, an "old two-storied, shingle-patched shanty . . . divided into a living room and wash house."[15] No matter how humble, this home sweet home had artwork, actually "gaudily colored prints" on a "soot-stained wall."[16] In contrast with Fowler's shabby dwelling, the home of another Montaukett present at the interment, former Queen Maria, widow of David Pharaoh, would have made East Hamptonite Martha Stewart proud. According to a visitor: "Poor as she is, she manages to keep a neat rag carpet on the floor of her cabin, an Argand lamp and porcelain shade on the table, while her children are better fed and clothed than any of the other Montauks."[17] Maria's four children accompanied her to Indian Field to bid farewell to Stephen Talkhouse, who would long be remembered for his multiple careers as a farmer, whaleman, hunting and fishing guide, champion walker, and Civil War veteran.

No matter how fast a Montaukett walked, however, he couldn't outdistance non-Natives when it came to the law. Once the courts ruled, that was it, as the Montauketts learned in the early twentieth century. The legal battle leading to a resounding judicial defeat for the Montauketts in 1909 went back to 1885 when Arthur Benson, a Brooklyn developer, eager to transform Montauk into a resort, with the help of the Long Island Rail Road (LIRR), persuaded the Montauketts still residing there to part with their land rights in return for an annual stipend and, supposedly, the privilege of returning to the area each spring. The stipends were never forthcoming and when the Indians, who had been relocated to Freetown, attempted to summer in Montauk, they discovered that their dwellings had been destroyed and they were regarded as trespassers. Viewing this as truly the last straw, especially since tribal, rather than individual, consent to the transfers had not been obtained, Montauketts, including those who had dispersed to places far removed from the East End, sued Benson and the LIRR. Led by Wyandank Pharaoh, son of David Pharaoh, the Indians waged an unrelenting legal battle despite the many obstacles placed in their path. At one point they even had to secure the New York State legislature's approval of their right to sue. When all was said and done, Judge Abel Blackmar ruled in 1909 that the Montauketts didn't have a case because the tribe did not exist! The judge told a packed courtroom in Riverhead that the tribe had "disintegrated"; in his opinion the Montauketts had "no internal government, and they live a shiftless life of hunting, fishing and cultivating the ground and often leaving Montauk for long periods to work in some menial capacity for whites."[18] The Montauketts appealed and the legal wrangling continued until 1918, but the judge's ruling stood for more than a century until the New York State legislature passed the 2013 Montaukett Restoration Act reversing Judge Blackmar's ruling. Governor Andrew Cuomo vetoed the legislation because federal criteria for determining tribal recognition precluded an objective evaluation by the state. The act could have also opened the door to legal challenges and delays in winning recognition, a process already complicated because a Montaukett splinter group had filed a separate claim for recognition in 1998, three years after the Montaukett Indian Nation submitted its petition. The latter group was not dissatisfied with the governor's veto, not only because the state's chief executive reiterated his support for recognition but also because the New York secretary of state was expected to intensify efforts aimed at obtaining state recognition of the Montauketts, a necessary prerequisite for federal recognition.

With the hindsight of over a century, it is glaringly evident that racism was a factor in Judge Blackmar's decision. The intermarriage of Montauketts and African Americans was interpreted as a dilution of the Native Peoples or, as Dr. John A. Strong has noted: "The ruling reflected an erroneous assumption about the connection between culture and race."[19] To the Montauketts themselves, skin color was neither the sole nor the primary determinant of identity and, as evidenced by the *Annual Report of the Montauk Tribe of Indians for the Year 1916*, they did indeed possess not only a distinctive culture but also an internal government. Describing the tribe's annual meeting, held in Sag Harbor in August 1916, the report stated:

> The evening session was called to order . . . by Wyandanch Pharaoh, Chief of the Tribe. All members of the Council were present. At this meeting there were over a hundred present. According to custom, the Chief of the Council addressed the people in regard to matters that will bring about a greater interest in Tribal matters and the need of every one to uphold his or her share of Tribal affairs.[20]

The push for tribal unity continued through the 1920s, but by the end of that decade council meetings were phased out. In that same decade, when developer Carl Fisher was about to begin building his Montauk Manor hotel, traces of the Montauketts' great fort, strategically located on the promontory where the new resort would rise, were found. Fisher agreed to relocate the approach road to the hotel to avoid disturbing the remains of the historic fort. But during World War II, when the military utilized the hotel, the army constructed a medical dispensary atop the Indian fort. In the 1970s, as preparations were being made to restore Montauk Manor, the dispensary was razed and the boulders of the old fort reappeared. The fort probably had palisaded walls constructed of wood when it was built, most likely in the mid-1600s, but given the value of wood, the walls may have been taken down and carted off when the fort was abandoned. In view of its location high atop Fort Hill, this spot was a likely place of refuge for the Montauketts whenever they anticipated an attack.

When the fort was erected, the principal threat to the Montauketts and other East End Native Peoples were New England Indians. Soon thereafter the Montauketts encountered a new enemy, Europeans eager to grab their property. Although initially allied with these newcomers whom they envisioned as protectors from the fierce mainland Indians, from the late nineteenth century onward descendants of the Montauketts viewed people of European ancestry as usurpers who had stolen their land. In the 1980s Montaukett descendants filed a claim to 10,000 acres of prime Montauk real estate. By doing so they challenged the 1885 decision by the Suffolk County legislature to allow Montauk to be auctioned, with the proceeds going to the proprietors of East Hampton, who had been utilizing Montauk as a common pasture going back to colonial times. With fewer than a hundred Montauketts remaining at that time and none of them of "pure" Indian stock, the legislature concluded that the Montauketts were extinct. Despite this ruling and the aforementioned decision of a Suffolk County judge in 1909, the Montauketts remained a viable Indian nation and, as they awaited federal recognition, they enjoyed a victory of another sort when East Hampton decided to acquire the Montaukett burial ground at Fort Hill for a cemetery.

## The Corchaugs

East Hampton was not the only municipality to preserve an ancient Indian site. In 1997 the Town of Southold purchased the site of Fort Corchaug. Although the Corchaugs, who had once dominated the North Fork, had departed by the late eighteenth century, their impressive fort dating from the 1600s had survived because of its isolated location on Downs Creek. For years the property had been eyed for development but the nonprofit Peconic Land Trust, which seeks to preserve open space on both sides of the bay, was able to put together a deal whereby the Town of Southold, New York State, Suffolk County, two Southold civic organizations, and a private donor chipped in to purchase the site. Like Fort Hill, Montauk, Fort Corchaug was a place of refuge where Indians took up residence when they perceived danger, but it was also the center of a very active wampum-making industry. The raw materials for fashioning the strings of shell currency known as wampum were close at hand, and clay pipes and brass artifacts unearthed by archaeologists indicate that there was direct or indirect contact with Europeans. William Wallace Tooker, a pharmacist, whose lifelong avocation was the study of Indians, traveled across the bay from his home in Sag Harbor in 1891 to inspect Fort Corchaug. Impressed by its protected location, he found an abundance of arrowheads, pieces of pottery, and shells and concluded that the field adjacent to Downs Creek, where the fort was located, had once been occupied by wigwams.

One can almost imagine the Corchaugs sauntering out of their dwellings to dip into the bay for a bountiful harvest of finfish and shellfish or jumping into their sturdy canoes to visit and perhaps conduct business with other East End Indians. The Corchaugs stayed in touch with the Manhansets on Shelter Island, the Montauketts, and the Shinnecock on the South Fork by using smoke signals. The puffy messages wafting aloft from Indian forts were, in a sense, akin to modern-day phone conversations transmitted via cellular towers. Whether these telecommunications skyscrapers dotting the East End landscape will be viewed with the same reverence as the remains of Indian forts centuries from now is unknown, but they are the latest manifestation of humankind's desire to stay in touch. So, too, is travel.

The bay was a nautical highway for the Native Peoples and served the same purpose for European settlers in the colonial period. With the exception of the Shelter Island ferries and the short-lived Greenport–Sag Harbor service of recent years, the bay is more of a playground than a nautical highway and people are still inexorably drawn to it. Just as the Native Peoples of the East End moved within sight of the water's edge in the summer, twenty-first-century urbanites and suburbanites migrate to second homes in communities bordering the bay. The allure of water is almost magical. Perhaps because we have come from the sea, we are constantly being drawn back to it, both in the here and now and in the hereafter. The purchase of local cemetery plots by relative newcomers to both forks is testimony to their desire to spend eternity in this very special place. The Native Peoples had similar ideas. An Indian gravesite on a hill within sight of Peconic Bay in Jamesport was excavated in the early twentieth century, and gravesites and other archaeological finds were discovered at Orient in the first half of the twentieth century. The Indian Museum in Southold and the Oysterponds Historical Society in Orient are the repositories of fascinating Indian artifacts and are well worth a visit.

## Gardiner's Island: Family Feud

Another very special place lying within the Peconic Bay estuary system is also worthy of exploration, but access is strictly by invitation, and that's the way it has always been since Lion Gardiner first set foot on the pristine isle that bears his name. A military engineer who was sent to the New World in 1635 to erect a fort at Saybrook, where the Connecticut River empties into Long Island Sound, Gardiner made the acquaintance of Montaukett chief Wyandanch, who journeyed across the Sound in the aftermath of the successful siege of a Pequot Indian fort by English colonists and mainland Native American allies. Following the Pequot War, Wyandanch made Gardiner an offer he couldn't refuse: tribute, similar to what the Montauketts had been paying the Pequots, in return for good relations and trade. Gardiner imposed a condition, however. Wyandanch would be required to surrender the heads of Indians who had slain Englishmen. Wyandanch complied and produced five heads. According to historian Roger Wunderlich: "The price of peace on Long Island was harsh, but the pact between Gardiner and Wyandanch, and the lasting friendship that followed, relieved eastern Long Island of the English-Indian carnage that persisted for forty years in New England."[21] In 1639 Gardiner, his family, and a group of would-be farmers, who were also handy with a gun just in case the pact did not hold, moved from Connecticut to Gardiner's Island. It was long believed that Lion paid Wyandanch with a big black dog, a gun, rum, and a couple of blankets, but this payment may be as apocryphal as the tale about Gardiner rescuing Wyandanch's daughter.

The young Indian maiden was supposedly kidnapped on her wedding night in 1654 during a cross-Sound raid by Narragansett Indians from the mainland. The bridegroom was slain and the grief-stricken bride remained abducted until Lion Gardiner, who had learned the Narragansett language while residing in Connecticut, did some fast talking and secured her release. A grateful Wyandanch, who had already transferred a nice chunk of East Hampton to Gardiner, threw in land upisland. As with previous transfers, the approval of James Farrett, agent for the Earl of Stirling, who had been granted Long Island by the Crown, was required. This was a mere technicality, however, because by this time Wyandanch had been declared Grand Sachem of Long Island by the English and any land deals he entered into were viewed as formal and final. As Roger Wunderlich noted: "One way to obtain the land was by force: the Long Island way, perfected . . . by Gardiner was to 'purchase' deeds from a super-sachem and have them confirmed by colonial writ."[22] Archaeologist Gaynell Stone, an authority on the Montauketts, views the relationship between Gardiner and Wyandanch as "probably pragmatic, of political benefit for both of them. Wyandanch was a figurehead supported by the English to make it easier to consummate their continuing land purchases."[23] Yet the Grand Sachem "became more powerful because he was backed by the threat of English force. Perhaps he had no choice, caught as he was between two aggressive forces, the Narragansetts and the English."[24] Wyandanch's ties to the English may have cut short his life. Although he died during an epidemic that carried off many of his fellow Indians, Wyandanch may have been poisoned. At least that was Lion Gardiner's conclusion.

By the time Wyandanch went to the great beyond in 1659, Gardiner was living in East Hampton. Upon his death in 1663, Gardiner's Island passed to his widow, who then willed it to their son, David. Like other scions of wealthy South Fork families, David had gone through a pile of his father's money before Lion Gardiner died, which is why Lion left everything to his widow. When she died in 1665 David became proprietor of the Isle of Wight, the name Lion Gardiner had given his island because of its topographical resemblance to the place of the same name in the British Isles. He presumably preferred this appellation because the Indian name Manchonake, meaning "place of death," was a real downer, although historically correct in light of an epidemic that may have killed Indians there in the early contact period. A 1668 patent from New York royal governor Thomas Dongan recognized the Isle of Wight as the lordship and manor of Gardiner's Island. For the next three centuries successive generations of Gardiners seemed to have lived quite happily in their island paradise, pirate threats and occasional military incursions notwithstanding. Then in the 1920s Lion Gardiner, the twelfth lord of the manor, sold all 3,347 acres of the island to another Gardiner but took back a mortgage. A great-nephew of the new owner inherited the property during the Depression, but when payments on the original mortgage were not forthcoming the island was put on the market. One potential buyer thought this pristine place, which had remained virtually unchanged, right down to the white oak forest, ospreys, and wild turkeys, for three centuries, would be the ideal spot for a resort, complete with casino and racetrack.

Sarah Diodati Gardiner thought otherwise. A direct descendant of the first Lion Gardiner, Sarah purchased the island and left it in trust for her nephew, Robert David Lion Gardiner, and his sister, stipulating that upon their deaths it would go to their children. When Robert Gardiner's sister died, her daughter, Alexandra Gardiner Creel Goelet, inherited her mother's interest in the island and, together with her husband and children, began spending considerable time there. The Goelets poured a great deal of money into Gardiner's Island, but Robert Gardiner, suspicious that they were going to develop the island, refused to pay his share of the upkeep. A nasty legal battle ensued and the flamboyant Gardiner was ordered by a judge not to set foot on the island for three years. In December 2000 the childless eighty-nine-year-old Robert Gardiner, who repeatedly threatened to adopt solely for the purpose of preventing his niece from inheriting the entire island upon his death, petitioned the East Hampton Town Board to designate the island a historic district and to upzone it from five- to twenty-five-acre residential lots. Upon the death of Robert Gardiner, in the summer of 2004, the island passed to his niece, who offered the Town of East Hampton a twenty-year conservation easement on 95 percent of the island. In return, the town was asked to refrain from upzoning the island or obtaining it through condemnation. With development still a possibility in the future, however, one can imagine the flamboyant Gardiner spinning in his grave, which, incidentally, is not on his beloved island but in East Hampton.

## Serene Shelter Island

While Robert Gardiner and the Goelets were slugging it out over the future of their island, on another sizable island in the Peconic Bay estuary, Shelter Island, Mrs. Andrew Fiske, resident of Sylvester Manor, was tossing out the welcome mat for a small army of archaeologists whose mission was to quite literally unearth the manor's past. In the process, they would learn a great deal about Shelter Island, where the Manhanset Indians dwelled until the late eighteenth century. Their dwellings were modest in comparison with the grand yellow house built in 1733 by the grandson of Nathaniel Sylvester, one of four merchants from Barbados who purchased Shelter Island in 1651. In time Nathaniel's heirs were the sole proprietors of the island. But the Manhansets were permitted to stay and work just as members of an outlawed religious sect, the Society of Friends or Quakers, were offered a haven from persecution on Shelter Island.

Before a church was erected on Shelter Island, the Sylvesters supposedly journeyed across the bay to worship in Southold. According to a nineteenth-century descendant, who spun elaborately embroidered tales about her ancestors, Nathaniel's grandson, Brinley Sylvester, and his wife, Mary Burroughs Sylvester, traveled in style in a barge rowed by a quartet of slaves. Weather permitting, Mrs. Sylvester donned a silk velvet cloak. Taken aback by both the elaborate barge and fashionable clothing, the Reverend John Youngs is said to have made a derisive comment about how proud Mrs. Sylvester must have been of her costly possessions. The lady responded by saying that what she was really proud of was the linen she made herself. Had she been around back then, Martha Stewart, the late-twentieth- and early-twenty-first-century doyenne of taste and style, would have beamed. Martha would have also liked another of the Sylvesters' vessels, a gondola that was said to have been painted sky blue and outfitted with silk cushions. Given the growing popularity of the bay area, perhaps a charter service featuring elegant gondolas has possibilities. Martha Stewart might be persuaded to customize the seats, choose the paint for the exterior, and maybe she and singer/composer Billy Joel, who, when he isn't making music, has been known to build some great boats on Shelter Island, could team up to construct a fleet of gondolas. A fanciful idea? Perhaps, but then again so was the idea of planting wine grapes on a potato farm in Cutchogue in the 1970s, thereby laying the foundation for a major wine industry. In any event, if the new nautical livery service materializes, Shelter Islanders will have something really great to look at in the near offshore waters—but so, too, did the Sylvesters in the colonial period.

From time to time the Sylvesters witnessed huge sailing ships coming from Barbados. A kind of nautical umbilical cord linked the island in the Peconic Bay estuary with the island in the Caribbean. According to Dr. Stephen Mrozowski, professor of anthropology at the University of Massachusetts, and supervisor of the Sylvester Manor archaeological field teams that conducted digs on the manor for nearly a decade, the manor was a "provisioning plantation" that supplied food and other necessities to the Sylvesters' sugar plantations in Barbados.[25] Given the global marketability of sugar, it made economic sense to raise as much of the crop as possible, using slave labor, rather than use the valuable land on the Caribbean island for other purposes. The end result was that the Sylvesters became very wealthy, in part because of slavery.

In her masterful book *The Manor: Three Centuries of a Slave Plantation on Long Island*, Mac Griswold notes that Nathaniel Sylvester imported large numbers of slaves to Barbados and had slaves on Sylvester Manor. Slave labor contributed to the manor's bottom line, enabling the Sylvesters to accumulate "personal objects, like jewelry, clothing and coins," found in the course of the archaeological excavation.[26] Evidence of early agriculture, including the cultivation of rye, wheat, and barley, was also discovered. The archaeological teams, which included Katherine Howlett Hayes, author of the excellent scholarly work, *Slavery before Race: Europeans, Africans, and Indians at Long Island's Sylvester Manor Plantation, 1651–1884*, learned that sheep, cattle, and pigs were present on Sylvester Manor and that wooden barrel staves were produced and sent to Barbados, where they were made into containers for molasses. Upon being shipped to the mainland of North America, the molasses was used to make rum, which was sent to Africa, where it was exchanged for slaves. Thus Sylvester Manor was part of a global trading network in colonial times. Although seemingly isolated, the manor was like the easy-off, easy-on destinations hyped on billboards on major U.S. highways. According to Dr. Mrozowski: "One of the reasons the Sylvesters chose this location was because there was a convenient outlet to Long Island Sound via what is today called Gardiner's Creek. Large ocean-going vessels would have been brought up right to a dock or landing."[27]

As the dig continued, which Alice Fiske viewed as a memorial to her late husband, Andrew, additional evidence of the manor's thriving economy was forthcoming. Much was learned about the manor's inhabitants, including Indians, some of whom toiled as slaves and others as indentured servants in the bay area in colonial times. Following Alice Fiske's death in 2006, this historical and archaeological data would prove useful for interpreting the 243-acre property for visitors to the Sylvester Manor Educational Farm, Inc. This nonprofit organization was established by Eben Fiske Ostby, who inherited the property from his uncle Andrew Fiske. While Alice Fiske was still alive, the ongoing archaeological work, which supplied data and artifacts for future interpretation of the site, necessitated digging up the property square foot by square foot. Yet, Alice took it all in stride, quite unlike Nathaniel Sylvester, who fretted about his property being unintentionally dug up by stray horses that had wandered over to Shelter Island from Southampton in the colonial period. The horses were either champion swimmers or beneficiaries of an extremely low tide or both. To the owner of Sylvester Manor, how they got there was less important than getting rid of them. He put the good people of Southampton on notice that he would destroy any horses whose owners did not collect them. Unneighborly? You bet. But from time to time in the nearly four hundred years since Europeans first settled the Peconic Bay area there has been sniping, some of it ongoing. For example, the towns of Southampton and Southold have been battling for more than a century over which community was settled first.

## And the Winner Is: Southampton versus Southold

Although both Southampton and Southold were settled in 1640, there may have been Europeans living, producing turpentine, and possibly manufacturing bricks in the eastern part of Southold in the 1630s. Even before the Reverend John Youngs and his followers left New Haven in October 1640, relocating to Southold, where the group came ashore at Founders Landing on Peconic Bay, Richard Jackson, a carpenter, built a home in Arshamomoque near Peconic Bay earlier that year. The fact that Southold town records for the first decade of settlement are missing makes it difficult to prove, beyond a shadow of a doubt, what was happening on the north side of Peconic Bay as far back as 1640 or maybe a bit earlier. But who knows? Anything is possible. Documents or material cultural artifacts substantiating Southold's claim that it was settled before Southampton may turn up in the future.

Given the threefold definition of history as past human events, the record of those events, and the technique of making the record, one is always mindful of the fact that, while the events themselves cannot be altered, new data requiring reinterpretation of those events may surface. Moreover, for those who subscribe to a theory postulated by true believers in the Montauk Project, a purported top-secret twentieth-century experiment in mind control and time travel, the past is, well, simply not the past! It's still out there somewhere and can be quite literally revisited by penetrating the space-time continuum. Putting aside the notion of transiting the ages and altering outcomes, however, there is always the very real possibility that our interpretation of the past may change when new evidence surfaces. Thus, at some point, the Peconic Bay's version of which came first, Southampton or Southold, may be resolved. Interestingly, as both communities prepared to celebrate the 375th anniversary of their founding in 2015, they formulated plans for joint celebrations.

In the final analysis, whether the community on the south side of the bay or the one on the north is declared the undisputed "winner," a more important question is whether either Southampton or Southold can preserve some semblance of its historic past and rural ambience. At the beginning of the twenty-first century, Southold was doing better than Southampton in preserving the agrarian environment familiar to the early settlers. But only time will tell whether enough of the rural ambience will endure into the future to enable bay area residents and visitors of the twenty-second century to experience what the East End was like in yesteryear. Southampton's efforts to preserve open space and Southold's attempts to keep the wide open spaces open through the acquisition of development rights and the encouragement of wine grape cultivation are positive signs. Still, the rapid pace of development in Southampton in the final decades of the twentieth century was a reminder that, when the hour hand on the clock nears eleven, there's just so much that can be done.

The clock is also ticking in Southold. Although the witty, insightful columnist Liz Smith differentiated Southampton from Southold by saying that, in the former place, they call it "sushi" but in the latter it's simply "bait," in the summer of 2001 the Southold Seafood Market began selling special rice for sushi. By the middle of the decade fully prepared entrees and an intriguing array of wraps were tempting a customer base that had expanded to include guests at the adjoining resort motel, once a nondescript place frequented by fishermen that was transformed into a spiffy postmodern inn in time for the 2004 season. A few miles west of the motel and seafood market, in the heart of Southold, a gourmet bread store flourished for a few seasons. Mind you, this is the fork where, in the 1980s, Italian bread was not that easy to find and garlic bread and bagels were considered exotic edibles from somewhere up west. All of this had changed by the early twenty-first century as had other things; for example, the paint store next to the pharmacy on Main Road in Southold had morphed into a decorators' headquarters, and down the street an architectural and ornamental hardware store had opened its doors to well-heeled newcomers intent upon sprucing up their second homes. Neither of these establishments remained permanent features of the hamlet's business district. But across Main Road, Complement the Chef, with its high-end cookware, Simon Pearce lamps, and elegant table linens, endured. The very existence of these stores underscores the gentrification of the North Fork. Until the real estate bubble burst, it was like a tidal wave sweeping across Peconic Bay from the Hamptons to the North Fork. The recession that followed the global financial meltdown of 2008 notwithstanding, even if a Category 5 hurricane were to blow through, leveling a large swath of the built environment, much of what would be destroyed would be reconstructed because lots of people want to live in this East End paradise, in spite of the vagaries of Mother Nature, and this has been the case for four hundred years.

## Saints, Sinners, and Just Plain Folks

Long before the late twentieth century, when the Nature Conservancy characterized the East End as one of the last great places in North America, the area ringing the Peconic Bay estuary system was a virtual paradise for the first European settlers who reveled in the bounty they discovered here. It was not only the productive soil and extended growing season—far longer than that of New England, where many of them had resided before crossing over to Long Island—but the freedom the area offered. Fast-forward almost four hundred years and we discover that things haven't really changed that much. It may not be religious freedom that newcomers are seeking (although practically every theological and philosophical belief system is represented on the East End), but rather the freedom to be your own person in an environment that inspires creativity, or the freedom to do your own thing even if it means doing nothing at all.

Relaxation had become a fine art on both sides of the bay by the turn of the twenty-first century, but the vocabulary of the first settlers probably didn't include the word. They were here to work. It was the only way they could survive, right from the first moment a boat carrying a group of English people landed at Conscience Point in the North Sea area of Southampton in 1640. These folks had journeyed from Lynn, Massachusetts, to the North Shore, somewhere near Manhanset, but the Dutch, who controlled western Long Island, prevented them from settling there. By the time these would-be colonists traveled from the region that would one day become Long Island's Gold Coast, resplendent with great estates, to the place where mansions would eventually dot the dunes, they were a tad weary. This would explain why one of the female passengers supposedly exclaimed, "For conscience sake we're on dry land" when the group finally scrambled ashore.[28] In the 1970s there was an attempt to make the large boulder where the first settlers landed the East End equivalent of Plymouth

Rock. The boulder was envisioned as the centerpiece of a historic park, complete with a full-scale replica of the ship that transported the first settlers, and recreations of the houses they inhabited. The proposal went nowhere but the settlers of the 1600s did. They moved from the shores of Peconic Bay to the present business district. After quite literally camping out for a while, probably in primitive little dugouts paneled with bark, they got serious about building real homes.

As time went on houses became larger and more comfortable. The Halsey House, a property of the Southampton Historical Museum, is an example of a substantial home erected by Southamptonites in the colonial period. Purported to be New York State's oldest wooden homestead in its original location, part of the house dates back to 1660. The structure underwent extensive restoration at the turn of the twenty-first century. Although it had been a museum since 1962, when it reopened in the summer of 2001 the house was so authentic that one almost expected to see the Halsey family greeting modern-day visitors. The Bowers-Rogers-Huntting House is another authentic Southampton residence. Built in 1708 on the foundation of a mid-seventeenth century structure, the house was a bed and breakfast (B&B) in the early twenty-first century. Historic or not, quaint old houses have been sheltering visitors to the Peconic Bay area for well over a century. With the advent of tourism in the nineteenth century, structures large and small became boarding houses and, unlike the Bowers-Rogers-Huntting House, with its bird's-eye view of all the goings-on in the middle of town, some were located in the more remote outlying areas of Southampton, including Red Creek in Hampton Bays. Settled in the 1660s and taking its name from the reddish color of the creek flowing into Peconic Bay, Red Creek was an island until its inhabitants linked it to the rest of Hampton Bays by erecting a causeway. Less isolated but still far from the center of Southampton in colonial times were Water Mill, where a mill was built on Mecox Bay in 1644, Bridgehampton, settled in 1654, and Sagaponack, founded in 1656.

Sag Harbor, which is partially in Southampton and partly in East Hampton town, was not settled until 1730. Early residents lived in the same neighborhood as today's trendy American Hotel. The area

was known as Turkey Hill back then and a few unpretentious dwellings may have been built right into the hill. These simple abodes were
replaced by sturdier structures in time and, after Sag Harbor amassed
wealth through whaling in the nineteenth century, magnificent homes
were built, many of which still stand. Thanks to its deepwater harbor and long wharf, Sag Harbor eclipsed nearby Northwest, so-called
because it was northwest of East Hampton.

Settled in 1651, Northwest was the port for East Hampton. The
town dock, believed to have been near the outlet from Alewife Pond,
was a hot spot of commercial activity. Ships loaded with timber and
agricultural products departed for places as distant as the West Indies.
Northwest may have been East Hampton's official port, but residents
of Southampton used it as well. It seemed as though everyone from
a wide surrounding area was beating a path to the Northwest wharf.
In response to all of this activity, taverns or public houses sprang up;
more homes, including that of Isaac Van Scoy, and a schoolhouse were
erected. In 2011 hikers on the Paumanok Path running through East
Hampton's Grassy Hollow Nature Preserve were afforded a glimpse
of the recently uncovered foundation of the Van Scoy residence. When
the Van Scoys lived there, Northwest was a viable community, and so
it remained until the nineteenth century, when its waters proved too
shallow for large whaling vessels. With the subsequent decline of maritime activity, farming sustained the community to a certain extent,
but by the end of the nineteenth century many of the farms had
been abandoned and land that had once been painstakingly cleared
for planting had reverted to forest. In the meantime, East Hampton,
which since 1652 had a direct overland link to Northwest via a road
called "the cartway," had become a thriving community. Founded in
1648, East Hampton expanded beyond the original settlement. Three
Mile Harbor and The Springs, bordering the Peconic Bay estuary,
were inhabited before the end of the seventeenth century. Amagansett, where the lifestyles of yesteryear are interpreted in the local historical society's charming Miss Amelia's Cottage, was settled by 1670.

Living in a community that stretched from ocean to bay, the good
folks of Amagansett were interested in the creatures of the deep blue

sea but cattle, sheep, and hogs were an integral part of the local economy as well. Cattle from Amagansett and elsewhere in East Hampton summered in Montauk, which East Hampton purchased from the Montaukett Indians in 1660. Nearly a century would pass before homes were built in Montauk. In the 1740s First House was erected to house shepherds in charge of the valuable herds of sheep and cattle. With the exception of horses on the Deep Hollow Ranch, nowadays about the only four-legged creatures one sees "on Montauk," to use the terminology of a bygone era, are the pampered pooches of second homeowners. Montauk may be more casual than neighboring communities in the Hamptons but the general absence of skyscraper hedges doesn't mean that there's no wealth in them thar hills. The likes of Ralph Lauren and Dick Cavett call the place home and in the summer of 2001, for a mere $50,000,000, one could purchase a colonial revival compound built in 1931 by the Arm and Hammer Baking Soda family.

Turn-of-the-twenty-first-century prices were lower on the other side of the Peconic Bay estuary system but the publication, in *Manhattan, Inc.* magazine, of an article touting the beauty and quaintness of the North Fork sent shivers up and down the spines of both permanent and seasonal residents. So, too, did a *New York Times* article describing the area as having "an exotic appearance like Provence without the mountains."[29] Soon after the piece appeared in *Manhattan, Inc.* the temptation to compare both forks during prime time, a Saturday in late July, proved irresistible. For someone who would rather switch than fight and hence avoids making left turns on either fork from Memorial Day through Labor Day, an exploratory journey to Water Mill, Sag Harbor, and Bridgehampton was as daunting as climbing Mount Everest. That there would be long lines of cars on Montauk Highway was a given, but being stuck behind and in front of SUVs on the South Fork is very different from being caught behind slow-moving farm equipment on the North Fork. The agricultural machinery is at least part of the local color; the steel and chrome behemoths driven by urbanites out for a weekend of sun and fun are intrusions upon a landscape that is becoming less and less reminiscent of the sort of thing that brought all of these people out to the East End in the first place. True, there are still farms south of the highway, as well as north on the Peconic Bay side of the South Fork, but they are being supplanted by postmodern architectural monuments to the rich and famous or just plain rich. To be sure, remnants of the past remain, but the fast-paced present has encroached upon them. The old Sagaponack General Store, known in the early twenty-first century as the Sagg Main Store, mounted a sign over the counter imploring customers to refrain from using cell phones. In the early 2000s the store was still rustic but outside there was near-gridlock on weekends. If the only available parking space was across the road, it wasn't a bad idea to make sure your insurance was paid up before you attempted to dart across.

In sharp contrast with the ambience of the South Fork is the relative tranquility of the North Fork. Oh, yes, gamblers rushing to the Orient Point ferry for the trip across the Sound to the Connecticut casinos can be every bit as impatient as the high-powered Porsche or SUV drivers on the South Fork. But, for the most part, the North Fork is an oasis of calm on a summer Saturday, particularly in late afternoon when the day trippers head west. At about "tea time" the situation in the Hamptons is quite the opposite, especially for the young, slim, and beautiful. After a day of sunning, swimming, and surfing, a night of partying is irresistible. If the late afternoon eastbound traffic on Montauk Highway is any indication, even those not fortunate enough to have spent the day at the beach are eager to sample the Hamptons' night life. Eastbound traffic on the North Fork, by comparison, is practically nonexistent as evening beckons.

The contrast between the two forks has been evident for as long as anyone can remember. Indeed, it extends all the way back to the mid-1600s when the first settlements were planted on the East End. Although many inhabitants were devout Puritans, the undertakers or organizers of Southampton were preoccupied not with religion but with dividing up the land for house lots and farms. The waterways, including Peconic Bay, were declared open to everyone. In Southold, where the meadows were held for common use, there was a distinctly religious focus from the time the first settlers began arriving in what is now Founders Landing Park. Contrary to local legend, the town's founders did not all hail from Southwold, England, nor had they all dwelled in New Haven for two years before setting out for Southold. They arrived at different times in a place that had been purchased by the New Haven Colony and their settlement remained part of that colony. Southampton and East Hampton, by contrast, were comparable to independent city-states for a number of years after they were settled. Seeking greater military protection, they ultimately joined the Connecticut Colony, a political entity separate from the New Haven Colony. Southampton became part of the Connecticut Colony in 1644 and East Hampton joined the colony in 1657. In 1665, a year after the English ousted the Dutch from New York, all of Long Island was placed within the New York Colony. Even Fisher's Island, a stone's throw from the Connecticut shore, was transferred to New York because it was part of Southold.

The Puritan religiosity that permeated the original settlement of Southold extended to the outlying areas stretching east to Orient, a picture-postcard hamlet with exquisitely restored homes, and west to Riverhead; and it persisted long after 1792, when part of Laurel and all of Jamesport, Aquebogue, and Riverhead to Wading River were spun off from Southold to form Riverhead town. Something else persistent was the presence of the founding families. As land beyond the original settlement was purchased from the Corchaug Indians, it was distributed among these families, many of whose descendants continued to work their inherited acreage for centuries. Some also lived in their ancestral homes. Within a dozen years of the establishment of a permanent settlement, Southold was a community of nearly three dozen thatch-roofed cabins. In Hashamomack, east of the village center, John Budd erected a much more impressive structure in 1699. Relocated to the village green of Cutchogue, the "Old House," now a museum, has a sizable kitchen plus a room called a "hall" downstairs and two spacious bedrooms upstairs as well as a third-floor attic.

A tad less grand but oozing historical charm is the John Booth house on Oaklawn Avenue, Southold. Arriving in Southold from

Barbados, Booth held religious views contrary to those of the Puritans and this doubtless explains why the Reverend John Youngs refused to baptize some of the Booth children. Booth's response was to withhold his tax for the minister's salary. Since church and state were one and the same in the early days of the settlement, the town fathers punished Booth by distraining or seizing his cattle. Given the acreage Booth owned in Cutchogue and Southold, where his holdings included property extending from Town Creek on Peconic Bay to Jockey Creek, also on the bay, plus much of Calves Neck and a half-dozen acres in the middle of town, he could well afford to acquire a new herd. He also owned New Suffolk, the charming nautical hamlet south of Cutchogue and opposite Robins Island. For a time, Booth had a share in Robins Island and, along with Nathaniel Sylvester, he purchased Shelter Island from the Manhanset Indians in 1652.

When he wasn't running around buying up East End real estate, Booth was happily ensconced in his three-room double Cape Cod house, which originally stood on Main Road near the Presbyterian Church. With four sons and most likely a few daughters in residence, the house was filled to overflowing but this was the 1600s, a time when both space and privacy were at a premium. Forget about double sinks in the master bath. Forget the bathroom altogether. Unlike the early twenty-first century, when prospective buyers and renters of North Fork properties turned up their noses at houses having fewer than two full baths, 350 years ago people were less particular and far less fastidious. They made do with backyard privies and indoor chamber pots; in northerly climes bathing was a rare luxury but in the summertime at least they could take a refreshing dip in the bay. But did they? Or were they simply too busy farming, fishing, and trading to devote an afternoon to swimming?

## Get Me to the Church on Time

And what about the women, who, on average, were pregnant every other year? Morning sickness aside, the fair sex was busy, busy, busy. Open hearth cooking, tending a kitchen garden, and child rearing filled their days. Talk about multitasking! Of course, with a life expectancy in the mid-thirties, people did not work until their "golden years." They usually expired long before, the women earlier than the men because of childbirth-related deaths. For some women death brought release from emotional as well as physical suffering, especially if their lawfully wedded husbands were anything like Captain John Underhill, who, like John Booth, lived in the center of Southold. Underhill's home was at Feather Hill, now the site of the Southold Free Library. After gaining fame as an Indian fighter during the Pequot War, Underhill "got around" in more ways than one. Charged with adultery, he left Boston and spent time in a number of places before heading to the Peconic Bay area, where he and his long-suffering wife Helena settled down. Mrs. Underhill may have regretted the sound advice she had given her husband about always wearing his helmet in battle. An Indian arrow actually pierced the dear captain's helmet but he escaped unscathed and lived to fight, and love, another day. Helena Underhill endured her husband's romantic wanderings several more times until her death. In time, the captain remarried a Quakeress, Elizabeth Feake. His last child was born only months before his death, at age seventy-four, upisland at Oyster Bay, where he had moved. Of note also is the fact that Underhill had exceeded by more than twice the average life expectancy, which, owing to infant and child mortality, was in the mid-thirties. He wasn't the only one to outpace the grim reaper.

Ezra L'Hommedieu, Yale graduate, authority on scientific agriculture, and prominent political figure who served in the Second Continental Congress, the New York Provincial Congress, the New York State Senate, and as a regent of the University of the State of New York, became a father, for the first time, at age seventy-two. Following the death of his first wife, Charity Floyd, sister of William Floyd, a signer of the Declaration of Independence, L'Hommedieu was a widower for eighteen years. Then, at age sixty-nine, he married thirty-eight-year-old Mary Catherine Havens, a member of a prominent Shelter Island family. He brought his bride to live in his spacious home on a bluff overlooking the town harbor in Southold. Mary and Ezra's daughter, who bore the same name as her mother, married at age eighteen. Her husband, Samuel S. Gardiner, was seventeen years her senior. Such May-December romances were not uncommon and they often involved prominent men. A case in point was that of Dr. Joshua Clark, a seventyish physician who took a seventeen-year-old bride. Dr. Clark was so anxious to remarry that he jumped on his horse one fine day in 1780 and headed from his home in Mattituck to Southold village, where he proposed, obtained the permission of the girl's parents, and exchanged vows, all within ninety minutes! Of course it helped that eighty-year-old Judge Samuel Landon lived a stone's throw from the bride's residence and was able to drop in at a moment's notice to officiate. Hardly anyone on the laid-back North Fork raised an eyebrow. Yet a century later, on the other side of the bay, when Henry P. Hedges, an East Hampton lawyer, judge, and author, remarried, it was a local cause célèbre because of the twenty-year age difference between the groom and his blushing bride. Addressing this in his memoirs, Hedges said:

> February 23rd 1892, Miss Mary G. Hildreth, then in charge of the Hampton library in Bridgehampton, and I were married. I was 74 years of age and this was noticed, under flaming headlines in the newspapers. It was a choice morsel for gossip. The novelty of discussion and the giggling of girls at length subsided. I reconstructed a new, quiet home, went on with work as before. Twelve years have gone by. No scandal of inharmonious life has ensued. The living cannot live with the dead. My second marriage occurred from no disregard of the memory of the first.[30]

Although the Hedges' nuptials spawned many a titillating tale and perhaps increased the sale of such products as "Life Elixir," touted in a local publication as a cure-all that "never fails to restore lost Manhood," he did not set a local precedent for late-life marriage.[31] In the eighteenth century the Reverend Samuel Buell, pastor of the church at East Hampton and founder, in 1786, of the prestigious Clinton Academy, the first private school chartered by New York State, married a lass who was a sprightly nineteen. The reverend was sixty-nine.

Let's just hope that Buell's newfound happiness curtailed the length of his sermons.

## That Old-Time Religion

Having honed his preaching style in New England during the Great Awakening, an eighteenth-century religious revival, Buell never ran out of energy in the pulpit. The same could be said of the Reverend James Davenport. On one occasion he spoke for almost twenty-four hours. His sermons, including those preached in the church in Southold, where he was pastor from 1738 until 1743, sometimes deteriorated into mere babble. Then there were his frequent absences. He periodically dropped everything and rushed over to New England to burn books and other items he deemed ungodly. The good people of Southold evidently deemed the reverend ungodly because they dismissed him as pastor of their church.

The Reverend George Whitfield, whose preaching inspired Davenport to embrace revivalism, journeyed to America from his native England repeatedly, and on his sixth visit traveled throughout New England and to both sides of Peconic Bay, where he preached at Southold, Shelter Island, East Hampton, and Bridgehampton. Much to his dismay, he missed the boat to Shelter Island, where he planned to stay at lovely Sylvester Manor. Instead, he ended up spending the night at the Orange Webb House, now one of the museum buildings of the Oysterponds Historical Society. This sizable house was moved by barge to a spot overlooking the bay in Orient in 1957. When Whitfield stayed there in 1763, the house was the inn of Constant Booth in Greenport, then known as Stirling. Making the most of his time before crossing the bay, Whitfield preached to a crowd so large that the lawn of the inn could not accommodate everyone. Some who came to hear him remained on the decks of boats moored nearby. Before leaving the house, Whitfield etched a quotation from Luke on one of the windows. In the course of his long career, the good reverend influenced many people, including Samson Occum, a Connecticut-born Mohegan Indian who became a minister to the Montauketts.

Occum preached in England to raise money for the establishment of Dartmouth College, which was originally envisioned as a school for Native Peoples. Another Indian inspired by Whitfield was Peter John Cuffee, who became a convert after hearing the awesome Whitfield. Cuffee's grandson Paul, ordained as a Congregational minister in 1790, became a famous preacher.

Whether among the Native Peoples or descendants of the European settlers, religion remained very strong in the Peconic Bay area. At the turn of the nineteenth century there was a revival in Bridgehampton. Between 1815 and 1818 much of the East End experienced revivals and for some places it came not a minute too soon, at least in the opinion of one godly man, who said of Shelter Island:

> This little spot of earth rising amid the flowing sea, and lifting itself above the highest wave, was a place to which the drunkards of other regions came and unhallowed fishermen drew up their nets, and hailed their wicked companions. . . . There a population not exceeding three hundred poured down their thirsty throats eleven hogsheads of rum annually.[32]

To use old-fashioned seafaring terminology, at least some of these people were "half seas over," and if they couldn't walk a straight line home from their favorite tippling place it was said that they were "making heavy weather of it."[33] By mid-century it was a different story. The temperance movement had taken hold on Shelter Island to such an extent that in 1851 there were "no paupers and no sale of intoxicating drinks."[34] Southold reportedly had twenty paupers and a hundred impoverished citizens, all because of alcohol. In Riverhead, where the movement had commenced in 1829 when seventeen men took the pledge to abstain from intoxicating beverages, fifteen of the eighteen inmates of the Poor-House had landed there because of booze. The place where they resided was located between the bay and the Sound on the road that ran from Jamesport to Northville. As they toiled away on the Poor-House farm, these "guests" of the government could scarcely have imagined that a century and a half later, bayfront homes not too far distant would fetch million dollar prices and new condos in a Soundfront complex in Northville would start in the mid-fours, increasing to over a million before the real estate bubble burst. Although scarcely as remote as it was during the period from 1832 to 1879 when the Poor-House was located here, the area is still somewhat off the beaten track. But you would never know it from advertisements touting the fact that both the condo complex and a community of upscale homes a few miles to the west were only twenty minutes from the Hamptons!

Long before the Hamptons acquired their mystique, the differences between the forks were almost imperceptible. Both areas were inhabited by sturdy farmers and fisherfolk who lived purposeful lives, largely devoid of amusements. Midweek church services and temperance meetings were about as close as most people got to a night on the town. Riverhead attorney James Tuthill's diary reveals that he attended temperance meetings both close to home and in New York City. Despite severe weather, he headed to Manhattan in February 1856 for a temperance convention. An astute observer of the urban scene, Tuthill felt sorry for the horses on the ice-clogged city streets and seemed to be happy to return to his home. Other bay area residents were glad to tarry in the metropolis, however. A half-dozen young Orient sailors, who worked on schooners involved in coastal trade, "met in New York and sallied forth to have a 'jolly good time.'"[35] They spent part of an afternoon and evening in drinking, attending the Bowery Theater, and "carousing generally."[36] Not feeling so great the next day they attended a total abstinence meeting on Division Street, took the pledge, and returned home "with the firm determination to form a total abstinence society and to stop the sale of rum."[37] The year was 1841. It's not difficult to imagine these lads strolling through the hamlet singing "Flow Gently Sweet Croton" (a reference to New York City's Croton reservoir and aqueduct) or any of the other temperance songs found in the collection of the Oysterponds Historical Society. Thanks to their efforts, a nascent temperance movement, which had begun in the 1820s, was reinvigorated. Although liquor was sold, surreptitiously, at the local pool hall, the citizens of Orient bought out the owner. This had the beneficial effect of assuring that farm hands arrived sober, rather than hung over, each morning, prepared to put in a full day's work.

Another byproduct of temperance was better health for former imbibers. Yet despite numerous instances, well documented in the newspapers of the day, of nineteenth-century bay area residents living well past the fortyish or so life expectancy of that period, a goodly number of people on both forks succumbed at an early age. Some were victims of contagious diseases. Augustus Griffin in his famous *Journal* recounts the sad story of the 1849 cholera epidemic. When the disease broke out in New York, commercial contact with the city ceased. According to Griffin:

> From early in July until as late as the middle of September, almost our entire fleet of vessels, say from sixteen to twenty, was laid up. It was hoped by all that our healthy village, at such a remote distance from any city, would escape. In this, we were disappointed. However, the disease that visited our village was not the cholera. It was dysentery of a very malignant type, combining many of the alarming symptoms of the former disease. Our physicians called it the cholera dysentery.[38]

The children of Orient were especially hard hit but not all adults escaped the disease. Victims ranged in age from toddlers to people in their late seventies. Evidently unaware of the situation, excursionists on board the steamboat *Statesman* from Sag Harbor disembarked at the Orient wharf and proceeded to stroll up an eerily quiet Village Lane where "seldom a house escaped, and, in some families, one half were prostrated."[39] When they ran into a local who "informed them of the state of the mortality existing among us, they seemed panic-struck, and they immediately left the place, with alarm depicted on every face."[40]

An examination of diaries in the collections of bay area historical societies and libraries reveals that epidemics certainly produced panic but that people were also concerned about debilitating illnesses, which took longer to snuff out the lives of victims. References to consumption or tuberculosis abound. What comes through very clearly in the diaries is that, faced with illness and the loss of loved ones, bay area residents of the nineteenth century found solace in religion. Like the Puritan settlers of the 1600s, many of the inhabitants of both forks two centuries later were devoutly religious. For that reason Daniel Hildreth never failed to note in his diary the anniversary of the death of his son Austin, who died in California, where he had gone to seek his fortune; in 1872, when another of Hildreth's children passed away, he wrote:

> On the 14th, my daughter Aurela died at eight fifteen in the evening. She died without a struggle and is going to join her sisters in heaven. Now we have only one child left. Aurela has left four children. . . . Aurela was thirty-nine years, eleven months, and two days old. . . . There were more people than I have ever seen at a funeral at a private house before. There were more than three hundred.[41]

In the close-knit farming communities of the East End such outpourings of grief were not uncommon, even in the late twentieth century. When the wife of a young North Fork farmer died in the 1990s, leaving behind several small children, so many people wished to pay their respects that the line snaked down the steps of the funeral home and onto the sidewalk. Some in that line were neighbors who remembered the pretty woman and admired her for juggling family responsibilities with a full-time job and part-time college. She earned her baccalaureate degree only a few years before she died. Despite a busy schedule that included a drive of more than an hour to a campus upisland, she persevered. Like her husband, who, on one of the rare occasions when the North Fork saw appreciable snow, plowed the driveway of someone he had yet to meet, an "upstater" who had just built a second home across the road, she was a good neighbor. Somehow life doesn't seem fair. This stunning young woman, with the perfect Princess Diana–style haircut, was the same age as Diana when she died and she passed away within months of the princess. Both deaths served as reminders of what Caroline Terry of Orient had written in her diary on New Year's Eve 1830: "Time still passes on his universal career and whirls our weeks and months & years away. Another annual period of our short lives is nearly completed; another of our fleeting years is bound to be joined with those that have long since gone down to oblivion."[42] Prentice Mulford, who returned to his native Sag Harbor after spending sixteen years in California, expressed a similar view when he mused about being "brought face to face with a past dead and buried."[43] He told himself:

> You know there is no use in looking across church for that interesting face once always seen there. . . . She is dead, and the other is a matron, stout, as to form, and rather coarse as to features. . . . The gray heads seated about you are those of men young when you left home.
>
> Well, this earth-life is ridiculously short. It is youth, then middle and old age, all huddled up together, and by the time a man begins to learn how to live it's time for beginning to die.[44]

## Walt Whitman and the Schoolhouse Scandal

Philosophical reflections of this sort were the thing that poured forth from the pen of poet Walt Whitman, who wrote that he spent "one of the happiest summers of his life on the shores of Peconic Bay."[45] Since Whitman's sister and her family lived in a house on South Street in Greenport, he didn't lack for a place to stay. When the house went on the market in 2014, it retained many of its original features, including wide plank pine floors. Whitman may have been more than a summer visitor. It is believed that, for a time in the early 1840s, he taught at the Locust Grove School, located between Peconic and Southold. This institution became known as the Sodom School after a local minister supposedly denounced Whitman from the pulpit for rumored homosexual acts with some of his students. The minister's sermon may have provoked an angry mob to tar and feather the twenty-two-year-old Whitman and ride him out of town on a rail. The author of a scholarly article published in the mid-1990s observed: "Whatever the status of the evidence, reports of a scandal persist."[46] Katherine Molinoff, who did extensive research on Whitman in Southold thirty years earlier, interviewed local people whose ancestors had some recollection of Whitman having been in the community but specific details were lacking. That people were loath to talk about such things is perhaps understandable given the nature of the community for, as Molinoff points out:

> The townspeople among whom Whitman lived were simple, devout, laconic, and very proud of family and town history. . . . Even poor families had shelves of treasured books, as well as The Book, and every child was given as much schooling as he could stand or the family could afford. Most boys, after finishing District School, attended at least for a time the Southold Academy.[47]

Like other private schools on the East End, the academy was not a purely local institution. Seeking pupils from the other side of Peconic Bay, the school advertised in the Sag Harbor *Corrector*. Prospective students and their parents were told, in 1835, that the location of the school was "peculiarly inviting" and the building was large and bright.[48] The ad also touted the "moderate" tuition and the fact that board could "be obtained in the vicinity on reasonable terms."[49] That same year, the newly established Riverhead Female Seminary advertised tuition of "$5 per quarter without any incidental charges."[50] A few years later Clinton Academy in East Hampton advertised not only "very moderate" tuition but the fact that "scholars from abroad can obtain good accommodations."[51] In those days, despite steamboat connections between the North and South Forks, the opposite side of the bay was definitely "abroad." Young men willing to venture to East Hampton for an education, however, were assured that they would "be fitted for entrance into any of the colleges in the United States."[52] For those who chose Southampton Academy, the inducements were board "in good families on reasonable terms" and "a good Library together with a Philosophical and Chemical Apparatus, connected with the institution."[53]

**Let the Good Times Roll**

For the students attending these and other schools on both sides of
the bay life revolved around the schoolhouse and local churches, but
there were occasional diversions. Boating, fishing, and swimming in
local waters were obvious leisure-time pursuits. More atypical but
always welcomed by both adults and young people were the agricultural fairs, picnics, or celebrations held in summer or fall. Good food,
music, and, often, a speech or two marked these occasions. The spirit
of these nineteenth-century gatherings lives on at such events as the
Cutchogue Fire Department's annual chicken barbecue. Although
the department's Ladies Auxiliary "cooked up" the idea for this fundraiser in 1957, it was a lady from the other side of the bay who really
put this happening on the map. Martha Stewart not only attended the
1997 barbecue but devoted a segment of her television program to the
event, "which, according to the commissar of culture herself, dishes
up the best barbecued chicken in the world."[54] Try though she did,
the irrepressible Martha could not obtain the recipe but thanks to her,
the year after the barbecue was featured on her show, all 3,200 tickets
were sold in a flash.

In Cutchogue and other places on both sides of the bay, local fire
departments are community focal points. In the 1800s they sponsored popular events, including firemen's drills, dances, and parades.
Around the time of Washington's birthday in February, there was
invariably some activity open to the public. Since this was downtime
for farmers, the scheduling of "blockbuster" events in the dead of
winter was understandable, but the tradition continues today with
firefighters' parades during Presidents' Day weekend. The Greenport
parade never fails to attract a crowd composed of locals and, increasingly in recent years, second homeowners yearning for authentic old-
time Americana.

The summer carnivals held by fire departments also pack in
throngs, and once again many of the patrons are folks seeking a past
that, for them at least, never existed. Nostalgia also accounts for the
hefty ticket sales for circus performances. Traveling circuses are a

summer tradition on the East End. An 1828 advertisement for a circus on the South Fork hyped a "shetland pony, only 36 inches" in height.[55] In 1831 the American Eagle circus advertised its Sag Harbor performances by highlighting "horsemanship without saddle or bridle by Mr. Howes who will leap his whip, garters, etc. and conclude by leaping a canvas TEN feet wide."[56] Prospective patrons were told that the performance would "conclude with the laughable scene of the clown turned barber and dentist, or wait half an hour and I'll shave you in a minute."[57] In addition to the full-fledged circus, there were also traveling menageries that visited the East End. Especially popular with the children of Bridgehampton were the dancing bears that "rose up on their hind legs and danced, a slow, lumbering step."[58] One man who remembered these huge creatures from his youth observed:

> Peddlers, wandering men and beasts; these were some contacts with the far-away outside world. Did they arouse a desire among the young and not-so-young to wander too and see these foreign places and creatures? In some, yes. But mostly we went indoors . . . returned to our play . . . and thanked God . . . we were safe and at home.[59]

There were, however, some youths who were eager to explore the world beyond the East End. In the 1800s going to sea, especially on one of the whaling vessels from Sag Harbor or another of the Peconic Bay ports that dispatched whalers, was a welcome adventure. Had he lived earlier in the nineteenth century George Sterling, whose brilliant career as poet laureate of California ended in suicide, may indeed have shipped out. The heyday of whaling was over, however, by the time he was born so he had to create his own excitement, which he did to the dismay of the citizens of Sag Harbor. On more than one occasion he was said to have ignited bathhouses and set them adrift in the harbor. Then there was the time he released a couple of hundred June bugs during a church service. Another stunt that was recalled, even long after he had departed for San Francisco, also involved a church, the Presbyterian Church of Sag Harbor. One Saturday evening George and some friends managed to shimmy up the steeple and attach a gigantic skull and crossbones. Well, boys will be boys and outrageous though the act was, the ringleader and his accomplices probably thought their sleepy little village, by then past its prime, needed a little excitement.

By the late 1800s, when George Sterling was growing up in Sag Harbor, the community was experiencing a decline. The whaling era, which had brought great prosperity to Sag Harbor, had been over for decades and, as a result, the place was no longer an economic power-house. In certain respects it was similar to what it had been a hundred years earlier, before the heyday of whaling. Francisco de Miranda, the Venezuelan revolutionary leader, passed through in 1784 and said, "the place is one of the worst you can imagine."[60] The Reverend Fitch Reed, who spent time in Sag Harbor in 1810, wrote that the approxi-mately 150 houses "principally stand on two or three streets which run back from the water."[61] Planned road improvements, in Reed's opinion, would go a long way toward enhancing a community "whose people are generally better informed than those of the country."[62] During the heyday of whaling Edward R. Merrall reported that the streets were not paved and that house rents were "nearly as high as in New York"; he also thought that Sag Harbor was "a pretty good sized place though very dull."[63] Annie Burnham Cooper who grew up in Sag Harbor in the late nineteenth century thought otherwise.

The youngest child of a prosperous former shipbuilder and mari-time venture capitalist who had squirreled away ample money to enjoy the good life in the post-whaling era, Annie always found something to do. Her diary contains notations about sailing, bathing, and fish-ing. On her eighteenth birthday she lamented the fact that she would soon be "too big to climb trees" but delighted in the fact that she could "ride horse back & go boating as much as I please."[64] Two years later she was being courted by a forty-three-year-old minister. Her father was not exactly thrilled by the man's frequent visits and Annie herself seemed perplexed by the minister's desire to "spend so much time on me, a green innocent, country maiden."[65] Six months later the minister was preparing to leave for Palestine and when he returned he became engaged to one of Annie's friends. Then the unthinkable hap-pened. The minister "cut his throat and jumped into a cistern where he was found dead."[66] In some circles his death was attributed to an illness that affected his brain but stories about "another woman & all sorts of scandal" circulated throughout the community.[67] Annie herself finally married in 1895. Discounting rumors that "he is a man of the world entirely," she exchanged vows with John Boyd but only after he agreed to respect her individuality.[68] The couple moved to Brooklyn but spent summers in a Sag Harbor cottage. Along with the adjoining larger home where Annie had spent her happy childhood, the cottage is included in Sag Harbor's historic district. In the 1930s Annie used the smaller house as a gallery for the display and sale of her lovely paintings depicting Sag Harbor scenes.

Annie's residency in Sag Harbor overlapped that of Margaret Olivia Slocum Sage, widow of financier Russell Sage. In the late nineteenth century Mrs. Sage purchased the impressive Greek Revival mansion built in 1845 by Benjamin Huntting, who had accumulated wealth in whaling. The house, which for many years has been the Whaling Museum, is directly across the street from the John Jermain Memorial Library, which Mrs. Sage erected and endowed in honor of her grandfather. She also donated a park to the community. Other famous nineteenth-century women with East End connections were First Ladies Anna Symmes Harrison, wife of President William Henry Harrison and mother of President Benjamin Harrison, and Julia Gardiner Tyler, wife of President John Tyler. Following the deaths of her mother and stepmother, Anna Symmes spent her childhood in Mattituck with her maternal grandparents and traveled to the other side of the bay to study at East Hampton's Clinton Academy. Julia Gardiner Tyler, a sort of accidental first lady whose husband became president following William Henry Harrison's death only a month after taking office, was born on Gardiner's Island and as first lady spent time in East Hampton. Despite financial problems resulting from the loss of the Tylers' Virginia estate during the Civil War, Julia had an enviable lifestyle. Like many of the fashionable folks who frequent the East End today, Julia's motto was "shop 'til you drop!" Were Julia, who was known as the "Rose of Long Island," around today she would surely be a dune-walking example of what in the early twenty-first century is called "Hamptons Festive," the style of attire preferred for occasions that are neither formal nor completely casual. "Hamptons Festive" wasn't limited to the South Fork. In the first decade of the twenty-first century it could be spotted at golf clubs on the North Fork and at catered events at Brecknock Hall, which was the restored stone mansion on the campus of Peconic Landing, the upscale lifecare community on the site of David Gelston Floyd's estate.

**Nice Little Places**

The owner of whaling vessels that sailed from Greenport, David Floyd, grandson of General William Floyd, a signer of the Declaration of Independence, erected the magnificent Brecknock Hall just north of Greenport. The house, completed in 1857, had three-foot-thick walls, Italian marble fireplaces, and interior woodwork done by ships' carpenters. Less grand but equally historic are the nineteenth-century homes built with whaling money in "Blubberville" between Peconic and Cutchogue. Nice as they were, Captain Selah Youngs, a hearty survivor of typhoons and near mutinies, decided to trade in his Main Street Sag Harbor abode for something a bit more private than Blubber Row. In 1849 he moved his family to a farm of nearly two hundred acres with a mile of waterfront on the bay in Mattituck. Is this enough to make a real estate broker drool or what? Actually in the 1800s such large spreads were not unusual. Cuyler B. Tuthill was born in 1874 on a hundred-acre farm that stretched from Main Road in Jamesport to the shore of Peconic Bay. The family home, built by his father in 1860, was "the typical eight room, two story and wing house."[69]

On both sides of the bay, from colonial times through the nineteenth century and beyond, putting additions on houses was commonplace. Like crops, the houses sort of grew and grew and rarely did anyone think about demolishing a venerable old homestead because it was too small or outdated. Whether on fashionable Nassau Point, Cutchogue, or on the South Fork, the twenty-first-century custom of buying a house because of its location and then razing it to build something more grandiose represents an attitudinal sea change for the East End. Years ago people simply made do. Even second homeowners in the bay area were content with what they had. At the turn of the twentieth century when author-actor James Herne's play *Sag Harbor*, described by the *Boston Herald* as "a simple romance of honest country folk," was packing in audiences in Boston, New York, and Chicago, things were less complicated.[70] Herne himself had enjoyed many a lazy, hazy, crazy summer's day on his boat *Gretchen* while sailing throughout the Peconic Bay estuary, putting in to Sag Harbor now and then or heading to his bayfront home near the old whaling port.

On the other side of the bay both permanent residents and summer people were flocking to minuscule cottages. Describing the pleasures of this type of vacation in an article titled "Camps along Shore at Southold," in 1904 the *Brooklyn Daily Eagle* declared:

> It is said that, grown-ups, as well as children, like "to hark back" to simple life and primitive customs. Our country people are indulging this instinct and getting more enjoyment out of it. It is not only a going back, however, but a sign of true development, when people open their eyes and find right at hand all that makes life worthwhile.[71]

Ella Hallock, who spent happy summers in a cabin in Southold's now ultra Paradise Point, was blissfully content and for good reason. Describing the area she said:

> Here were ideal conditions—high ground, woods and water, with all their beauty and life. Standing on the southeastern shore, we looked eight miles across the bay, whose waters are accounted by yacht-clubs as affording the finest sailing; by sea-captains, the safest harbor; and by fishermen, the best fishing-grounds, that can be found on the eastern coast of our country. As to its beauty, we learned later, it has no rival in this nor any other land. "Why go to the Bay of Naples or to the coast of Scotland with Peconic Bay at our door?" has become a saying with travelers.[72]

The Hallocks' little cabin became so popular with relatives and friends that they ultimately enlarged it. But in the late 1920s, a quarter-century after discovering the place, Ella proudly declared that "we have tried to be true to the original principle. Simple life has been maintained . . . because care has been taken in all our additions to multiply our joys without increasing our burdens."[73]

Across Peconic Bay, in Southampton, the simple life was being enjoyed in Noyac where a development called "Peconic Bay Estates" was launched with the publication of an elaborate real estate booklet in 1912. Beginning with a question, "Have you ever seen Peconic Bay?" to which it provided an answer, "If so, you must have been charmed by the first sight of it," the booklet went on to tout Southampton as a place that "holds the most exclusive element of New York society."[74] Having said that, the booklet quickly added that Rose's Grove, where the new development was to be built, "is still democratic" and there was "no class distinction."[75] An added bonus was the excellent highway running from Southampton to Rose's Grove. The section of the booklet dealing with the history of the area discussed the earliest inhabitants of Southampton, stating: "The Shinnecocks, one of the most peaceful Indian tribes, had chosen that dimpled shore for their camping ground. Nowadays, the Shinnecock nation is all but extinct. But the traditions that clustered around the waters of the Peconic shall not become extinct as long as man passes the printed word from generation to generation."[76]

Hyperbole may have been acceptable when launching a new waterfront development a century ago. A slick real estate ad or brochure, punctuated by superlatives, may have drawn potential buyers but in the final analysis it was the location that cemented the deal. For many people seeking a country home, there was no better location than the beautiful Peconic Bay area.

## Not So Dear Deer

For the most part, life in this special place was delightful but from time to time there were problems, such as the overpopulation of deer on Shelter Island. When a "wholesale slaughter" of the animals was announced in 1916, the *New York Times* published an editorial urging a postponement until a plan could be worked out to capture the deer and relocate them to private game preserves or state wilderness property in other areas.[77] Within days a deer relocation scheme was devised and fifty men from the New York State Conservation Commission arrived on Shelter Island to force the deer into a corral created with wire fencing. The deer pound on beautiful Mashomack Point overlooking the bay was to be a holding area until the animals could be transported to off-island locations. Some of the deer had other ideas, though. According to one of the many reporters who covered the event, once the deer sensed what was happening, "the excitement began."[78] A mini-flotilla consisting of the *Olive*, the Conservation Commission's vessel, and several other speedboats secured the ends of the line that had been stretched across the island and positioned themselves "to watch for deer that took to the waters of Peconic Bay."[79]

Although a few deer were lassoed by men in the boats, others got away. As conservation officials approached, a buck who hid in a swamp "until only the tip of his nose was above the level" sprang into action and with one leap outwitted them.[80] Not even the wire fencing of the corral and a phalanx of twenty men could stop a determined doe who headed straight for them. Struck by the clubs of her would-be captors, she "left a good deal of hair" on the briars but she escaped.[81] At that point her captors "broke into cheers for the brave doe that had eluded them."[82] At the end of the two-week effort to rid the island of deer, even the farmers, who had requested state help because of crop destruction caused by the animals, had done a complete about-face. The fact that several captured deer had died of fright and others of broken necks turned public opinion against the Conservation Commission.

There was also the not so little matter of fleeing deer causing problems in Sag Harbor and environs. A huge buck who had led numerous other deer out of the corral "was espied making for Sag Harbor."[83] He was captured but others made it across, much to the dismay of the

Conservation Commission, which pulled out all the stops to round up these four-footed Olympic swimmers. The scene was truly chaotic. "A person cruising into Sag Harbor through the fog that mantled Peconic Bay early this morning might have thought an invading army was making a landing for a march upon New York City," observed a reporter.[84] Hampering the efforts of the conservation people were the motion picture cameramen who took to the water. Curiosity seekers also posed a problem. So many people flocked to Shelter Island that the North Ferry from Greenport had to improvise to accommodate them. A *New York Times* article with a Greenport dateline noted that the owner of the ferry running between Greenport and Shelter Island was doing such a booming business that he would "probably declare a 100 per cent dividend tomorrow."[85] The number of people wishing to cross to Shelter Island was so great that the enterprising ferry owner lashed a barge to the ferry to accommodate the extra passengers. When the roundup ended, the *Times* published an editorial headlined "A Failure Truly Pathetic."[86] There are some who would come to the same conclusion concerning attempts to deal with the proliferation of deer on the East End in the late twentieth and early twenty-first centuries.

Widely believed to be carriers of ticks that cause Lyme and other diseases, deer have been regarded as a serious health threat. Moreover, as the number of vehicular collisions involving deer increased and as a larger percentage of farmers' crops and homeowners' landscaping became breakfast, lunch, and dinner for the growing deer population, Bambi no longer seemed cute. Clearly something had to be done. At least that's what the towns of East Hampton and Southold concluded. With the goal of reducing the deer population by 3,000, these municipalities agreed to bring in sharpshooters employed by the U.S. Department of Agriculture. The plan was to have these professionals cull the herd during February and March 2014. Almost immediately there was an outcry, just as there was opposition to a New York State Department of Environmental Conservation (DEC) plan, unveiled in 2014, to reduce the population of mute swans because of their aggressive behavior and destruction of aquatic vegetation. The scope and timing of the DEC swan extermination plan were quickly modified, however. In late January the *East Hampton Star* ran page-one articles about both the swans and a major protest rally staged by opponents of the deer cull. The placards and shouts of the nearly three hundred participants, together with lawsuits seeking a restraining order, sent a clear message to the Town of East Hampton, which withdrew from the program. Not long before, *Dan's Papers* had published a piece about lions being flown in from South Africa to deal with the deer problem. Regular readers realized that this was one of Dan Rattiner's clever spoofs but thanks to social media, the story went viral, with the result that people all across the United States actually thought East Hampton had let lions loose to kill deer.

Unlike East Hampton, Southold proceeded to bring in federal sharpshooters. Not everyone was in favor of the operation. Some residents preferred a contraceptive initiative, something that had been utilized on Shelter Island; others favored an extension of the regular bow hunting season. Rounding up deer and transporting them to the Adirondacks was also suggested despite the dismal failure of the 1916 attempt. Interestingly, in the early twentieth century Frank M. Smith, who discovered a borax mine in Death Valley and marketed its contents as a household cleaner, had a deer park on his Shelter Island estate. Located near South Ferry, the estate also had its own fish hatchery, the country's first set of "autographic footprints" or impressions of his children's feet in concrete slabs, and a deep-water mooring for the owner's ocean-going yacht.[87] Each summer Mr. Smith traveled from his home in California to Long Island by rail, in his private car, accompanied by a retinue of Chinese servants. Following his death, his widow had the mansion demolished, a not uncommon practice during the Great Depression when even the rich sought to reduce taxes on properties they were not using.

## Hanging On, Making Do, and Trading Up

Although the Depression did not exactly result in a demolition derby for East End real estate, projects such as the rumored plan of financier

Otto Kahn to create a top-drawer summer colony in Northwest did not materialize and houses, large and small, languished on the market. Bargains abounded. Among them was the Cedar Island Lighthouse overlooking Gardiner's Bay and Shelter Island Sound and protecting the entrance to the port of Sag Harbor (see fig. 2). Decommissioned by the federal government following the installation of a tower beacon nearby, the 1868 lighthouse was sold at auction in 1937. The price was $2,000 and the buyer was a New York lawyer who leased property across from the lighthouse for a game preserve. In the 1960s Suffolk County purchased the historic lighthouse. Although the victim of fire in the mid-seventies, the lighthouse is the nautical focal point of the 800-acre Cedar Point Park in Northwest but, unlike the Montauk Point lighthouse, which was designated a National Historic Landmark by the U.S. Department of the Interior in 2012, Cedar Point Lighthouse awaits full restoration. Elsewhere in the Peconic Bay estuary is Bug Light off Long Beach, the site of Orient State Park (see fig. 3). The original lighthouse, built in 1871, was burned by vandals in 1963 but, thanks to dedicated volunteers, a full-size reproduction was built in a Greenport shipyard and placed on the site of the original lighthouse in 1990 (see fig. 4). Today Bug Light, which can be

2. Cedar Island Lighthouse, Sag Harbor. Courtesy of Suffolk County Historical Society, Riverhead, N.Y.

3. Long Beach Bar Light (Bug Light), Orient. Courtesy of Oysterponds Historical Society.

booked for overnight stays, is maintained through the cooperative efforts of two organizations: East End Lighthouses and the East End Seaport Museum.

Long before Bug Light became a unique B&B, back in the thirties, the Depression notwithstanding, lighthouses and other components of the nautical ambience of the Peconic Bay area cast a magical spell over people, especially newcomers. English writer and adventurer Robert Powell extolled the virtues of the region in his book *I Sailed in the Morning*, published in London. In 1937 he spent a blissful summer in Greenport, "a very pretty little town."[88] He loved the friendliness of the people and the festiveness of the local watering holes, where there was lots of singing, something he was unaccustomed to in the United Kingdom. Despite the protracted economic downturn, America's standard of living, in Powell's opinion, was "years in advance of England."[89] In the Peconic Bay area where agriculture and

4. Bug Light rebuilt. Courtesy of Oysterponds Historical Society.

fishing were mainstays of the economy people had enough to eat in the thirties even if they didn't have much else.

Things improved in the forties and, after World War II, waterfront areas where fishing boats had once dropped anchor, as well as farm fields, were sprinkled with second homes. In the 1940s African Americans purchased summer homes in the Eastville section of Sag Harbor. At the turn of the twenty-first century a 1925 Sears mailorder house was being restored to serve as the headquarters of the Eastville Community Historical Society. The early years of the new millennium also saw renewed interest in the slaves' burying ground in Orient where slave owners Seth Tuthill and his wife Maria elected to be buried alongside their slaves who were manumitted in the early 1800s. Across the bay on Shelter Island there is a slaves' cemetery on Sylvester Manor. Among those interred there, in an unmarked grave, may be Matilda, a slave freed in the late 1700s who went on to build a small house with borrowed money, which she repaid. Matilda was not alone in her desire to have a place of her own, though in her case she wasn't permitted to own the land upon which her house stood. In her day and subsequently, the little place in the country has been an objective worth seeking. This was especially true in the mid-twentieth century when people were drawn to such places as Cutchogue, described in an early forties real estate brochure as "complete in happiness," or The Springs, one of East Hampton's bay communities.[90] In the latter place contemporary saltboxes "even frailer than the rickety" originals were built along with modern homes whose designers were "creative and imaginative."[91]

Development in The Springs and many other relatively undiscovered bay area communities was hastened by the building of the Long Island Expressway. In a 1954 article dealing with Shelter Island the *New York Times* noted that the completion of "the projected Brooklyn-Riverhead Expressway" would reduce the travel time between New York City and "the shores of Peconic Bay" by an hour, to approximately two hours.[92] The paper offered a very plausible explanation for the development spurt affecting Shelter Island, observing that the development of the island was not unique. It was, instead, an aspect of "the gradual vanishing of the private resorts that once flourished" to serve the wealthy; the newcomers were upper-middle-class people "who can pay up to $50 for a foot of waterfront land and build $25,000 houses."[93]

In the mid-fifties that was a pretty hefty price but enough people were willing to pay it for the exclusivity of dwelling on an island. In the interest of maintaining their splendid isolation, second homeowners were vehemently opposed to a Suffolk County plan to bridge the bay between Greenport and Shelter Island. This mid-twentieth-century proposal was quickly shelved, but one gets the feeling that some of the impatient South Forkers who use the less crowded roads of the North Fork and the Shelter Island ferries to reach their homes on Fridays might like the idea of bridges to and from Shelter Island. Noisy altercations and fistfights on the ferry line at Greenport in the summer of 2001 tried the patience of weekenders and locals alike, but everything is relative.

Wealthy Europeans renting on the South Fork find the East End uncrowded compared with the Riviera. Some foreign visitors don't mind renting homes a bit of a distance from the ocean, not that the prices are cheap, mind you. For example, in the summer of 2001 a seventeen-bedroom, ten-bath home in the Devon area of Amagansett was offered for $400,000 for the season. Rentals were not snapped up all that quickly because of a stock market downturn, but on both forks the season was far from a bust. Of course, a few years earlier, when the bulls ruled Wall Street, prospective renters who did not commit by February were out of luck or had to adjust their sights a bit lower. During those heady days prior to the dot-com bust, real estate throughout the East End was so hot that an elegantly dressed young-ish matron who strolled into a Cutchogue real estate office in early spring, seeking a rental for the chef she planned to bring out to her North Fork estate for the summer, was told that there wasn't much left in any price range. What was milady to do? The main house would be filled with family and friends, with the overflow in the guest house. Maybe industrialist Ira Rennert had the right idea. Build big, really big. His oceanfront estate on former farmland in Sagaponack was in the process of being constructed in the early years of the new century. With 66,000 square feet in the main house, counting the basement, there would surely be enough room for help, including a chef.

Although zoning battles related to the Rennert project were pro-tracted and acrimonious, the development of practically every major piece of land and some smaller choice waterfront properties was preceded by sometimes heated debate. Whether Barcelona Neck in East Hampton or Miamogue Point in South Jamesport, there was a hue and cry when large developments were proposed—single-family homes on Barcelona Neck and condominiums in South Jamesport. Muted at first but increasingly more vociferous as the years went on was opposition to the destruction of historic buildings. At the turn of the twenty-first century Greenport, whose mayor, David Kapell, was attempting to restore the community's historic ambience, was ground zero in the preservation battle. When the owner of the Hanff House, located on a pricey piece of waterfront property since the eighteenth century and maybe earlier, applied for a permit to demolish the deteriorating structure, his petition was denied. Preservationists wanted to see the house saved because of its unusual timber-frame construction. Some local residents had another reason for opposing what they viewed as "demolition by neglect."[94] They believed that George Washington stayed here in 1756. George did get around, as did Ben Franklin, who passed through the North Fork. On their way to Boston, Thomas Jefferson and James Madison stayed at Peck's Inn on the site of the Southold Free Library in 1791 after visiting William Floyd in Mastic, where they received a vocabulary of the Uncachogue Indians. Whether Greenport's Hanff House was the inn where George Washington rested his weary bones before crossing over to New England is really not the issue. What's at stake not only here but elsewhere in the Peconic Bay area is preserving enough of the past to ensure the future ambience of a rapidly evolving region. Admittedly not everything can be saved. A county-owned house, near the bay in Southold, where Helen Keller and her teacher Anne Sullivan are believed to have stayed for at least one summer in the 1930s, was deemed unsalvageable in 2010. Preservationists were dismayed. Yet residents of historic districts sometimes objected to strict regulations limiting what they could do to their own homes.

Just as the preservation of the region's historic architecture has come to the forefront in the bay area in recent decades, so, too, has preservation of the natural environment. Unlike the Native Peoples of the precontact period who lived lightly upon the land, increased population is taxing the area's resources, maybe not to the limit just yet, but that day may be fast approaching. The Peconic Bay estuary and contiguous upland areas cannot support unlimited growth. Yet, given the desirability of the area, people are going to be drawn to the East End to live, to play, and to work. Increasingly, the newcomers will be people of means who, should they be so inclined, can stretch out in leather seats on a Hampton Jitney deluxe bus. For a time, their dogs and cats could be transported to the South Fork on the Hampton Petney, a van service instituted in the summer of 2001. Besides having their own compartments on the air-conditioned Petney, the animals were provided with complimentary bottled water and gourmet snacks. The "people" bus and pet van made the same stops so well-heeled owners could be reunited with their four-footed friends the minute they and their Vuitton luggage disembarked. Despite the popularity of the service, there were no plans for a North Fork equivalent.

In the early twenty-first century, dogs in the back of a pickup truck were a common sight on the North Fork. On the other side of the bay, this would be considered cruelty to animals. So, too, would leaving a dog outside much of the time or putting it in a plain old garden-variety doghouse lacking air conditioning. Oh, well, this is yet another difference between the two sides of the bay, a water-way that, in the precontact and colonial periods, served to unify and connect people on opposite shores. As the twenty-first century progresses, and more people flock to the East End to live part-time or full-time, to play and even to work, the inhabitants of both forks are going to have to become reacquainted in a common effort to preserve and enhance the rural and nautical ambience that brought them here in the first place. It's time to roll up sleeves, even designer sleeves, and get to work!

# 2

# At Work

## Making Ends Meet

On the day after Labor Day in 2000, two North Fork natives standing in line at Southold's Bagel Café on Route 48 (known by locals as the North Road) chatted amiably about changes sweeping over the East End. One of the ladies remarked how sorrowful she had been some years earlier when the first traffic light had been installed on Main Road. Her friend, lamenting the recent appearance of yet another light, this one at the intersection of Horton's Lane and Route 48, sort of half-smiled and said, "That's progress."

Meanwhile, on a nearby beach, a twenty-first-century entrepreneur scanned the shore with a metal detector searching for treasure inadvertently left behind by summer people. The pickings were slim that morning, but the beachcomber persevered knowing full well that he wasn't likely to find any long-buried jewels or coins deposited by Captain Kidd. Finding the dear captain's booty would be the equivalent of winning the lottery. In actuality, the New York Lottery's "dollar and a dream" slogan inspires East Enders to plunk down their hard-earned money for tickets, and occasionally it pays off. The gigantic jackpot won by a waitress at a North Fork luncheonette at the end of the twentieth century confirmed that it could indeed happen here. While the "gazillionaires" on the South Fork have no need to queue up for lottery tickets, the working class and retirees on both sides of Peconic Bay are lotto devotees, judging from the gray hair and overalls in evidence at ticket counters.

There are, however, other ways of generating revenue on the Twin Forks. Some of those people wearing overalls were deriving their paychecks from one of the most remunerative occupations of the 1990s and early 2000s: building.

Thanks to end-of-century prosperity, carpenters, plumbers, and other construction workers, who counted pennies during the recession of the early 1990s, smiled all the way to the bank less than a decade later. It seemed as though everyone wanted a house on the East End, preferably a new one, but a fixer-upper would do, especially if it was directly on the waterfront. As megamansions transformed the Hamptons from a place of genteel wealth, with preppy "uniforms" and accents to match, into a glitzy, international playground, construction workers were in such demand that they had to be imported from "upisland."

With resumption of the South Fork building boom following the economic meltdown of 2008, the Hamptons seemed poised to become "Suburbia by the Sea" as more people made their South Fork homes their principal residences. Telecommuting has made it feasible for some lucky Hamptonites to work at home, at least part of the time. This is also happening on the other side of Peconic Bay, even in sparsely populated North Fork corridors that did not have electricity until the 1920s or cable TV until the 1990s. In the early twenty-first century, however, high-speed Internet is more readily available thanks to competition between cable and phone companies.

What will they think of next? Rest assured, whatever it is, the shrewd locals will embrace it, perhaps warily at first; but like the pioneers who migrated from New England to the East End oh so long ago, if it increases productivity, they'll go for it. A case in point: faced with declining revenue from farmstand operations, occasioned at least in part by the unwillingness of multitasking two-career couples to cook Martha Stewart–worthy veggies from scratch, North Fork farmers morphed into agritainment entrepreneurs at the turn of the twenty-first century. This trend gained momentum throughout the decade to the point where farmstands featuring more than the usual array of produce were thriving. If families enjoying a day in the country, or merely following wine trail signs after a busy morning of hitting the outlets in Riverhead, would not plunk down money for cauliflower, Brussels sprouts (on the stalk, no less), or the ever-dwindling supply of Long Island potatoes, maybe they would pay to be entertained. Hence the corn mazes from Labor Day until Halloween, along with pumpkin picking, pumpkin decorating, and hayrides.

There is even an innovative "murder mystery on the farm" tour. The mystery the tour is based on, which was solved long ago, unfolds during a wagon tour of the historic Wickham farm that hugs Peconic Bay in Cutchogue. A brainchild of the family's younger generation, the tour was introduced in the 1990s at the justifiably famous Wickham Fruit Farm farmstand operation on Main Road. Any day but Sunday, one can purchase picture-perfect fruits from the Wickhams' own orchards plus baked goods, including doughnuts that were so highly touted by the islandwide Cablevision Channel 12 in October 2003 that the very next day the place was overrun, mainly by upislanders. Biting into a heavenly doughnut or a nice crisp apple from the Wickham orchard on an equally crisp autumn day is a real treat, but it may be wise to save the refreshments until after the murder mystery tour. Better to lose one's appetite and then recover it after the tour than to wolf down farmstand goodies and develop a queasy tummy while listening to the gory details of murders that occurred on that very farm. If listening to the tales isn't scary enough, seeing the size of the ax used to replicate the murder weapon can be startling even if the tour guides refrained from hacking away at a big pumpkin to simulate what occurred on the night of June 2, 1854. Happily, murder is pretty rare in the bay area, which is why the 1998 slaying on Shelter Island, the first in the island's nearly 400-year history, made headlines nationally. A century and a half earlier, the peaceful farming community of Cutchogue was equally shaken right down to its sandy foundation by the brutality of the killings on the Wickham farm.

The complete story of the Wickham murders is ably told in *Murder on Long Island: A Nineteenth Century Tale of Tragedy and Revenge* by Geoffrey K. Fleming and Amy K. Folk, a richly detailed account placing the event in a contextual framework that lends relevance to events of our own day. Upon learning of the tale, a reader may ask why anyone would want to harm James Wickham, who moved to the Cutchogue farm after retiring from the New York City grocery firm Wickham and Corwin. The brutal murder of Wickham was compounded by the slaying of Frances Post Wickham, his young wife, and an African American teenage boy, Stephen Winston, who worked on the farm. Wielding a poleax used in erecting fences, the murderer, Nicholas Behan, who had worked on the farm for several years prior to his recent firing, broke into the house. According to the *New York Herald*, he "entered the premises by pushing up a kitchen window."[1] The paper noted: "A very furious dog is kept in this kitchen, and the fact of the dog not making any noise showed it was some one he well knew."[2] Using a back staircase in an annex to the main residence, Behan, whose name was given as Beheehan in *New York Times* articles, reached the room of the young boy, who "was struck several times on the head, which left him insensible and bleeding freely."[3] With the boy unable to alert the master and mistress of the house, the murderer passed through a doorway separating the annex from the main part of the building and crept down a hallway to the Wickhams' bedroom. There he began hacking away at James Wickham, literally cutting his head into pieces. When Frances screamed, Behan knocked her brains out but not before her cries awakened two live-in Irish servant girls asleep on the third floor. They barricaded themselves in their room and waited until the intruder left. Then they began screaming loudly enough to be heard by neighbors who came to the rescue. When the girls emerged from their hiding place, they headed to the Wickhams' blood-splattered room. Sobbing uncontrollably, one of the girls, Ellen Holland, fingered Behan, whom she accused of making unwanted advances toward her, as the likely culprit.

The *New York Herald* put a somewhat different spin on the story, saying that Ellen and Behan, whom the paper initially called Nichols Dane, had "become intimate, and he wanted to marry her until some difficulty arose between them, and she accused him of stealing $10 from her."[4] Ellen told Mrs. Wickham about this and intimated that she would quit her job unless Behan was dismissed. Frances Wickham sided with the girl and persuaded her husband to terminate Behan. "This . . . produced a very bitter feeling on his part towards the family, and particularly against Ellen, to whom he declared he would have satisfaction, and even went so far as to threaten personal violence," according to the *Herald,* which contended that Behan intended to "ravage the girl Ellen and then kill them both."[5] Behan admitted his rape-murder-suicide plan upon his capture, in a swamp near the bay. As his captors closed in, he attempted to slit his own throat with a razor but managed to inflict only a minor wound, which was treated by a local physician to whom he confessed his unspeakable crime. Behan had remained at large for days after the murders as every able-bodied man from miles around searched houses, barns, and other buildings in a cordoned-off area stretching from Long Island Sound to Peconic Bay.

When the suspect was finally apprehended, he was quickly transported to the county seat, Riverhead, to prevent an angry mob from taking justice into its own hands. The subsequent court proceedings were the nineteenth-century equivalent of the O. J. Simpson trial. The courthouse was packed, and area hotels were filled to overflowing with out-of-towners who journeyed to Riverhead in hopes of witnessing some of the courtroom drama. The jury took twenty minutes to convict the accused. Before the verdict was announced, the "signal bell in the cupola" of the courthouse was rung. Immediately "citizens were running from every direction toward the Court House."[6] Inside, Behan, who sometimes danced the Irish jig in his cell, was "continually smiling." During the sentencing, his behavior was bizarre; the *Herald* observed, "The criminal looked at the Judge with an air of vindictiveness," and he "exclaimed, in a rough voice: 'Thank you, Sir! and when I die (pointing to his head) I will leave you my hair to make you a wig!'"[7] Behan's hanging attracted more onlookers than any other public execution in the history of Suffolk County and, to make sure things did not get out of hand, militiamen from Sag Harbor were on duty throughout the day.

If motion pictures had existed back then, Hollywood would have had a field day with the Wickham murder case. Even a modern-day flick based upon this historical drama might end up being shown at the autumnal rite known as the Hamptons International Film Festival. Each fall Hollywood moguls and other film business folks gather in East Hampton for what has become an annual event. It's not quite Cannes but in a couple of years, who knows? While the beautiful people descend upon the Hamptons to view, review, and talk about motion pictures, ordinary mortals flock to the other fork for less glamorous pursuits. After a day in the country, their autos and SUVs piled high with pumpkins and cornstalks, day trippers begin the westward trek home. In contrast with "Hollywood East" on the South Fork, the North Fork is more like Old MacDonald's Farm, especially in the fall, and maybe that's not such a bad thing. Even Martha Stewart opined at the end of a program devoted to the North Fork that the area's farms should be preserved so that future generations can see what American agriculture was like. Peter Van de Wetering would agree; his computerized Jamesport greenhouses, imported from his native Holland, set a new standard for efficiency in the rapidly expanding wholesale nursery business. Van de Wetering thinks the place should be declared a national park. Now that's an interesting idea, but how would the dwindling number of farmers feel about being ogled and photographed by tourists on nonpolluting electric trams? They'd probably feel like bears in the national parks out west. Oh, well, it's only a suggestion—for now, at least.

### Hand to the Plow

Still, today's East End farmers have to keep their eyes open for new income-generating activities while, at the same time, abiding by state and local regulations governing agriculture. Given the excellent soil and climate of the area and the extensive use of irrigation when needed, abundant harvests are not unusual. Thanks to Grapes and Greens, a state-of-the-art food storage and processing facility in Calverton, opened in 2013 with partial funding from New York State, farmers can store produce in an ideal environment. Instead of losing a significant percentage of what they previously harvested and stored in sheds and cellars, farmers have more produce to sell. Vineyards are also using the new facility to store grapes and wine. It remains to be seen whether better crop storage will enhance farmers' bottom line to the point that they can forgo participating in what is commonly known as agritourism, despite the often hefty component of entertainment. Yet, it may enable them to do more of what some of them prefer, namely interacting with the land and with Mother Nature rather than with tourists. Well into the twentieth century agriculture flourished on both sides of Peconic Bay, and the Long Island potato was the king of the crops. These days homegrown spuds are becoming so rare that Sang Lee Farms in Cutchogue once displayed a sign proclaiming "Southold potatoes." It surely looked as though these humble little spuds might become as trendy as the "mesclun by mail" advertised by Sang Lee Farms. In a simpler bygone age the area surrounding Sang Lee Farms was a sea of potatoes. The vagaries of nature notwithstanding, when the white flowers appeared on the potato plants, farmers' mental cash registers began clicking. In 1920 the New York State Department of Farms and Markets noted that the major potato growing area in Suffolk County was the East End, where "two narrow strips of fertile land . . . divided by Peconic Bay" were extremely productive and prosperous as evidenced by the presence of "the two strongest rural savings banks in the state . . . beside many commercial banks."[8] (See fig. 5.)

In 1925 Orient, at the tip of the North Fork, had a record-breaking potato crop. Even the poorest acreage in that community yielded in excess of 300 bushels, while on the very best land 450 to 500 bushels per acre were produced. Nary a spud went unsold, according to a press account: "Every day a fleet of trucks calls at the farms to pick up the filled barrels and transport them cityward; others are shipped by vessels from local docks not far from the farms; still others are shipped by rail from Greenport. England is a large buyer."[9]

It was a similar situation in the Hamptons. In contrast with today, when subdivisions are encroaching upon farmland, in the 1940s it was just the opposite. "Southampton Fights Potato Farm 'Invasion,'" proclaimed a *New York Times* headline in 1944.[10] Government

5. Eagle's Nest Farm, Orient. Courtesy of Oysterponds Historical Society.

subsidies to expand agriculture during World War II accounted for the enthusiasm with which farmers purchased foreclosed properties and expanded cultivation to the boundaries "of the large estates."[11] The Town of Southampton was concerned that the estate owners, who were the largest taxpayers, would "move to rival resorts."[12] An ordinance prohibiting agricultural expansion into the estate area was drafted, and restrictions were imposed upon property already under cultivation. A prohibition on the use of motorized equipment "on Sundays and before 7 A.M. and after 8 P.M. on weekdays" was instituted.[13] Such legislation would have warmed the hearts of veterans of the North Fork corn wars of the late 1980s. Homeowners whose property adjoined farmland, overrun in the early hours of the morning not so much with farm machinery but with boom boxes of hired hands picking corn for farmstands, restaurants, and the New York market, would have loved Southampton's forty-year-old legislation.

Getting back to potatoes, though, the boom times of the 1940s and the postwar years, when East End potatoes were shipped to such distant places as Venezuela on Norwegian ships that loaded up at Greenport, came to an end in the late 1950s. Roy Latham of Orient, a celebrated naturalist as well as a farmer, informed a friend in September 1958 that "we still have acres of potatoes in the ground. It has been impossible to sell them and they are worth little when they are sold."[14] A year later Latham wrote to the same friend, saying, "We are a long way from finishing digging potatoes yet. . . . Mean year all the way through. A number more local farmers are planning on quitting next year. If I was a young fellow I would too."[15] (See fig. 6.) Low wholesale prices, too low to even cover production costs, sent farmers to Washington, D.C., in 1961 to petition for government purchase of the surplus crop. In the 1970s Suffolk County's farmland preservation program helped some potato cultivators remain in business by purchasing the development rights to their farms. By putting money into the hands of cash-strapped farmers, the program ensured the future of agriculture on the East End. Although the total acreage devoted to potatoes dwindled for the remainder of the twentieth century, the humble spud remained Southold town's biggest crop into the 1970s. Even at the turn of the twenty-first century, there was some potato cultivation on both forks. In comparison with fifty years earlier, when 60,000 acres in Nassau and Suffolk were used for potato cultivation, potatoes were being raised on only 6,000 acres, nearly all in Suffolk County, in the year 2000.

During the harvest season in 2000 the *Southampton Press* ran a front-page story featuring a Bridgehampton farmer who had 120 acres of potatoes under cultivation. The headline on the article, "East End Potato Harvest Is Best in Years," appeared in large type beneath an appealing photo of the farm and its owner.[16] The light-blue denim the farmer wore for the photo op complemented the grayish clouds darting across a backdrop of blue sky almost the same color as the farmer's coveralls. Well, it is the Hamptons after all and even agrarian entrepreneurs have to be color-coordinated! Wonder what the owners of new homes in Bridgehampton's potato farm subdivisions thought

6. Beebe and Latham, Orient, 1890. Courtesy of Oysterponds Historical Society.

about this? If they're like a lot of the folks who have migrated from "upisland" or from that other island, the one across the East River, they probably loved it. Working farms do add to the ambience of the East End, even if they stir up a bit of dust. That beige film on the Jag or Mercedes can be a trifle annoying but a trip to the car wash takes care of the problem.

The challenges facing modern-day farmers on the Twin Forks are more daunting. The law of supply and demand still governs what they receive for their crops. A good harvest does not necessarily translate into a decent income unless other areas raising the same crops have poor yields. What's a poor farmer to do, especially in good years devoid of the recurring potato blights that caused many farmers to abandon potato cultivation? The number of spuds that can be sold to the makers of Long Island potato chips is, after all, finite. One approach is to take a leaf from the book of those gazillionaires on the south side of the bay. Diversify, diversify, diversify! Actually the days when farmers put all of their eggs in one basket, so to speak, have been gone for some time. From the middle of the past century onward, East End farmers have been hedging their bets by planting a variety of crops, often the things people like or used to like to buy on farmstands, such as cauliflower.

Historically, cauliflower was right up there with potatoes as a megacrop on the East End. An entry in the diary of Daniel Hildreth, a nineteenth century Water Mill farmer, notes that cauliflower was introduced in Southampton town in 1876. Nearly a decade earlier, in 1867, the venerable Riverhead Agricultural Society induced its members to experiment with cauliflower seeds that the society had imported. The rest, as they say, is history. The crop was so successful that in 1914 growers banded together to create the Long Island Cauliflower Association, which attracted wholesale buyers to its Riverhead auctions until 1989. In 1922, in a single day, between 6,000 and 7,000 barrels of cauliflower were sent to market from the North Fork. This was the biggest one-day shipment ever. A half-century later, in 1976, a Jamesport farmer received a record price of .0875 cents a head for cauliflower sold to the A&P. By that time cauliflower was no longer in the ascendancy, production having peaked in 1949 with 5,500 acres in cultivation. By 1990 only two hundred acres in Riverhead township were devoted to cauliflower production and the Long Island Cauliflower Association's packing plant had closed a few years before.

While cauliflower production dwindled in Riverhead and elsewhere throughout the Peconics, the cultivation of cranberries, once a thriving business in that town, ended completely. Wild cranberries dotted the marshes along stretches of the Peconic River, and in the late 1800s cranberries were planted in Calverton and elsewhere in Riverhead town. The A&P marketed Riverhead cranberries under the "Blue Diamond" label. Local women were employed as pickers each autumn. They were paid by the pail and no one considered it a full-time occupation but, rather, a chance to be outdoors doing productive work with friends and neighbors while generating a little extra income. Children also pitched in but they could be employed legally only if they were between the ages of twelve and fourteen and presented proof that they had been in school for a minimum of eighty consecutive days during the school year. Younger children, ages eight to twelve, were barred from working during the school year. Employers who did not abide by these rules were subject to a $50 fine, a huge penalty for the late 1890s. Cranberry cultivation remained important through the mid-twentieth century but a cancer scare involving a chemical weed killer used on the plants led to diminished sales, presaging the demise of cranberry growing on the East End in the 1970s. In the early 1990s, however, a one-acre bog planted within hailing distance of Great Peconic Bay on the Wickham farm in Cutchogue signaled the reintroduction of cranberries.

Outlasting cranberries as an East End crop were strawberries. The *Suffolk Times* reported, in 1859, that "a gentleman left at our office, one day last week, a mammoth strawberry, measuring four and a half inches in circumference!"[17] The size of the berry, raised in Greenport, was so impressive that the newspaper asked, "Can our Riverhead or Jamesport friends beat that?"[18] Actually, communities on both sides of the bay were growing strawberries and the yields were excellent. An incredible 15,000 quarts per acre were reported for Mattituck in the early 1950s. Now that's a lot of strawberry shortcake! So much, in fact, that you almost have to have people over to enjoy it, which is exactly what the Mattituck Lions Club began doing. The organization's annual fundraiser started out as a small local affair and grew into a three-day event featuring carnival rides and a mammoth craft show plus strawberry shortcake, served under a huge tent. Locals, upislanders, and offislanders show up by the thousands. A good time is had by all with the possible exception of the local police department, which has to go on gridlock alert for the weekend. Ah, shades of the Hamptons on the north side of Peconic Bay! Besides the annual Mattituck festival, strawberry picking at local farms, farm stands featuring strawberries and strawberry jam, and ubiquitous bagel shops and delis offering strawberry cream cheese are all part of strawberry season. So, too, is strawberry wine featured at some North Fork vineyards.

## Raising a Glass

The cultivation of wine grapes and the making of wine have become big business on the East End, enabling Suffolk County to remain the number one agricultural county in New York State in terms of the value of its crops. In the early twenty-first century there were tasting rooms on both forks. By 2014 more than fifty vineyards, wineries, and tasting rooms dotted the North Fork Wine Trail, a well-traveled route, with excellent signage, stretching east from Riverhead. The Ternhaven winery, which for a few years had a tasting room on Front Street in Greenport, even erected a sign proclaiming, "Last winery before France." The East End wine industry is in its fifth decade, having been launched in 1973 by Alex and Louisa Hargrave, a highly educated and very farsighted young couple, who bought an old potato farm in Cutchogue where they planted European wine grapes. The soil and climate of the East End were ideal for wine grape cultivation, something Francis Fournier, a French Huguenot immigrant, discovered in the eighteenth century. Fournier lived in Aquebogue in the mid-1700s, and after the American Revolution he moved to the other side of Peconic Bay where he developed a vineyard at Southport, now called Red Creek. Although he did not have his own vineyard, Daniel Hildreth made wine in the nineteenth century. Writing in his diary on August 17, 1871, Hildreth noted: "I went with wife, Ida, and Alice, granddaughters to Shinnecock Hills blackberrying. Got one bushel; the day hot and dry, berries very thick. I made them into wine; they made 10 gallons."[19] In 1873 Hildreth made seventy gallons of wine in one day. A year later he made thirty-one gallons of elderberry wine. Precisely one hundred years later a meeting was held at Cornell Cooperative Extension in Riverhead to discuss the potential of wine grape cultivation on the North Fork. Vintners from upstate New York met with Long Island farmers who, by then, were searching for a replacement for potatoes and cauliflower. When the farmers learned that the estimated profit for vineyards was $1,000 per acre, their ears perked up because, at the time, each acre planted in cauliflower was returning only $66 in profits.

Ultimately it wasn't the old farming families that became wine barons but rather newcomers with deep pockets. Robert Entenmann, whose family made its fortune producing baked goods, began raising horses on property in the eastern part of Riverhead. Then he planted wine grapes and opened the Martha Clara Vineyards. In 2001 the Martha Clara tasting room on Sound Avenue, opposite the Hallockville Museum Farm, made its debut. That same year the $6,000,000 Italianate-style Raphael winery in Peconic welcomed its first visitors. To the immediate west of Peconic, in Cutchogue, Prince Marco Borghese purchased the venerable Hargrave Vineyard in 1999 with the understanding that Louisa Hargrave would stay on for a while to act as a consultant to Prince Marco and his wife, Ann Marie. The Borgheses operated the vineyard successfully until their deaths, weeks apart, in 2014. Fifteen years earlier when they had plunked down something in the neighborhood of $4,000,000 for the Hargrave land, home, and winery, the price of good farmland on the North Fork had shot up from $4,000 an acre in the late 1970s to upward of $20,000 per acre. At the time of the sale to the Borgheses, a page-one article in the Metro Section of the Sunday *New York Times* praised the Hargraves, saying that "as a consequence of their early gamble, the North and South Forks are home to 25 producers, with 2,786 acres of vines owned or leased by them and small-scale growers. In 1998, 221,000 cases of wine were made."[20] A custom-crush winery was erected in Mattituck at the turn of the twenty-first century to accommodate small growers lacking their own winemaking facilities. The idea was borrowed from California's Napa Valley, and it was interpreted as a sign that the Long Island wine industry was not only here to stay but had reached the next stage of development. Further evidence of this was seen in the purchase of Laurel Lake Vineyards by a group of Chilean investors and acquisition of Bedell Cellars by the CEO of New Line Cinema. Established winemakers on the Twin Forks were also buying additional acreage. In 2000 the manager of Wolffer Estate Vineyard in Sagaponack purchased ten acres of farmland a few miles north of downtown Riverhead and close to Schneider Vineyards, which, at the time, was the East End wine industry's westernmost outpost. A little more than a dozen years later New York Governor Andrew Cuomo was among 1,200 guests at a gala celebration at McCall Wines in Cutchogue to mark the fortieth anniversary of Long Island wine country. Earlier that summer *National Geographic Traveler* highlighted the attractions of the North Fork. With all of this favorable publicity, it was no surprise that more investors were attracted to Long Island's wine country, including a private equity firm that purchased Lieb Cellars vineyard and winery in Cutchogue and the Premium Wine Group's custom-crushing facility in 2013.

Major acquisitions of wineries had taken place previously. In the 1990s physician/vintner Dr. Herodotus Damianos, whose Pindar Vineyards in Cutchogue was one of the first on the East End, crossed over to the South Fork, acquiring the former La Reve Winery in Water Mill and renaming it Duck Walk Vineyards. Although Dr. Damianos took an active role in the Southampton operation, this Renaissance man—whose death in 2014 marked the end of an era in the East End wine industry—was as knowledgeable about literature and other subjects as he was about wine. He was also a fixture at Pindar Vineyards, where the vines stretch from sea to shining sea, which on the North Fork means from Peconic Bay to Long Island Sound. For years the good doctor's companion in the tasting room, where the vineyard's popular tours end, was Hobson, an oversized feline, who would have been equally at home in a bookstore, a more traditional setting for cats. Whether napping next to the cash register or snuggled between cartons elsewhere in the tasting room, the laid-back Hobson was just the opposite of his bouncy owner. Yet, like the soil and microclimate of the North Fork, especially Cutchogue, which Dr. Damianos informed visitors has more sunny days than anyplace else in the entire Northeast, Hobson and his owner were a great team. In addition to the two vineyards owned by Dr. Damianos, there were seventeen others on the North Fork and two others on the South Fork at the turn of the twenty-first century. A decade later, the membership of the Long Island Wine Council numbered thirty-seven on the North Fork, including such Damianos enterprises as Duck Walk North in Southold and Jason's Vineyard in Jamesport, and six on the South Fork.

Grape vines stretching as far as the eye could see were not only aesthetically pleasing but also, to the delight of East End residents, preserved open space, preventing the Twin Forks from becoming a megasuburb like much of the rest of Long Island. Yet, one of the issues so evident upisland, namely traffic congestion, emerged as an unexpected challenge on the North Fork toward the end of the first decade of the twenty-first century. Although accustomed to fall pumpkin-picking tie-ups on Sound Avenue and Main Road (Route 25), the two principal roads traversing the North Fork, natives and second home-owners alike were taken aback by the cars, limousines, party vans, and full-size motorcoaches lining up to enter vineyard parking lots. At some vineyards prominent signs warned that buses and limos were not welcome, or at least not without an appointment, but most vineyards had no such prohibitions.

Consequently, on weekends, when many vineyards feature live music on outdoor patios and decks, weather permitting, it was not uncommon to see vehicles that were unable to find spots in designated lots parked along the road, a practice that raised safety concerns, especially at Vineyard 48 in Cutchogue. This popular destination, which attracted large crowds, elevated what can only be called agritainment, rather than merely agritourism, to new heights. According to owners of nearby residences, who took their complaints to the Town of Southold and the New York State Liquor Authority, the winery's DJ dance parties, ear-splitting music, and inappropriate behavior of patrons who wandered onto adjacent property compromised the quality of life in the surrounding area. At issue was whether Vineyard 48 had become a nightclub, something that is prohibited in an agricultural conservation zone. This is what the Town of Southold claimed in its litigation against the vineyard. The New York State Supreme Court issued temporary restraining orders ending the dance parties and limiting parking at the vineyard. A week before Christmas in 2013 the New York State Liquor Authority dumped the proverbial coal into the vineyard's stocking by voting to revoke its liquor license. Pending an appeal, the vineyard was still operating with a temporary extension of its license in early 2014. A day before the Liquor Authority vote, the Southold

Town Planning Board adopted a resolution denying Vineyard 48's pending request for an outdoor pavilion and a hundred new parking spaces. Following a November 2014 ruling by a New York State Supreme Court judge that Vineyard 48 could retain its liquor license, the Town of Southold planned to appeal.

Some of the issues that surfaced regarding Vineyard 48 were not unique to that winery. Overflow parking on the side of the road, for example, occurred at other vineyards, especially in the early years of the popular Jazz on the Vine Winterfest event, a six-week-long tourism promotion initiative, begun in 2008, and featuring live jazz at wineries and discounts at area B&Bs and restaurants, but a concerted effort was made to direct visitors to nearby venues if a particular vineyard parking lot was full. By 2014, Winterfest, then known as Live on the Vine, featured various types of music in addition to jazz and numerous venues. Tickets were required for many events and parking was regulated.

Winterfest traffic was manageable, but the announcement of the NoFo Rock and Roll Festival featuring artists who had performed at Woodstock in 1969, to be held at the Peconic Bay Winery in 2011, conjured up images of traffic jams all the way back to the Long Island Expressway from the site of the winery, which is just across Main Road from the King Kullen Shopping Center in Cutchogue. Although an estimated 2,600 people were in attendance over the course of the two-day festival, rather than the 15,000 projected, the event stirred up a huge controversy. Residents questioned why the Town of Southold had granted a permit for the festival and wondered whether the staging of music festivals constituted a legitimate use of agricultural land. In the opinion of some it did not. They objected to the constant musical performances and to weddings and other special events, which sometimes stretched late into the night, disturbing nearby residents who likened amplified music to the noise of low-flying helicopters transporting well-heeled weekenders to the Hamptons. Efforts to alter the flight pattern over the North Fork were still a work in progress at the end of the first decade of the new century as were attempts to bring about a meeting of the minds between winery owners and their neighbors, some of whom insisted that, if the wineries were to continue offering food and entertainment, they should be taxed as something other than farms. In general, whether they grow grapes or other crops, owners of farmland have a great deal of leeway. Occasionally, they are called on the carpet by the authorities, as in the case of Vineyard 48 or the legal action taken by Riverhead in 2014 against an indoor farm market selling a larger percentage of items not produced locally than the town code permits. At the very time Riverhead was mounting a legal challenge to the farm market, Suffolk County was considering changing regulations governing farmland whose development rights the county had purchased. Such previously prohibited usages as larger farmstands, public crop picking, and corn mazes would be allowed by revised regulations.

Just as more farms were poised to embrace agritourism, wineries were finding ways to generate revenue that do not involve large-scale agritainment amid the vines. Some wineries have found niche markets for their products in such faraway places as Denmark, Japan, and Singapore. One North Fork vineyard began marketing skin preparations made of residue from grape pressings. Another vineyard was renting half-acre plots to wine enthusiasts eager to perform some of the lighter tasks involved in tending vines. At harvest time, these avocational vintners could sell their grapes or have them made into wine. Some vineyards created wine clubs and VIP tasting rooms to ensure repeat business. In 2013 the Peconic Bay Winery reserved its Cutchogue location for its wine club, special events, and winemaking. The winery's tasting room operation for the general public was relocated to Empire State Cellars, a large space in the Tanger Outlet Center in Riverhead, which features wine and beer from throughout New York State.

In the second decade of the twenty-first century the North Fork was poised to become a craft beer destination drawing visitors to the Greenport Harbor Brewing Company, which opened a spacious brewing and tasting facility in Peconic in 2014. In Riverhead a concentration of breweries, including the Crooked Ladder Brewing Company, the Moustache Brewing Company, and the Long Island

Beer Company, had the potential to transform the old county seat into a beer lovers' mecca. For those who preferred something stronger than beer the place to go was LIV or Shinn Vineyards for North Fork vodka.

Distilleries and craft breweries were definitely a draw but they were eclipsed by wineries where agritainment events and bachelorette parties are likely to continue. As Long Island wines garner more and more awards, both nationally and internationally, however, in terms of visitation to tasting rooms, true wine connoisseurs may eventually outnumber the merrymakers. By 2012, when the *Wall Street Journal* named a semidry Riesling produced at the Paumanok Vineyards in Aquebogue as one of the top dozen in the United States, the East End was well on its way to becoming a world-class wine region. That same year, with the start of construction on an Agriculture Consumer Science Center as an addition to SUNY Stony Brook's Calverton Business Incubator, vintners and farmers could look forward to research assistance. Besides a microbiology laboratory, training and conference facilities were planned for the new facility.

**Moonlighting**

Whether vintners or farmers, East Enders striving to generate new sources of income in the early twenty-first century were embracing a longstanding tradition. On both sides of Peconic Bay, supplementing one's income has long been part of the East End's agrarian lifestyle. Farmers on both forks engaged in a variety of land- and sea-based activities, including duck raising. The practice of earning some extra change by breeding ducks may have begun on Long Island as early as the 1820s; at least that's what eccentric English author and political radical William Cobbett noted in a book published in London. Cobbett had lived in the United States for a time and became notorious for exhuming the bones of Revolutionary War activist Thomas Paine and running off with them. His intention was to return Paine's remains to his English birthplace, where he thought Paine would be revered instead of reviled, as he was in the more conservative post-Revolutionary America. The bones eventually disappeared and Paine was pretty much forgotten. Cobbett had better luck with another of his projects, raising ducks in New Hyde Park, where he resided in 1817–1818. He fattened his own ducks by keeping them in a pen and feeding them vegetables, but he wrote that ducks were often fed horseshoe crabs.

Ducks remained a sideline for farmers rather than a full-time pursuit until the late 1800s. Following the introduction of the succulent Pekin duck in 1873, the industry really took off. On the South Fork there were duck farms at Water Mill, Flanders, and Hampton Bays. No wonder the "Big Duck," that impressive piece of folk art that once served as a roadside store and is now a tourist information site and gift shop, is so at home on the road to the Hamptons. Riverhead had nearly a dozen duck farms in the early twentieth century, with production totaling a million ducks in 1915. In 1945 Riverhead was home to the world's largest duck farm. The operation's owner, Hollis V. Warner, was featured in a lengthy article in the *New Yorker* magazine. The piece noted that half of the ducks raised in the United States "spend their lives in one clattering, thirty-square mile section of Long Island. There are about seventy-five farms in this area which extends from Brookhaven . . . to Aquebogue on the Great Peconic Bay. The largest of them is on the bay, near Riverhead."[21] Two decades later, with duck raising in decline because of new regulations governing runoff of nitrogen, Warner converted his duck sheds on the 360-acre Indian Island at the mouth of the Peconic River into housing for migrant farm workers. It was there on an August day in 1967 that seventy-two-year-old Hollis Warner and a woman described in press accounts as a convicted prostitute were shot to death by Warner's forty-one-year-old son, John.

By the time the Warner family tragedy played out, the industry that Hollis Warner had once dominated was shifting to the Midwest. In 1987 the Long Island business all but disappeared with the closing of the Long Island Packer's Plant in Eastport. Nevertheless, the Crescent Duck Farm in Aquebogue was still functioning. According to owner Douglas Corwin, "The only way we've survived is by trying to differentiate ourselves. The biggest thing is breeding year after year to develop better strains."[22] The cost of upgrading water treatment, creating artificial wetlands, and undertaking odor-abatement measures notwithstanding, the Corwin operation was financially successful. "We probably get about the best price in the country," Douglas Corwin told a *New York Times* reporter in the mid-1990s.[23] He also noted, with justifiable pride, that Crescent ducks were on the menu at the finest New York City restaurants.

Unlike duck raising, which started out as a sideline and then became a full-time pursuit for some farmers, wood cutting was, historically, a part-time activity. Farmers not only cleared and sold wood from their own land but also purchased the right to cut trees on other people's property. As long as railroad locomotives were fueled by wood and houses were heated by wood stoves, the woodcutters of Long Island prospered. Until the changeover to coal for heating, New York City was the major market for the island's wood. Wood sloops bound for Manhattan set sail from Riverhead, Flanders, Noyac, and Northwest Harbor and Abrahams', Barnes', Settlers', and Fireplace landings. Although some of these vessels were as small as fifteen tons, the *Lillie Ernestine*, "the largest schooner to sail out of the Riverhead area," was 250 tons.[24]

More enduring than wood as an income-generating sideline for East End farmers was seaweed. It littered the shores of Peconic Bay and was there for the taking. Whether used for insulation or in barnyards, seaweed was in demand, its fragrance notwithstanding. Of course, years ago bay area residents were accustomed to the smells of nature. That was their aromatherapy! In the sanitized East End of today, however, odors, as opposed to fragrances, are unacceptable, so much so that they make front-page news. In the late summer of 1999 the *East Hampton Star* ran a page-one article detailing public concern about foul odors wafting through Sag Harbor (or "Gag Harbor," as some of the locals were calling it). The sewage treatment plant was suspect, but the real cause of the problem was the buildup of excess seaweed in the vicinity of Havens Beach. This "parfum de Sag Harbor" dissipated within days but, while it lasted, dining al fresco was not an option.

Odiferous seaweed was the subject of another *East Hampton Star* article in 2010. Juxtaposing past and present, the paper noted that historically seaweed was there for the taking by the residents of the East End towns. Yet some people objected to the idea of strangers crossing their property to reach the beach. A landowner in the Northwest area of East Hampton insisted that he owned the beach and could prevent the public from accessing it. In 1861 he was sued by the town trustees, who maintained that the Dongan Patent, granted by New York colonial governor Thomas Dongan in 1686, had guaranteed access to the beaches to all residents. The landowner fought back by hiring attorneys, and in the process drove himself to the poorhouse because the ensuing legal battle lasted twenty years. More than a century later, the trustees took a different position on beach access to gather seaweed. In 2010 when a commercial nursery sought permission to scoop up seaweed for use in organic horticulture, its request was denied because of the potential environmental impact. Aside from the threat to endangered piping plovers if the seaweed were gathered during the birds' nesting period, seaweed anchored the sand and for that reason its removal was viewed as detrimental.

Returning to the subject of how farmers earned extra income, in addition to the sometimes odiferous seaweed, another source of revenue was salt hay. Whether salt meadows or marsh grass were the property of individuals or owned by shareholders or by the town, farmers harvested the hay for fodder for milk cows and cattle. George Case, whose family owned "a small submerged island in the middle of Hay-waters Creek" in Cutchogue, "where the salt grass grew, lush and lovely," described the challenge of helping his father and grandfather harvest salt hay.[25] Case pointed out that a team of horses would be driven into the creek, "to a spot . . . as was compatible with safe sea, and horsemanship. Then, the man with the scythe would go overboard, and start mowing. I was left in charge of the horses," he said, adding:

and warned to watch that they didn't lie down, in the water, to escape the stings of flies, and outrageous fortune, or wander away from the safety of sandy bottom, to where the mud was deep, and dangerous. By the time Gramp had mowed, and moaned a few rounds, Dad would have arrived, with the float, on which the sloppy stuff was then piled, and thence transferred to the wagon. Thence 'twas but a short pull, to the Skunk Lane Thoroughfare, provided the tide hadn't risen too high for passage across the channel, at the North side of the Creek.[26]

Although salt hay was used by livery stables and for packing china and other breakable items, it was not the most desirable form of nutrition for milk cows because dairy products made from cows fed a steady diet of salt hay had a distinctive taste that many consumers found unacceptable. Switching over to English hay solved the problem but, for the most part, dairy farming on the East End was phased out in favor of potato and vegetable cultivation in the late nineteenth century. Interestingly, around the turn of the twenty-first century, the Captain Kidd Dairy in Mattituck, renamed Catapano, for its new owners, began marketing homemade milk and goat cheese. A few years later, in its new location in Peconic, Catapano was marketing a line of beauty creams and soaps as well. Elsewhere on the East End, Cream of the Hamptons ice cream was a big hit with devoted consumers who rated it higher than Häagen-Dazs. Cows providing the raw materials for these yummy treats are doubtless fed gourmet hay rather than grasses cut from local marshes.

Before leaving the subject of salt, a mention of the salt works established by John Mitchell in eighteenth-century North Haven is in order. Mitchell used windmills to pump saltwater through log pipes to cisterns that "would settle out particles of wood, stone and sand."[27] The remaining brine was then pumped to evaporating pans where salt cakes formed. In addition to the Mitchell salt works, there was a similar operation in Sag Harbor that supplied salt to whaling vessels and to communities across Peconic Bay on the North Fork. In the second half of the nineteenth century, however, cheaper salt from mines in upstate New York replaced the more expensive East End variety.

Windmills, which were an integral part of the Peconic Bay area salt business, were also essential for processing grain. In colonial times East End townships offered land grants to millers willing to relocate to the area. An experienced miller was such an asset that the town fathers of Southold, in 1706, voted to give land totaling four acres to a miller willing to relocate from Boston for the purpose of operating a mill where townspeople could grind their grain. In the nineteenth century a gigantic mill called "The Great Western," which had been built in Brooklyn Heights and then moved to Jersey City, was dismantled and transported to Southold Harbor on Peconic Bay. Four Southold men formed a corporation to buy the mill from the New Jersey Railroad and Transportation Company, which had purchased the land occupied by the mill. The railroad had plans for a terminal on the site so the mill had to go. Getting the gigantic structure from the Hudson to Peconic Bay proved to be a real challenge. Two packet boats were needed to transport the various components of the mill, including the imported English stones. Writing about this undertaking in the *Long Island Forum* in the mid-twentieth century, Dr. Clarence Ashton Wood said that, when the boats arrived in Southold harbor, massive pieces of the mill "were thrown overboard and towed ashore."[28] Other components were transported up Jockey Creek or went by wagon to the mill site. Describing the special features of the mill, Dr. Wood said, "The Great Western was at once the lion of the place inasmuch as the sails were made of iron. They were reefed and always kept in the wind by means of fans. Another feature was a machine for hoisting the grain and returning the flour."[29] The Great Western was a prominent feature of the landscape for three decades until its destruction, by fire, in 1870.

Moving mills around was not uncommon on the East End. In 1898 an Orient mill, built by the famous Nathaniel Dominy, an East Hampton clockmaker and miller, was purchased by former congressman John Starin, owner of the Starin Line steamship company. The mill was placed on a barge and towed to Starin's Glen Island theme park in Westchester County. Still in place on Eastern Long Island are

Pantigo Mill on the grounds of the Home Sweet Home Museum in East Hampton; the Hook Mill, built by the Dominy family, on Main Street in East Hampton; and the Gardiner Mill near the East Hampton North burial ground. Like Hook Mill, the mill at Water Mill is now a museum. Southold's former Red Mill, which was moved to Shelter Island in 1840, is on private property, as is the mill on Gardiner's Island. In recent years a number of North Fork farmers have been using windmills to pump water for irrigation and some wineries have installed wind turbines. A 121-foot-high windmill, the largest on Long Island at the time, was completed at a nursery in Laurel, on the North Fork, in 2009, but large-scale projects to harness wind power to produce electricity that could be distributed to customers of the Long Island Power Authority remain controversial.

## Manufacturing

In the twenty-first century, even prior to the massive blackout of August 2003, the electrical utility industry generated opposition, as well as kilowatts, but there was a time when all sorts of industries were welcome. Although overshadowed by farming and fishing in the nineteenth century, industry was an important component of the economy, especially in Riverhead and environs. Swampy areas of the Peconic River yielded bog iron, which was transformed into anchors and other products in Riverhead foundries. In the eighteenth century there was an iron works on the Peconic River a few miles west of the county courthouse. Solomon Townsend acquired the business at the end of the century and began manufacturing gigantic ships' anchors for the U.S. Navy and scythes for the agricultural market. In the early twentieth century the site of the Townsend Forge was home to the Suffolk County Ice Company's huge icehouse.

Cigar manufacturing was another important industry in the early 1900s. Its beginnings can be traced to the nineteenth century, when Riverhead was home to companies manufacturing goods as diverse as soap, chocolates, buttons, flannel, and agricultural equipment, including the riding potato planter invented by S. Terry Hudson, whose home is now part of the Hallockville Museum Farm. Perkin's Woolen Mill, which turned out high-quality cloth, was "Suffolk County's biggest industry" by 1866, and carriages designed and manufactured by Charles M. Blydenburgh were sold not only in this country but abroad.[30] The precursor of Henry Ford in some respects, Blydenburgh designed a carriage "more comfortable and more attractive than others then in use, and not too expensive for the ordinary user."[31] Like Ford's cars, Blydenburgh's carriages had names. The first was the Suffolk and the second, the Montauk, "was well received and carried the name of Montauk to the countries of South America and even down under to New Zealand."[32] A model of the Montauk was featured at a world's fair in New Orleans in 1885. Another of Blydenburgh's carriages, the Roanoke, took its name from an agricultural district north of downtown Riverhead. Other carriages were called the Duall, the Hyland, the Speedway, and the Outing. One can imagine local folks taking these vehicles on jaunts to the surrounding area, including the hamlet of Aquebogue, a few miles east of downtown Riverhead.

Although small in comparison with Riverhead proper, Aquebogue was a popular destination because it had a number of stores, which were accessible not only by land but also by sloops coming up Meeting House Creek from Peconic Bay. Jasper Vail, whose general store and tavern were located across Route 25 or Main Road from Aquebogue's Steeple Church, provisioned sailing vessels. Vail had an interesting way of making change. He would split a dollar bill into two even pieces and return half of it to a customer whose purchase totaled fifty cents. Franklin Wells also ran a general store and a lumberyard. From the roof of the three-story building, which served as his home as well as his place of business, Wells, with the aid of a telescope, could see wood schooners approaching Indian Island. Arrangements were then made to have the lumber unloaded onto a scow and floated up Meeting House Creek to his dock. At various times in the nineteenth century, other businesses flourished in Aquebogue. Merchant John Downs sold grain, vegetables, and meat, shipping some goods to New York once the Long Island Rail Road (LIRR) was in place in 1844. Two decades earlier, Benjamin Corwin Jr. catered to a more local clientele who purchased items in his store ranging from tea and rum to books, paper, and candles. Such eclectic inventories were common in general stores on both sides of the bay. The account book of the Southold store of Samuel S. Vail, preserved in the manuscript department of the New York Historical Society, lists gin, rum, whiskey, tea, textiles, tobacco, and nails among the things sold between 1813 and 1830. It is not inconceivable that items manufactured at the Greenport Pottery were also available at Vail's emporium. The raw material for the crockery made in Greenport was high-quality clay found along the shore of Peconic Bay.

Clay was also the main ingredient in the bricks manufactured near the bay in the vicinity of Mill Creek, between Greenport and Southold. Although there had been brickmaking here on a small scale going back to the pre-Revolutionary period and on Robins Island in the nineteenth century, two large-scale brickmaking businesses, one started by DeWitt Clinton Sage in the 1880s and the other by Captain Charles Sanford at the turn of the twentieth century, dominated the industry. The Sage brickyard turned out 24,000,000 bricks per year at its peak. Both operations loaded their products onto boats in Peconic Bay for delivery to customers in New England, and the Sanford brickyard used the Long Island Rail Road to take its bricks to customers upisland. Competition from Hudson Valley brick manufacturers, who installed state-of-the-art machinery, the growing popularity of concrete block, and the ruination of the clay beds along the bay because of saltwater intrusion during the hurricane of 1938 all contributed to the demise of this once-thriving Peconic Bay industry.

On the other side of the bay, in Sag Harbor, where the Kiss Art Pottery Company used local clay to manufacture its products in the early 1900s, industry had come to represent an increasingly important part of the local economy. A half-century earlier, coinciding with the decline of whaling, the Montauk Cotton Mills had been established to manufacture flannel cloth and other textile products using cotton shipped from the South via the bay. From a profitability standpoint, the Mills were a terrible disappointment, but they survived for three decades until they were destroyed by a fast-moving fire in 1879. The fire was reported by the captain of a schooner that had come into the bay. As the night was very calm, the boat was unable to reach Long Wharf and remained some distance offshore. Smelling smoke, the captain jumped into a small boat and rowed ashore, where his nose led him to the factory. Although a fire alarm was sounded immediately, the combination of highly combustible cotton and oil used to lubricate the factory machinery spelled disaster. The *Sag Harbor Express* described the magnitude of the fire, saying, "The flames shot with . . . rapidity through the building."[33] The end result was that the roof collapsed "less than three-fourths of an hour from the time the alarm was sounded."[34] A few hours later little remained except "a heap of smoldering ruins."[35] Describing this milestone in Sag Harbor history, historian Harry D. Sleight said:

> When it burned it had a capacity of 10,000 spindles, ran 216 looms and was driven by a steam engine of 175 horse power. It manufactured 45,000 yards of print cloth weekly. The number of hands employed was 110 and the payroll amounted to $2,200 per month. No attempt was ever made to rebuild the cotton mill.[36]

Two years after the fire the Joseph Fahys and Co. watch case factory opened on the site of the textile mill. A French immigrant, Fahys had learned to manufacture high-quality watch cases by working as an apprentice in New Jersey. He then bought his employer's company and opened new factories in New Jersey and Brooklyn before being lured to Sag Harbor by a tax abatement engineered by a citizens' committee established in the aftermath of the fire to woo new business to their community. The chairman of the committee "took the matter into his own hands and by personal solicitation . . . raised subscriptions to an amount considerably over $6,000. The money subscribed can be devoted to paying the taxes on the new property for a period of ten years should such property be erected here."[37] The committee met with Joseph Fahys in New York City and made him an offer he couldn't refuse. Within a year he moved to Sag Harbor, where he employed Eastern European immigrants who put down deep roots in their new community, establishing cemeteries in the late nineteenth century and in 1900 founding Temple Adas Israel. In addition to the watch case factory, Joseph Fahys had a major financial interest in the Alvin Silver Company, the Sag Harbor Brick Works, the local water company, and the steam ferry running from Sag Harbor to New England (see fig. 7).

In the 1930s the Bulova Watch Company took over the Fahys watch case factory. During World War II Bulova turned out timing devices for ammunition before reverting, in the postwar period, to watch production. The plant closed in the 1970s. Thereafter attempts to transform the historic red brick building into condominiums failed for the remainder of the century because of toxic contamination of the site by chemicals used in the manufacturing done there through the years; but in 2001 new plans for condo apartments in the historic factory building and townhouses elsewhere on the property were announced. Concerns about population density, the need to remediate toxic waste, and the onset of the Great Recession proved to be major obstacles but they were eventually overcome. In 2014 the historic

7. Fahys Watch Case Manufactory, Sag Harbor. Courtesy of Suffolk County Historical Society, Riverhead, N.Y.

structure welcomed the first occupants of its forty-seven spacious lofts and the adjacent seventeen bungalows and townhouses that, together with an underground garage and recreation center, constitute the new Watchcase complex.

## Down to the Sea in Ships

Just a stone's throw from the revitalized watch case factory is Sag Harbor's thriving waterfront. On this site, where pleasure craft now drop anchor to allow their passengers to come ashore to meander through the quaint streets, enjoy a drink or a meal at one of the fine restaurants, or attend a performance at the Bay Street Theater, the sound of hammers once filled the air as shipwrights built sturdy boats for whaling and commerce. In the 1790s Prior's Shipyard was turning out vessels. A few decades later, Benjamin Wade was engaged in shipbuilding, while Stephen Howell and the Hunttings were building vessels near Long Wharf. James and Edward Smith were crafting sailing ships in North Haven where the Budd Shipyard was located. When the ship *Hannibal*, built at the Huntting shipyard, was launched in 1819, the *American Eagle* declared that "she glided off in the handsomest style . . . greeted with cheers from the numerous spectators on the shore."[38]

Although not as closely identified with shipping as Sag Harbor, Riverhead had a number of boatyards along the Peconic River. The Dimon Shipyard built sailing vessels and steam yachts. Dimon also made "a handsome little sharpie for Mrs. Anna Ostrander."[39] The vessel was outfitted with "nifty cushions and carpet . . . and a pretty awning." Named the *Ethel*, the white and gold sharpie was fashioned of cedar "with hardwood brass trimmings, all highly polished."[40] Its launching was a gala time, witnessed by a large crowd of spectators. Following the traditional champagne christening, the attractive little vessel slid into the water and Mrs. Ostrander and friends went off "for a sail down the bay."[41] Jamesport, in the eastern part of Riverhead township, also built ships. One of those vessels, the schooner *Presto*, built in Jamesport in 1856, was offered for sale two years later.

According to an ad in the *Suffolk Times* the vessel "carries 325 tons, has just been thoroughly overhauled."[42]

Boat launchings seem to have been quite the spectator sport on the East End. An 1866 notation in the diary of Henrietta Terry Conklin of Southold mentions witnessing the launching of the schooner *Elmmer Wooley* in Greenport. The April 1880 launching of a barkentine built in the Smith and Terry shipyard attracted a crowd of 4,000! According to an account in the archives of the Oysterponds Historical Society in Orient:

> The scene at the launching was most exciting and impressive. The weather was most favorable. . . . A fresh breeze was blowing from the west, which continued to increase during and after the launch. . . . Wharf and shipyard and vessel were crowded with spectators. All were full of anxious expectation and none were disappointed.[43]

The launching did not go as planned. The barkentine managed to slide down the ways but it became grounded on a shoal and had to be helped by a small steamboat, which threw it a line. The services of a second steamboat were required to tow the newly launched vessel to the wharf. Occasional mishaps like this failed to dampen the enthusiasm of East Enders for ships and shipbuilding.

With its deepwater harbor and easy egress to Peconic Bay and Gardiner's Bay, Greenport was an ideal place for shipbuilding. According to historian William B. Minuse, the descendant of Suffolk County shipbuilders, during a fifty-year period between the 1830s and the mid-1880s, "18 builders constructed 121 vessels: 57 sloops, 57 schooners, 4 brigs, 1 bark, 1 barkentine and 1 steamer."[44] Beginning in 1880 the venerable Preston's started outfitting ships. Today, Preston's still caters to boaters, as does Wm. & J. Mills and Co., makers of sails and canvas, which also opened in 1880. Mills's practical and attractive canvas bags are snapped up by landlubbers who visit the company's Greenport showroom, and Preston's delights boaters and nonboaters alike with an interesting array of merchandise. Through this retail outlet and its mail order catalogue Preston's serves customers in the

United States and abroad. After perusing the Preston's catalogue, one client, eager to select some new furnishings for his vacation home in Bermuda, flew into the Westhampton airport in the 1990s and was limo-ed to Greenport. The customer, H. Ross Perot, enjoyed his quick shopping spree and promptly headed back to his private jet.

A century before H. Ross Perot paid a visit, Greenport was building boats for the United States Life Saving Service. If capsized, these trusty vessels could clear themselves of water in sixteen seconds. The Greenport Basin and Construction Company, whose government contracts during the world wars of the twentieth century are discussed in a subsequent chapter, built schooners, sloops, and steam yachts, including a number with such interesting names as *Now Then*, *Vanish*, *Rialto*, *Fra Diavolo*, and *Freelance*. Fishing vessels were constructed at the Stirling Harbor shipyard of Tuthill and Thorn and at the Greenport Ship Company in the early twentieth century. A hundred years earlier, fishing vessels were being crafted in East Marion by Jerry Brown. In the late eighteenth century the whaling vessel *Minerva* was built in Orient. Shelter Island had a shipyard on West Neck Creek. The sleek and fast *Paragon*, which outran Napoleon Bonaparte's blockade of England to deliver a consigned cargo to Liverpool, was built here. In the late twentieth century thirty-eight- foot cruising boats, which singer and composer Billy Joel had a hand in designing, were built at the Coecles Harbor Marina and Boatyard on Shelter Island. In the nineteenth century specialty craft were built in Southampton by William French. His *Sarah Helen*, constructed in 1835, may have been the first three-masted schooner. The boat was built on property adjoining French's Hill Street home. When completed, it was dragged by oxen to a creek leading to Shinnecock Bay. A second, smaller vessel, the *Phantom*, was also built on Hill Street. For a time, both vessels plied the route from the East End to New York.

The New York connection was important for the economic well-being of the Peconic Bay area but so, too, was foreign commerce. Merchant ships entering American waters at the port of Sag Harbor, which was designated an official port of entry in 1789, carried all sorts of marketable goods. After duties were paid at the home of customs collector Henry Packer Dering, these goods found their way into the regional economy. Whaling vessels also carried treasures from afar back to Sag Harbor in the nineteenth century. In the colonial period, as noted previously, North Sea and Northwest, rather than Sag Harbor, were the important ports on the South Fork. Oil harvested from whales taken in nearby Atlantic waters was transported overland to Northwest in East Hampton for shipment to Boston. Ships also departed for New England from the port of North Sea. With the advent of larger cargo vessels, however, Northwest and North Sea were eclipsed by Sag Harbor, which was Bridgehampton's outlet to the world. Sag Harbor offered not only deeper water but also an impressive new pier. Built in 1770 by investors from Southampton and East Hampton, Long Wharf was an immediate hit. For a half-dozen years prior to the American Revolution the products of nearby forests, plus fish, cattle, horses, beef, pork, and assorted other items, were loaded onto ships at Long Wharf for export to New England, the West Indies, and points in between. In 1808, and again in 1821, the wharf was expanded. During the whaling era Long Wharf produced enviable profits for its shareholders, but with the end of that colorful epoch commerce declined and so did revenue. Just before World War I Sag Harbor lost its designation as an official port of entry. Customs matters were handled across the bay in Greenport for a little while and then everything was transferred to New York City. Long Wharf, which had been acquired by the Long Island Rail Road as a winter berth for the steamboats it purchased from the Montauk Steamboat Company, subsequently became the property of the Village of Sag Harbor, which in 1947 transferred the wharf to Suffolk County. In 2011 the county was eager to divest itself of the wharf, then on the National Register of Historic Places, by turning it over to the village. The historic structure was formally transferred to Sag Harbor two years later.

Although Sag Harbor was, far and away, the most important port in the Peconic Bay estuary, other communities had similar aspirations. One wannabe was Jamesport. An 1833 advertisement in the Sag Harbor *Corrector* announced that "an application will be made to the Legislature of the State of New York . . . for the passage of an act to incorporate a Company to be called 'The Miamogue Wharf & Ways Company' with a capital stock of Two Thousand Dollars, with the privilege of increasing the stock to Four Thousand dollars."[45] The wharf and a general store materialized thanks to James Tuthill and his brothers but James' Port, which had more than three dozen homes by the early 1840s, failed to become the major seafaring center James Tuthill envisioned. James' Port simply could not compete with Sag Harbor's deeper water and its superior location closer to the open sea. The James' Port wharf, where numerous whaling vessels were to have tied up, was used by farmers to ship their products to market. When a winter storm destroyed the original dock, a cooperative formed by local farmers built a new wharf; but this dock took second place to the Long Island Rail Road for transporting agricultural products to market.

Jamesport was hardly alone in its efforts to generate revenue from seaborne commerce. A notation in the Long Island News column of the Sag Harbor *Corrector* attested to Southold's ambitious plans. "Southold is going to build a wharf at a cost not less than $7,000," the paper informed its readers in 1872.[46] Four years later the steamer *Coit*, one of the vessels of the Montauk and New York Steamboat Company, made its first run to Southold, which was the last stop, following Orient, Greenport, Shelter Island, and Sag Harbor, for boats from New York. The *Coit* dropped anchor at Founders Landing in Southold, where entrepreneur Jonathan B. Terry had erected a wharf in the 1850s for his commission business. He then branched out into steamboats. Like Sag Harbor's Long Wharf, the Founders Landing wharf was acquired by the Long Island Rail Road, which transferred it to the Southold Park District in 1908. The wharf, extending far out into the bay, remained intact until a severe hurricane in 1954. Soon thereafter what was left of this venerable piece of Peconic Bay history was taken down.

To the east of Founders Landing, in the Village of Greenport, the Long Island Rail Road wharf also deteriorated in the twentieth century before being rebuilt. Like Sag Harbor, Greenport's wharves were busy places in the nineteenth century, particularly during the whaling era, and when that bright, shining moment faded into history, the village's docks accommodated commercial fishing vessels. Boats tying up in Orient were as likely to be transporting farm produce as fish. The farmers/entrepreneurs in the Hallock family even had their own steamboat, the *Halyoke*, which carried agricultural products to market, provided weekend excursions for tourists, and, in the winter, ferried coal from New Jersey.

### The Romance of Whaling

As important as wharves and shipping were for the economy of the Peconic Bay area for hundreds of years, they lacked the romance associated with whaling. Of course, in the 1600s, when South Fork settlers imitated the example of the Indians and converged upon Atlantic beaches whenever one of the gigantic mammals drifted ashore, whaling wasn't all that glamorous. Even when some of the folks in East Hampton formed whaling companies and employed Indians to go out in boats to drive whales ashore, the industry lacked the enchantment it would acquire in the nineteenth century when Long Island whaling ships traveled to the distant Pacific and the polar regions in search of their elusive quarry. With the possible exception of the captain, and his wife, if she accompanied him, a practice discussed in Joan Druett's charming books, crew members of whaling vessels found little romance in a job that entailed interminable periods of waiting around until a whale was spotted and nonstop work once it was. If the voyage was successful, which it usually was because ships stayed out for two or three years until they had enough whale oil and bone to ensure the profitability of the trip, the surviving crew members were hailed as conquering heroes when they finally got home. Whether regaling lovely young maidens with tales of danger and adventure or purveying exotic trade goods from the South Seas, the returning sailors were seen as superstars.

Sag Harbor, where most of the male population was involved in one way or another with the industry, whether serving on whaling ships or building, outfitting, repairing, or provisioning them, was truly a mecca for sailors, including men from exotic places who signed on as replacement crew. All told, Sag Harbor sent out more than a hundred whaling vessels between 1760 and 1871. The industry, whose history is chronicled in Dorothy Zaykowski's masterful book, *Sag Harbor: The Story of an American Beauty*, declined in the mid-nineteenth century when whales became more elusive and voyages longer and less profitable. The use of kerosene for lighting was another factor in the demise of whaling. The discovery of gold in California also contributed to the industry's decline. During the Gold Rush whaling ships transported prospectors to the West Coast, and Sag Harbor whalers were among the vessels abandoned in San Francisco's harbor.

Although by far the most famous, Sag Harbor was not the only East End community that sent out whaling vessels in the 1800s. New Suffolk's *Gentleman* and Orient's *Minerva* were involved in whaling, while Greenport dispatched more than a dozen whaling ships between 1830 and 1858. The *Potosi*, the first whaler to depart from Greenport, was gone for only seventeen months before returning with bone and oil worth $15,000. The ship was wrecked in the Falkland Islands on a subsequent voyage but the entire crew and part of the precious cargo were saved. The *Claudio*, whose name survives in the famous Greenport restaurant overlooking the bay, returned from an eighteen-month voyage with a cargo valued at $22,000. The *Washington,* which is believed to have sailed from Jamesport on one of her voyages, departed from Greenport in July 1843 with Captain Edwin Peter Brown of Orient vowing to return in a year. Exactly one year later, to the day, he made good on his promise after venturing as far as the Indian Ocean and New Zealand.

The record for the longest voyage by a Greenport whaler belonged to the *Phillip I*, which rescued more than two dozen Chinese, including a government official, whose vessel had lost its mast. The *Phillip I*'s captain was treated like royalty when he landed his Chinese passengers in Napa Kiang in 1856. More than a decade before, in 1845, Captain Mercator Cooper received a cordial welcome from the Japanese when he returned shipwrecked sailors he had taken aboard his Sag Harbor whaling vessel, the *Manhattan*; but Japanese officials, who were fascinated by two members of Cooper's crew, a Shinnecock Indian and an African American, made it clear that the *Manhattan* should not tarry in Japanese waters.

Rescuing people was only one serendipitous aspect of whaling. Once out on the high seas, captains and their crews had to be ready for anything, including the birth of a baby. Among the wives who accompanied their spouses on whaling voyages was a Mrs. Babcock from Greenport. Whenever she boarded her husband's ship, this very practical lady took along baby clothes in case she became pregnant. Although expectant mothers were often dropped off in Hawaii to await the births of their children and the return of their spouses, which sometimes took a year or longer, Mrs. Babcock gave birth at sea. The baby died but instead of burying the child at sea, the grief-stricken parents preserved the little body in a wine cask. The child was ultimately buried in Greenport. Martha Brown, who accompanied her husband, the aforementioned Captain Edwin Peter Brown of Orient, on a whaling voyage aboard the *Lucy Ann*, which sailed from Greenport in 1847, gave birth to her second child, a son, in Hawaii and endured a difficult voyage home. Storms, bedbugs, cockroaches, and illness marred the journey but the *Lucy Ann* eventually made it back to Greenport. Safely ashore and reunited with her daughter, who had been left behind with relatives, Martha put her foot down and declared there would be no more whaling voyages for her husband but, contrary to her wishes, he continued to sail for several more years. By the time he settled down on his parents' Orient farm, the whaling industry was in decline. At least one Greenport whaler, the *Sabina*, had pointed the way to new opportunities by transporting people to California for the Gold Rush. The final whaling voyage began in 1858 when the Greenport ship *Minerva* set sail, never to return. An important era in the history of the Peconic Bay area had ended. but now and again East End residents were reminded of those glorious days.

In the mid-1870s, for example, a couple of Riverhead men out for a day of clamming on the bay were almost struck by a whale that beached itself at Simmons Point. Using boat oars to finish off the whale, they had their prize catch towed to the Riverhead town dock, where it was exhibited. In 1882 a whale caught in the Atlantic off the Hamptons was towed to Cedar Point in Peconic Bay, disemboweled, and put on display. For a quarter, sightseers were transported from Sag Harbor to Cedar Point to gawk at the gigantic mammal. East Enders had to act fast if they wished to see the whale, however, because its next stop was New York City. En route to the Big Apple, the whale was embalmed and then cork chips were inserted to plump it up again in preparation for exhibiting it, for a fee, of course, under a gigantic tent on Beekman Street in the vicinity of the present-day South Street Seaport.

Six decades later, in 1944, a ten-foot-long baby whale stranded on a sandbar in Peconic Bay off Mattituck was nudged back into the water by kindly locals wielding a pole. That same year a six-ton killer whale beached itself at Orient. Towed to Tuthill's dock in Greenport, it was displayed for several days until a scientist from the Cold Spring Harbor Laboratory upisland carted the head off for research. The rest of the unfortunate creature was towed down the bay and allowed to float away. In 2014 a dolphin that had wandered into the bay was found dead in Southold's Goose Creek and was retrieved by the Riverhead Foundation for Marine Research and Preservation. That same year, a whale paid a brief visit to Greenport harbor before departing for deeper waters. Through the years the handful of marine mammals found in the Peconic Bay estuary, including the whale that appeared in 2003, were merely footnotes to a bygone chapter in East End history. The whaling era had, for the most part, ended by the mid-1800s, but for the remainder of the nineteenth century Long Islanders continued to go down to the sea in ships. They just didn't venture as far from home. There was no need to because they were no longer seeking the peripatetic leviathans of the deep but, rather, a tiny fish that paid more than an occasional visit to Long Island waters.

## Harvesting the Bays in Yesteryear

Known as menhaden, mossbunkers, or simply bunkers, these small bony creatures, which are sometimes called "garbage fish," are not good eating but they certainly increased crop yields when spread on the farm fields of the East End, something Southold's scientific farmer Ezra L'Hommedieu discovered way back in the 1790s. Forty years later there were nearly three dozen companies taking menhaden during their spring and fall migrations. Composed of local farmers, these companies used money put up by five to ten shareholders to purchase boats and equipment, including the huge seines or nets employed in taking bunkers. Each company had its own charter and name, which was often whimsical, such as the Coots, Night Hawks, Canadians, Turks, Skunks, Owls, and Dragons. Besides buying shares in the company, the members did all of the work, and hard work it was.

Although catches were generally enormous (e.g., 67,000,000 "taken on the Bay" in 1869, according to the *Republican-Watchman* newspaper), there were some years when menhaden were in short supply.[47] The year 1867 was a particularly bad one, ostensibly because there was an oversupply of eager bunker fishermen who embarked upon their search for menhaden very early in the spring when the fish were spawning. Since it was generally believed that "the first schools contain the largest fish," some people tried to get a jump on the season, which traditionally began in April or early May, depending upon the migration of the bunkers.[48] A compilation of the catch of one menhaden fisherman for the years 1852–1880 revealed that "in the early years of the fishery the season began later and ended earlier."[49] In 1882 Eugene R. Blackford, president of the New York State Fishery Commission, informed the United States Fish Commission that overfishing of menhaden was reducing the number of other species that fed upon bunkers.

In 1899 bunkers themselves were in short supply. The *Brooklyn Daily Eagle* reported that "the recent experience of the fishing fleet of the American Fisheries Company has not borne out the favorable omens of a good season, which the earlier weeks of cruising foreshadowed."[50] The situation was so bad that the company, located in Promised Land, had "decided to lay off a number of the boats and the crews have been discharged for the season and paid off."[51] The crews in question were employees of the American Fisheries Company rather than the farmers/fishermen of old, and this was not the only change occurring in the menhaden industry.

Another was the way the fish were taken. Until the early 1840s the seines were dragged ashore but thereafter a capstan turned by horses did the laborious work. Another advance came when the practice of counting the catch was abandoned in favor of selling them by the wagonload to farmers who had their wagons measured. Since it was determined that an individual bunker occupied twenty cubic inches, by dividing the volume of any wagon by twenty cubic inches, it was possible to come up with a fair approximation of the number of fish for which a farmer should be charged. Farmers weren't the only people interested in these bony little fish. When it became evident that menhaden oil could be used in place of whale oil, the demand for bunkers became so great that farmers were sometimes priced out of the market. To extract the oil, so-called pot works, where menhaden were boiled, were established throughout the Peconic Bay area, starting in the late 1840s with Judge Marcus Osborn's operation at Jessup's Neck, now the site of the Morton National Wildlife Refuge. The fragrance wafting through the air was anything but delightful, and a steam factory established by Greenporter Daniel Wells on Shelter Island in 1850 was moved from Chequit Point to a more remote part of the island a few years later for that reason. In the 1860s the fishy smell became less of a problem because menhaden processing was done on factory ships to which local fishermen delivered their bunker catch. This was only a brief respite, however, because the introduction of steam- powered fishing vessels in that same decade permitted the rapid delivery of menhaden to processing plants on shore. Describing a state-of-the-art steam-driven plant, located in what is now Gerard Park, East Hampton, a reporter said it was "one of the most complete factories on the bay."[52]

Similar establishments dotted the waterfront of not only Shelter Island, where there were plants at Dinah's Rock, Hay Beach (which was sometimes called "Bunker City"), Ram Island, and elsewhere, but also in Southold at Pine Neck and Paradise Point, in Orient at Long Beach (now the site of Orient State Park), Napeague Harbor between Amagansett and Montauk, and in East Hampton at North-west, Promised Land, and Accabonack. Although Brooklyn and Man-hattan businessmen were principals in some of these businesses, East End seafarers were also prominent. One of the most interesting locals was Captain Jacob Appleby, owner of bunker factories on both sides of the bay, at Paradise Point and Napeague. The son of a New York City butcher who amassed a fortune by investing in Manhattan real estate, Jacob Appleby ("Captain Jake") went to sea as a young man and even-tually became captain of a whaling vessel. He was also involved in the slave trade after it had become illegal and narrowly escaped pros-ecution. Always controversial, Appleby was sued by his siblings for actions he had taken as a trustee of their father's estate. This proved to be the least of Captain Jake's problems, however. More important than financial matters relating to the estate was the dissolution of the captain's second marriage. After the death of his first wife, he had remarried, but the second Mrs. Appleby dumped her husband after a quarter-century of marriage. Why, you might ask? Well, it turned out that the lady had a very good reason, actually three good reasons, for it seems that the dear captain had a trio of other "wives" and four chil-dren, three of them with a woman known to her neighbors as "Mrs." Appleby! None of this seemed to faze Captain Jake, who lived to the ripe old age of ninety-one, dying around 1907.

In contrast with the colorful Captain Jake, Edward Hawkins, who passed away at his Jamesport residence in 1908 at the age of eighty, was quite conventional. With two of his brothers, Edward Hawkins had bunker factories on Shelter Island and upisland in Jamaica Bay and a fleet of factory ships. Despite their business partnership, two of the brothers, Edward and Simeon, ran against each other for the state senate. Simeon, the incumbent and a former state assemblyman, lost to brother Edward.

By the time Edward Hawkins passed away, smaller menhaden processing operations were being supplanted by large-scale factories. One of the biggest, the Triton Oil and Fertilizer Company's new plant at Promised Land, opened in 1911. This factory could process 5,000,000 menhaden a day but it was the last such plant erected at

Promised Land. Aside from the fact that the malodorous fragrances wafting from menhaden factories were incompatible with the East End's burgeoning tourist industry, periodic scarcity of the bony little fish in local waters beginning in the 1920s contributed to the demise of the industry. By the 1960s, when the last bunkers were processed at Promised Land, planes were being used to spot migrating menhaden and the oil, which by then was an ingredient in myriad products, including lipstick and linoleum, was being extracted elsewhere.

Commercial fishing for other species also underwent a transformation in the twentieth century. The introduction of new, better-equipped, and far costlier vessels, combined with longer trips to more distant fishing grounds, transformed an industry that a century before had been not only local but also, for many fishermen, part-time. Farmers' diaries from the nineteenth century reveal that fishing was an important sideline. Although much of the fishing was simply a way for farmers to augment their income, going back to the mid-eighteenth century, there was large-scale commercial fishing. In 1744 Benjamin L'Hommedieu Jr. formed a partnership with a half-dozen other Southold men to fish for porpoises and other species. In the 1790s Orient fishermen journeyed to Newfoundland for cod. At the turn of the nineteenth century Orient men worked on commercial fishing boats in New London, Connecticut, and environs. Before long, sturdy fishing smacks built in Peconic Bay communities were venturing up and down the East Coast.

Closer to home, fishermen were using pound traps, long nets draped from slender poles, and fykes (long bag-shaped nets). Fykes were placed in the bay early in the year although fishermen, well aware of potential ice damage to lines and anchors, waited until after the January thaw to put their equipment into the water. Then the fishermen waited until runs of fish entered the area, filling the fykes. The next step was to load the fish into smacks for the first leg of the journey to market. The catch was then transferred to steamboats or rail cars for the trip to New York's Fulton Fish Market. The railroad was so eager to corner the market on transporting fish that it acquired a tugboat that was dispatched to tow fishing smacks to the railroad dock in Greenport. The LIRR's successful efforts to grab a major chunk of the fish-hauling business indicates just how important the fishing industry was by the late nineteenth century. Although fishermen had some lean years when nothing seemed to be biting and very little filled their traps, on the whole business was good. It was not unusual for a lone fisherman to catch upward of 500 bluefish and enough sea bass to fill more than a hundred barrels, and this was all in a day's work.

From time to time, fishermen got more than they bargained for, such as the case of the fish with the oval sucking disk on its head. This strange creature was snared near Greenport in 1889. That same year a 400-pound sunfish was landed at the dock in Greenport and tropical fish were found in traps in the bay. Dr. Clarence Ashton Wood, who detailed some of these unusual catches in a series of articles for the *Long Island Forum* in the mid-twentieth century, described what may have been the strangest fish ever spotted in the Peconic Bay estuary system. According to Dr. Wood this creature was spotted by people on the *Prospect* ferryboat when the vessel was traveling between Greenport and Shelter Island. Eyewitnesses said they saw "a sea-serpent at least 75 feet in length. They said it swam past the boat faster than the speed of a steamboat. They claimed that its three coils, larger around than a barrel, were clearly visible."[53]

Although this may sound like quite a fish story, there were other reports of strange creatures. The captain of the steamboat *Halyoke* swore that he had seen "a serpent with a crested head" and an undated press clipping in the collection of the Oysterponds Historical Society in Orient describes the capture of a "reptile 22 feet long" in a fish trap off Montauk.[54] The clipping bears a handwritten notation that this occurred "when Taft was President," which would mean sometime between 1909 and 1913.[55] According to the article the strange-looking creature was decomposed because it had been in the trap for several weeks. The fishermen who made the discovery said that it had large dual fins on each side of its body, which enabled it to swim "with great rapidity."[56] Although the decomposed body "was permitted to drift away with the tide," the head and tail were displayed in Montauk.[57]

Montauk was also the place where a pair of Greenport fishermen took a ninety-two-pound striped bass in December 1899. Stripers were an important part of the commercial fishery well into the twentieth century. So, too, was the controversy surrounding the use of nets for commercial fishing, something that sport fishermen opposed as far back as the 1880s according to Captain Frank Tuthill, president of the Fishermens and Gunners Protective Association. When the good captain headed to Albany in 1924 to lobby against proposed legislation outlawing the use of nets, he told a reporter how the controversy between sport and commercial fishermen had begun four decades earlier when Seth Green and Robert Roosevelt, fisheries commissioners, had no luck catching bluefish in Fire Island Inlet. Upon returning to shore the two men decided to purchase some blues from pound fishermen. Furious over what they viewed as the exorbitant price of ten cents per pound, "they swore that they'd have a bill passed at Albany that would stop all pounds."[58]

Convinced that there were enough fish in the sea for everyone, Tuthill opined that regardless of the nets there would "still be fish enough left for the sport fishermen."[59] Since fish migration isn't wholly predictable, the captain felt that even if nets were outlawed, there would be some years when sport fishermen wouldn't have much luck, nor would commercial fishermen. The seventy-one-year-old Tuthill, whose father and brothers were commercial fishermen, had begun fishing at age fourteen and was completely enamored of what he did for a living. "We fished not only to make a living but because we loved the work. . . . And if I had my life to live over again I certainly should go a fishing," he told a reporter, adding, "I have seen all kinds of seasons. Some years we hardly pay our way because the fish are so scarce. Another year, for no apparent reason, we may be swamped with 'em."[60] Speaking about sea bass, Captain Tuthill said he remembered that in 1861 they were scarce. Five years later and again in 1890 they were abundant. In the latter year he was "one of three men who caught 1,040 sea bass in four hours."[61] As far as Tuthill was concerned, fish came and went and no one could control their movement.

Isn't that the truth? In 1925 a boy fishing for snappers in Northwest Harbor, East Hampton, probably thought so. A budding naturalist, the lad was fascinated by the behavior of all kinds of creatures and for that reason could not resist wading into the water to observe two dogfish that seemed to be chasing each other around. After standing motionless for approximately ten minutes, he was able to grab one of the playful fish by the tail. The fish, weighing 25 pounds, put up a good fight but the boy was able to drag it ashore, where his companions helped him subdue it.

## Modern-Day Baymen

Impressive though they are, stories about nontraditional ways of snaring fish, supersize fish, and other anomalies are of secondary importance when compared with the gratifying, albeit challenging, life of commercial fishermen, which Peter Matthiessen recounted so beautifully in his book *Men's Lives: The Surfmen and Baymen of the South Fork*. Three decades before Matthiessen's book appeared, the East Hampton Town Baymen's Association was founded "to promote fraternity among its baymen members and to educate the public about the environmental concerns of men who make their living on the water."[62] Writing in 1989, Arnold Leo, secretary of the East Hampton Town Baymen's Association, stated: "For the most part, the baymen come from families that date back to early times in the history of East Hampton. Among the older members of the fishing community today are men who speak with the English dialect of their English forefathers."[63] Their equipment was also a throwback to an earlier age as "the types of fishing nets they employ . . . come from earlier centuries. The baymen are living history.[64]

Leo went on to say:

Unfortunately, they are now an endangered species. This has come about because, on the one hand, development of waterfront property has resulted in badly deteriorated marine environments . . . and, on the other hand, pressure from sportsfishing lobbies has resulted in increasingly strict regulation of commercial fishing which serves no purpose of conservation but only tends to place certain key fisheries (such as striped bass) in the hands exclusively of sportsfishermen.[65]

Unlike the early twentieth century, when "few if any sportsmen sold their catches," according to Leo, by the 1980s, "the practice is for sportsmen to sell whatever they can of their catch."[66] These entrepreneurial sport fishermen were, therefore, in competition with the baymen and both groups were intensely interested in the striped bass. Although this popular fish had all but disappeared from local waters between 1916 and the early 1930s, they resumed their annual migration through the area and kept on coming, usually in larger numbers, according to Stuart Vorpahl Jr., president of the East Hampton Town Baymen's Association. In a letter written in 1970 to New York State Senator Earl Brydges, opposing a bill that would have limited commercial fishing for striped bass, Vorpahl declared that commercial fishing had taken place from the time the East End was settled whereas sport fishing had emerged only in the past quarter-century. In his opinion, the demands of the sport fishermen were excessive.

The sport fishermen appeared to have won a victory in 1975 with the passage of a bill outlawing netting of striped bass anywhere in New York State. This legislative initiative evoked the spirited opposition of commercial fishermen's wives. The East Hampton Baymen's Ladies Auxiliary issued a press release appealing to women throughout the state to oppose the legislation if for no other reason than it would result in much higher prices for this popular species since the fish would be brought in from other states. The release also noted that the out-of-state catch would be frozen and of lesser quality than what New Yorkers were accustomed to eating.

A decade would pass before striped bass from New York State waters disappeared from dinner plates, and when it did the culprit was contamination from PCBs dumped into the Hudson River at an upstate General Electric plant. Three decades of this sort of waste disposal caused the Food and Drug Administration (FDA) to conclude that the striped bass in the Hudson were too contaminated for human consumption. Reacting to the FDA, in 1985 New York State banned the taking of striped bass in state waters except for Eastern Long Island. In 1986 the exempted area was included in the ban, with the result that commercial fishermen from the Hudson, where the striped bass went to spawn, to those in Eastern Long Island, where river bass migrated, were deprived of an important part of their livelihood. Adding insult to injury, the brown tide (explored later in this volume) in the Peconic Bay estuary system reduced shellfish harvests, thereby further diminishing the income of baymen who, typically, spent part of the year taking shellfish from the bay. Calling upon the state, in 1986, to "conduct full scale PCB testing of marine waters in 1987," Arnold Leo expressed hope that such tests "might result in reopening the striped bass fishery in 1988."[67] In his statement Leo pointed out that the baymen were "in rough waters as a result of the ban on taking striped bass and the loss of scallop stocks to the brown tide. Many baymen have left the mending of nets and the small winter fisheries to take construction or other wage jobs," he said.[68]

At the same time that they were battling New York State over the reopening of the striped bass fishery, baymen were taking on General Electric in court. Although legal action was initiated in 1985, the fishermen had to wait for another three years before being granted the right to sue as a class. As their case wended its way through the courts, the baymen attracted a powerful ally, singer/composer Billy Joel, a native Long Islander who in the 1980s moved his wife, model Christie Brinkley, and daughter Alexa Ray from Manhattan to East Hampton. Genuinely concerned about the plight of the baymen, who are often called Bonackers because of their concentration in The Springs or Accabonac area of East Hampton, where their ancestors settled in the 1600s, Joel publicized their cause by recording "The Downeaster Alexa," a song he had composed, and donating proceeds from concerts to the East Hampton Town Baymen's Association. He also participated in a 1992 protest staged by East Hampton commercial fishermen to oppose the state's approach to the reopening of the striped bass fishery.

Beginning in 1990 the New York State Department of Environmental Conservation (DEC) permitted sport fishermen, who were not required to have fishing licenses, to catch one striped bass at least thirty-six inches long each day during a season lasting seven months. Commercial fishermen, who had to be licensed and who were required to tag the fish they caught, were permitted to take a collective total of 128,000 pounds of bass between twenty-four and twenty-nine inches during a three-and-a-half-month fishing season, but the use of haul seines and otter trawls, favored by commercial fishermen, was prohibited. Compounding the problem was the size of the fish. They were too big to be caught in pound traps, another mainstay of traditional commercial fishermen. To focus attention on this situation, which the baymen felt favored sport fishermen, the East Hampton baymen sued the DEC in 1990 and two years later, on a beautiful July day, they defied the DEC by putting a seine into the ocean off Amagansett. Twenty people, including Billy Joel, received summonses for taking striped bass from this net after it was hauled ashore. The protest, viewed by a thousand people, caught the state's attention and within a month the DEC issued new regulations permitting commercial fishermen to keep striped bass up to thirty-nine inches long. The annual quota was also increased from 10 percent to 48 percent for commercial fishermen, and the state announced that the commercial season for striped bass would be lengthened by two months the following year. In the mid-nineties a modified haul-seine fishery was permitted.

Although things seemed to be looking up for the commercial fishermen, there were new challenges. Sport fishermen pressed for state legislation classifying the striped bass as a game fish, meaning that it could be taken only for recreation and not sold. Bills were introduced in Albany for this purpose but they went nowhere, much to the relief of the commercial fishermen. More good news came when the class action lawsuit against General Electric (GE) was settled. In 1993 GE and the fishermen agreed to an out-of-court settlement providing $7,000,000 to the fishermen for income lost as a result of GE's pollution of the Hudson River. The accounting firm that disbursed the payments to the fishermen failed to enclose 1099 forms with the checks, however, with the result that the recipients thought the GE money was not taxable. This was not the case and the fishermen were hit with retroactive tax bills in 1997. Dan Barry, writing in the *New York Times*, described the impact of belated taxation upon men who had used their share of the settlement to acquire new boats and other equipment and pay off old debts. He said the compensation the fishermen received had been spent and, since the number of striped bass commercial fishermen could take was limited by the state, they were compelled "to chase lobsters for their income."[69] To Barry it appeared that "every day . . . another bayman leaves this centuries-old profession to drive a truck or pound some nails."[70]

Stuart Vorpahl was one bayman who wasn't retreating from the water, however, even after his 1998 arrest for fishing without a license. According to the *New York Times*, "Mr. Vorpahl has never had a license, and has maintained for years that he does not need one."[71] The newspaper went on to state that Mr. Vorpahl asserted that a patent issued by New York colonial governor Thomas Dongan "granted the inhabitants of East Hampton the right to hunt and fish within the town's borders subject only to the powers of a group of town trustees."[72] According to Mr. Vorpahl, who was himself a trustee, only the trustees could impose fishing regulations.

In the early nineteenth century the role of town trustees was clarified by the New York State legislature when a dispute over seaweed occurred in Southampton. Reacting to a claim to underwater land, undivided property, beaches, and meadow land by Southampton's proprietors (i.e., the original purchasers of land in that town), their heirs or assigns, the legislature, in 1818, passed a law allowing the proprietors, through their trustees, to supervise, sell, lease, and divide mill streams and undivided land but beaches and underwater land were not included. In fact, the law specifically stated that "waters, fisheries, sea-weed and productions of the waters, shall be managed by the trustees . . . of the Town of Southampton, for the benefit of said town."[73] The law also said that "nothing herein contained shall in any manner affect or alter the right, title or interest of any person, or the inhabitants of said town to any of the before mentioned premises."[74] In East Hampton the town trustees in 1828 established fines for non-residents who took oysters from local waters without the consent of the trustees. In the 1880s East Hampton prevailed in a number of suits aimed at voiding documents purporting to be trustee deeds to underwater parcels. By this time underwater land had become quite valuable. As companies displaced individual baymen on the Great South Bay, fishermen headed east in search of shellfish. In 1884 New York State enacted legislation transferring underwater land in Peconic Bay to Suffolk County. The county then appointed an Oyster Commission to lease the underwater parcels. Seed oysters planted on the bay bottom would quite literally become the foundation of a major industry; but clams and scallops, which were called "escallops" in the 1800s, remained an important source of revenue for baymen.

A U.S. Commission of Fish and Fisheries study of fishing communities in 1880 had noted that attempts were being made to cultivate oysters in Peconic Bay but that clams and scallops dominated the shellfish industry. In The Springs, where there were "forty professional and ninety semi-professional fishermen," the catch for the fall and winter of 1879–1880 was "10,000 bushels of scallops" in Three Mile Harbor.[75] Greenport had an equivalent scallop yield and, like The Springs, a harvest of crabs and lobsters as well. The undisputed scallop capital of the East End, however, was New Suffolk, which, according to the U.S. Commission of Fish and Fisheries, "has been built to accommodate the scallop trade."[76]

Describing every facet of the business, the commission's report stated:

> The scallop fleet numbers sixteen sloop-rigged boats, ranging from 5 to 15 tons each, the aggregate being about 120 tons. Seventy men are engaged in fishing for scallops; while twenty men, thirty women, and eighty children are employed in opening the product, making a total of two hundred persons, the majority of whom are

Americans, engaged in this industry. . . . The fleet averages 100 bushels (in shell) per day, or 18,000 during the season. They "open out" half a gallon of meats to the bushel of shells, making 9,000 gallons which, at an average of 60 cents a gallon, net the producers about $5,400. They are shipped in boxes to commission merchants in New York. . . . The scallops are caught with dredges (pronounced drudges by the fishermen), similar to those used in taking oysters, except they have no teeth. . . . Scalloping has been practiced here twenty-five years, and it is claimed that the discovery that the species was eatable and marketable originated here.[77]

Fascinated by the role played by women and children, the author of the report noted that women "ordinarily open from 15 to 18 gallons per day, according to the size of the scallops, and it is not uncommon to see a woman standing at her place working while she is rocking the cradle with one foot. . . . The work is all done in frame buildings and the people stand in a row at a bench. Children often come down after school and open 5 or 6 gallons."[78]

This may not seem like big business but for the time it was and it continued to grow, prompting the Town of Southold to seek an attorney's advice about title to lands under water. In his opinion, published in 1893, Charles S. Street reaffirmed Southold's rights to Peconic Bay based on a patent granted by royal governor Sir Edmund Andros in 1676 but stated that the Town of Riverhead, which was split off from Southold in 1792, "is the owner of the . . . lands under water within its boundaries."[79] Street also advised "that an act be passed by the Legislature of the State providing for a board of trustees for the town of Southold, with power to manage its lands under water, subject to directions made at town meetings, all the proceeds of town property to be applied towards the expenses of the town."[80] Following enactment of the legislation, the board of trustees announced that it was "ready to receive applications for grants of lands under water."[81] At the same time, the board declared, very emphatically, that "in the name of the Town of Southold" it claimed "all rights to lands under water which the Town owns under and by virtue of the colonial patents, and the rights to manage, lease, convey, or otherwise dispose of them."[82] That's telling them, but not everyone was listening, especially across the bay in the Town of Southampton.

At the turn of the twentieth century, Southampton officials did some historical detective work aimed at figuring out the exact location of the town's northern boundary. Southold countered by laying claim to the entire bay all the way across to Southampton. Among the evidence presented by Southold was what purported to be the long-lost original deed to the town, which turned up in the court records of the New Haven Colony in 1901. According to this document, the original settlers did not purchase their land from the Indians but rather from the New Haven Colony, which sold them everything from New Haven to the South Fork of Long Island. According to historian Harry D. Sleight, this "explains how Governor Andros, knowing these facts, came to grant all these waters to Old Southold in his patent of 1676."[83] Expounding upon this, Sleight said, "When Governor Andros stuck his seal into the wax on that document the water rights it described became Southold's beyond a question by the highest form of title known to the human race."[84] Nevertheless, in 1903 the state supreme court in Riverhead ruled against Southold on the basis of the fact that, for two hundred years after the issuance of the Andros Patent, the town failed to claim ownership of the bay. The court had ruled previously that the Town of Southampton did not own the bay, and in 1897 the court had decided that while East Hampton did own its harbors, it had no claim to Peconic Bay or Gardiner's Bay.

While the question of ownership of the bay bottom was being considered by the court, large scallop beds were discovered near North Haven and in Napeague Harbor. A 1900 newspaper article announcing these finds explained the allure of this shellfish, which it described as "one of the most prized articles in the category of epicure."[85]

Another article appearing that same year described all of the shellfish activity off Barcelona Neck and Northwest in East Hampton. It noted that scallops were still abundant despite the number of sloops out dredging. There was, however, a running battle between the baymen taking scallops and oyster companies leasing underwater parcels for cultivation. The oyster companies employed guards to keep the scallopers away from their beds, which were delimited by poles secured with big rocks. Pieces of canvas bearing the names of the owners were secured to the tops of the poles.

Companies and individual baymen were doing well early in the new century. A front-page story in the *Brooklyn Daily Eagle* in 1904 noted that a hundred boats from Jamesport and other places were scalloping on the bay and that some of them took "150 bushels each."[86] On a Friday in November, 329 gallons of scallops were loaded onto the train in Jamesport. The *Eagle* also said that some of the boats were working round the clock and one of the female workers opened forty-five quarts of scallops in one day. A decade later the *Riverhead News* reported that scallopers were "coining money" with each boat generating between $10 and $50 daily.[87] In the 1920s off Mattituck it wasn't unusual "to see . . . a hundred boats" on the first day of the scalloping season.[88] By the late twenties it wasn't the number of boats on the bay nor the quantity of shellfish taken from the bountiful waters that were making headlines but rather the recurring issue of ownership of the bay. When the New York State Land Commission transferred land under Sterling Creek, an arm of the bay in Greenport, to an individual who planned to fill in the property and then use it as a building lot, the Town of Southold, citing the Andros Patent, challenged the Land Commission in the courts.

Legal battles over the bay notwithstanding, during the 1930s the economic challenges posed by the Great Depression and the churning up of the bay bottom by the hurricane of 1938 contributed to a decline in shellfishing. Within a few years, however, the industry rebounded. In 1940, 500 people were employed in oystering in Greenport alone. The community's numerous oyster companies included Lester and Toner, Cedar Island Oyster Company, Robert Utz and Sons, M. C. Rowe Company, American Oyster Company, Sea Coast Oyster Company, Modern Oyster Company, Greenport Oyster Company, and the Radel Oyster Company. In nearby East Marion a General Foods Corporation subsidiary, the Blue Point Oyster Company, opened that year. In 1941 Greenport oysters were placed aboard refrigerated railroad cars for a cross-country trip prior to being planted in the Pacific Ocean.

In the years after World War II the demand for Peconic Bay shell-fish could not always be satisfied because pollution closed portions of the estuary system. The New York State Department of Environmental Conservation (DEC) kept a watchful eye on the waterway and sometimes, when pollution abated, the DEC reopened closed waters. In 1978, for example, an area of the bay bordering the towns of River-head and Southampton near Suffolk County's Indian Island Park was conditionally reopened after having been closed for fifteen years. Following periods of heavy rain, resulting in runoff from roads and duck farms, the newly reopened waters were temporarily off-limits for shell-fishing. But despite these periodic interruptions, local baymen were ecstatic about the DEC's action. The reopening of these waters was the impetus for the formation of the Riverhead Baymen's Association.

In the 1980s baymen throughout the Peconics joined forces to oppose a plan put forward by the New York State Urban Development Corporation (UDC) to lease underwater land owned by the state or Suffolk County. The state hoped to encourage aquaculture, but similar leasing proposals advanced by Dr. Lee Koppelman, director of the Long Island Regional Planning Board, and by Suffolk County legislators had been shot down a few years before the UDC entered the picture. At a 1984 hearing in Riverhead on the state's proposal, a hundred baymen turned out to oppose the plan. Although less than one percent of the bay bottom would have been involved, the baymen feared that this would be only the beginning of a program that would ultimately result in big companies dominating the shellfish industry.

Besides fending off proposals they perceived as threats to their livelihood, baymen had to deal with a disappointing Department of Environmental Conservation reseeding program involving the transplantation of 6,000-plus bushels of clams from Little Neck Bay in Long Island Sound to bays and creeks in Suffolk County. With Little Necks selling for up to $100 a bushel in 1986, baymen hoped to generate some badly needed income. The clams the DEC transplanted, however, were not the prized Little Necks but ordinary chowder clams selling for a mere $10 a bushel! Compounding the problem was the fact that baymen were more dependent than ever upon clams because of the ban on taking striped bass and the appearance of the brown tide, which decimated the scallop population of the bay. Although the brown tide will be discussed at length in the last chapter, it should be noted that in 1987 the Long Island Oyster Farms, which since 1843 had been transplanting oysters from New Haven Harbor to Peconic Bay, announced that it was withdrawing from the area and would be selling its underwater land. The brown tide was the principal reason for the company's decision.

If a large and well-established company had to pull out, how long would it be before individual baymen were forced off the water entirely? Even after the brown tide abated, earning a living on the water remained difficult. As Stuart Vorpahl Jr. told the court in a memorandum of law drafted to support a motion for the dismissal of charges in his fishing without a license case: "Without a fishing license we can't catch striped bass, and with a license we are allowed less than one fish per day with an unworkable size limit, which means we can't catch enough to earn a living, and this is what commercial fishing is all about."[89] Vorpahl also noted:

> The N.Y.S. commercial fishing license is an imposition of no validity or applicability to the fishermen of the East End . . . as well as practically all of the conservation laws which are of great hindrance to us. These laws are imposed upon us, primarily as social-political enactments. . . .
>
> The political "conservation" agenda of today, which theorizes that we must be regulated by government to protect ourselves from ourselves, is without any foundation or merit.
>
> We have a continuous fishing history on Eastern Long Island of at least three hundred years, with many years of scarcity of fishes and years of abundance. This very natural set of conditions, which are true rulers of our fisheries, will never change.[90]

The real issue, governmental jurisdiction over the bay, is something Vorpahl, an acknowledged expert on the Dongan Patent, confronted in the early 1990s when he was twice charged with fishing without a license. Both charges were dismissed because, according to Vorpahl, the court did not wish to tackle the question of bay ownership. The 1998 charge led to a trial in East Hampton but there was a hung jury. New York State then attempted to have the case moved to a different jurisdiction. In August 2001 Southampton was selected for a retrial. The following February all charges were dropped on a technicality but in the future baymen may once again face arrest. Should that occur, perhaps a jury will have the final say on the validity of the Dongan Patent. When that day comes, state regulations governing commercial fishing could be set aside but, in the meantime, the continued participation of people like Vorpahl in the economy of the Peconic Bay area is questionable because commercial fishermen see themselves as victims of the government. In their view, the federal quotas imposed under the Magnuson-Stevens Act of 1996, which was reauthorized in 2006, were unrealistically low. They simply did not reflect the rebound in certain fisheries.

To make the point, commercial fishermen from the East End, along with recreational anglers, joined fishermen from other parts of the United States at a rally outside the Capitol in Washington, D.C., in March 2010. Among the 5,000 protesters were Peconic Bay captains who fished commercially in the winter and ran party boats from spring through fall. These men were quick to point out to elected representatives that they were literally being driven out of business by quotas based upon outdated estimates of fish populations that had rebounded to sustainable levels. As one fisherman put it, no one was going to pay $100 for an excursion on a party boat if he was only allowed to take home two fish. In 2013 Senator Charles Schumer of New York, recognizing the outdated data sets used to determine the allowable catch for fluke by commercial and recreational fishermen in each state, proposed new legislation requiring the Atlantic States Marine Fisheries Commission and the Mid-Atlantic Fishery Management Council to establish identical size and number limits for neighboring states. This was implemented in 2014, but Peconic Bay party boat captains were dismayed to learn that the date selected for the opening of the fluke season was the one that had previously applied to the New England states. Since it was two weeks later than the traditional New York State date, the Peconic Bay captains feared that the fish would have migrated beyond the East End of Long Island by the time the season began.

A challenge of a different sort had confronted recreational fishermen a few years earlier, in 2010, when licenses were mandated by New York State for sport fishermen. Some of the state's recreational anglers bought the $10 licenses; others held off awaiting the outcome of a lawsuit filed by several East End towns against the New York State Department of Environmental Conservation on the grounds that the DEC lacked the authority to impose this requirement without the consent of the municipalities. The legal challenge was successful and the New York State legislature repealed the license requirement in 2011. Nevertheless, one can't help but wonder what lies ahead for recreational anglers, party boat captains, and commercial fishermen. To keep on doing what their ancestors had been doing, generation after generation, baymen may end up spending time not just on the water but in court. Although the charges were dismissed following a nonjury trial in the fall of 2011, a sister and brother from one of the oldest fishing families, the Lesters, required legal counsel to fight charges brought against them by the New York State Department of Environmental Conservation of violating legislation governing fishing and selling fish.

Despite the favorable outcome of the Lesters' trial, in the early years of the twenty-first century the dwindling number of baymen was testimony to the changing nature of work on the East End. Whenever a bayman ties up his boat for the last time, a piece of Long Island's proud maritime heritage disappears. Like the whales that were once numerous off the South Shore, the fraternity of baymen had many members a hundred years ago; but a century hence, or sooner, commercial fishermen may be as rare as whales in these waters. As the pace of development quickens on both sides of the Peconic Bay estuary system, and as tourism continues to expand, on both the North and South Forks, it is not inconceivable that the Stuart Vorpahls of the East

End will be driven off the water. Without intelligent management of the estuary's vast resources and rational planning for the contiguous upland areas, the East End may become a glorified theme park. Picture something like Disney's California adventure park, which debuted in 2001. Can't you just see salaried "baymen," whose costumes resemble the real thing, taking tourists out on the water for a little seining or crabbing? Instead of fast food in the East End theme park, there will be shoreside clambakes, preceded or followed by winery tours and visits to working farms staffed by guides in designer overalls.

To keep the tourists coming in the winter there could be courses in conversational Bonac, the centuries-old dialect of the baymen. Students will learn to end conversations with "Yes, yes, bub," the way real Bonackers do.[91] Visitors could also be treated to demonstrations of such cold-weather activities of yesteryear as fyke fishing and trapping of minks, muskrats, raccoons, fox, and possum, the very animals that constituted the source of off-season income for Stuart Vorpahl's father, who "used to have so many furs that they would bundle them up and . . . put them on the railroad and go into the city to a fur auction."[92] After listening to charming tales about the activities of the locals and sampling gourmet cider, hot chocolate, or cappuccino, tourists could head to the gift shop to purchase fleece sweatshirts sprinkled with cutesy little animals. It can't happen here! Is that what you're thinking? They said the same thing about fast food restaurants coming to Southold town, but after a protracted battle a Cape Cod–style McDonald's opened on Main Road in Mattituck in 1995. You just never know! The economy of the Peconic Bay area has been tourist-dependent for 150 years. During that century and a half, the last whaling vessels sailed off into history, farms have been gobbled up for development, and the baymen have become a vanishing species. No one can predict the future, but what has already transpired points the way to greater changes in the years to come. Welcome to Peconic Bay, U.S.A., part theme park and part living museum!

# 3

# At Play

## The Paint Box Brigade

In the early years of the twentieth century, spectators on both sides of Peconic Bay witnessed a most unusual sight: a scow pulled by the sailboat *Tortoise*, whose owner, American Impressionist artist Henry Prellwitz, had transformed it into a motorboat for a very special house-moving mission. The dwelling in question was an architectural gem Henry and his artist wife, Edith Mitchill Prellwitz, had spotted on the bay side of Main Road in Aquebogue one fine day in 1911 when they were motoring out from New York City. Built in 1814 by Joshua Livingston Wells and modeled on New York City townhouses of the period, the home towered over the typical farmhouses in the area and was dubbed "High House Josh" by its neighbors. This doesn't seem to have bothered homeowner Wells, a successful carriage, stagecoach, and agricultural equipment manufacturer.

As for the Prellwitzes, they found it positively charming. Enamored of the house, they snapped it up and then proceeded to have it completely dismantled and moved to their private garden spot in the North Fork hamlet of Peconic. Oak timbers, shingles, trim, foundation bricks, and any other materials that could be incorporated into the rebuilt house were placed in wagons and transported to Aquebogue Creek. From there the numbered pieces were towed to Peconic and reassembled "in a clearing" amid oak and cedar trees close to Peconic Bay.[1]

The Prellwitzes' historic new home was a replacement for a North Fork residence they had purchased in 1899 after leaving the Cornish,

New Hampshire, art colony where their tiny home had been struck by lightning. Happily ensconced in their "new" North Fork abode, Edith and Henry produced some lovely paintings reflecting the tranquility of the bay area. Henry, in particular, "devoted his later paintings to capturing the essence of the North Fork," according to art historian Ronald Pisano, who noted that "he was interested primarily in the different effects of light, weather and season."[2] Presumably Henry derived some inspiration for his paintings from jaunts he and Edith took on their tandem bike and also carefree days aboard the *Tortoise*.

When Edith wasn't out and about enjoying the local scenery, she was hard at work producing still lifes, portraits, and landscapes. Assessing her achievements, Ronald Pisano observed, "During her lifetime, her paintings were compared favorably to the work of leading American artists of the day," a group that included William Merritt Chase, a fellow resident of the Peconic Bay area, John Singer Sargent, and Mary Cassatt.[3]

Trained at the Art Students League and in Europe, the Prellwitzes, who died in the 1940s and are buried not far from Peconic Bay in the North Fork hamlet of Peconic, were largely forgotten for the next fifty years. In the 1980s exhibitions of their paintings at the Long Island Museum of American Art, History, and Carriages in Stony Brook and in Washington, D.C., revived interest in this talented couple and in the Peconic art colony that flourished on the North Fork in the late nineteenth and early twentieth centuries. Marine painter Edward Moran, who had a studio in Greenport, and two of his sons were members of the colony. Another member was Benjamin Rutherford Fitz, a descendant of an old Southold family, who was a pioneer and leader of the emerging North Fork artistic circle. Taking time out from his landscape and figure painting, Fitz, together with his brother, fashioned a sharpie called *Daphne*. Not long before his death, Fitz presented the boat to fellow artist Edward August Bell. The "staunch little yacht" was "used for the next several summers traveling about the local bays and inlets."[4]

Irving Ramsey Wiles, who like Bell and the Prellwitzes had honed his craft at the Art Students League, was induced by Bell, as had the

Prellwitzes, to head for the North Fork. In the summer of 1895 Wiles conducted art classes in the 1815 Overton homestead on the corner of Route 48 and Peconic Lane in Peconic. A few years later he set down permanent roots in the community. Building a home called "the Moorings"—"most likely after the fact that he moored his boat, *The Flapper*, there [on Indian Neck Lane in Peconic]"—he enjoyed "the fishing and boating activities on Peconic Bay and nearby waters."[5] Wiles's final resting place, not far from his beloved home, had been an unmarked grave until 2013 when Geoffrey Fleming, director of the Southold Historical Society, personally funded the design and erection of a headstone to mark the burial site of Irving Ramsey Wiles, his wife, and his daughter, Daphne, who was also an accomplished artist.

Like an artist of a later generation, William Steeple Davis, who spent practically all of his seventy-seven years, until his death in 1961, in his native hamlet of Orient depicting sailing vessels, Wiles positively adored sailing. This passion, plus exposure to Edward August Bell's tales of countless happy hours on Peconic Bay, may explain why Wiles agreed to conduct art classes in Peconic.

During the summer of 1895 Wiles and his fifteen or so students journeyed to the south side of the bay once a week to the studio of William Merritt Chase for his artistic critique. The renowned Chase, with whom both Wiles and Edward Bell had studied at the Art Students League, had been conducting summer art classes at Shinnecock Hills since 1891. The idea for a summer art school in Southampton seems to have originated with Mrs. William Hoyt, a summer resident and artist. Mrs. Hoyt acquired the property for Art Village, composed of a studio and housing for students. She was helped by wealthy friends, including Samuel L. Parrish, who would, in time, establish the art museum that became a cultural focal point of the growing summer colony and would remain so until 2012, when it moved into a spacious new building in Water Mill. William Merritt Chase and his family resided a few miles away in a hilltop home designed by noted architect Stanford White. "The number of children subsequently increased to eight and it is related that Chase hoisted a signal on a staff whenever a child was born. The emblem was a red Japanese paper fish with its mouth open to catch the wind and float out like a kite."[6] When Hazel, his fourth daughter, was born, the little girl "said to be the first white child born on Shinnecock Hills, was given the name 'Neamug,' meaning 'Between the two waters'; this was the Indian name for the Shinnecock Canal and was also descriptive of Chase's home situated between the Peconic and Shinnecock Bays."[7] The landscape paintings Chase did while residing on the East End feature the surrounding waterways, countryside, and his own children. These timeless works of art enhanced his reputation as an American Impressionist.

Another artist who captured South Fork scenes in the late nineteenth century, English-born Thomas Moran, was already famous for his gigantic painting *The Grand Canyon of the Yellowstone* when he brought his three children and his Scottish wife, artist Mary Nimmo Moran, known for her etchings, to East Hampton in 1878. The Morans built a home they called "the Studio" on Main Street across from Town Pond. In addition to the house, there were various outbuildings, including a bathhouse, which the Morans stored on their property during the winter and transported to the beach for the summer. A 2010 report analyzing the auxiliary structures on the property noted that the pine bathhouse, with its two changing rooms, was the only known intact building of its type and period in East Hampton. The restoration of the bathhouse was completed in 2012 but the considerably more challenging job of restoring the Studio, which will be open to the public for tours and serve as a venue for cultural events, was ongoing two years later.

When he wasn't accompanying his family to the beach, Moran was painting East Hampton's windmills and other local scenes. Whether East End artworks or later depictions of Venice, Moran's paintings were "full of sunlight . . . the Long Island paintings" having "the moist light typical of this area, tempered with tree shadows."[8] Thomas Moran helped popularize the Hamptons as did members of the Tile Club, a group of New York artists who amused one another by painting small pictures on tiles during their informal weekly gatherings in the city. Tilers, whose warm weather travels were chronicled in *Scribner's Monthly*, spent several summers capturing the beauty of East

Hampton on canvas. The Tile Club descended upon East Hampton beginning in 1878, the year Moran arrived. Four years earlier Winslow Homer had produced East Hampton scenes for *Harper's Weekly*. In the 1890s American Impressionist Childe Hassam carried on the tradition of popularizing the Hamptons.

Artists continued to flock to the area right through the twentieth century. In the aftermath of World War II, The Springs, a charming northern district of East Hampton, along the shore of Gardiner's Bay and Accabonac Creek, became a mecca for such masters of modern art as Jackson Pollock and Lee Krasner. Influenced by these artists, many other people seeking beauty and tranquility beat a path to the South Fork. In her article "Back to Nature: The Tile Club in the Country," Connie Koppelman observed:

> By 1873 there were eight boarding houses and one hotel on the main road into East Hampton. Local residents, at first reluctant to allow any change in their lifestyle, considered boarders peripheral to the economy of the village. . . . Gradually, the more conservative residents perceived the economic benefit that could accrue to individuals and to the town if the resort idea were further promoted. . . . By the 1890s the summer people had begun to exert an influence on the development of the town. The new vacation industry blossomed with a concomitant need for architects, builders, carpenters, stores, and services of every description. The vacation business became the principal occupation of the village.[9]

## Getting There

It's hard to imagine the emergence of tourism as a major component of the economy without the nineteenth-century artists who put the area on the map. Yet, the canvas- and paint-box-toting visitors of the late 1800s were not solely responsible for this development. It was, after all, one thing to paint a pretty picture of a rural landscape and quite another for people to enjoy the real thing. For that, good transportation was needed. To a certain extent, even before artists made the East End famous, there was a decent system of waterborne transport. Sailing vessels and steamboats linked the East End with New York City and New England, and on Peconic Bay commercial boats plied between the North and South Forks on a regular basis. As early as 1823 there was weekly service, on Saturdays between Sag Harbor and Southold. A vessel departed from Southold at 7 a.m. and returned from Sag Harbor at 4 p.m. with newspapers, letters, and packages. Six years later, the packet boat *Dandy* made two weekly trips between Sag Harbor and Southold and was available for special charters.

In the early 1830s the packet *Dread* linked Southold and Sag Harbor on Wednesdays and Saturdays. By 1833 a new packet boat named, believe it or not, *Electricity* departed from Southold for Greenport and Sag Harbor on Tuesdays and Thursdays. On Wednesdays and Saturdays the boat sailed to Sag Harbor from Town Harbor, Southold, and returned the same day. The following year the new packet boat *Eclipse* had a similar schedule. In 1837 the *Cinderella* was making three trips per week between Sag Harbor and Greenport. James' Port Steamboat Company was also founded in 1837. In 1838 a large advertisement in the Sag Harbor *Corrector* announced the debut of the steamboat *Olive Branch*, which would "ply between Jamesport, Sag-Harbor and Greenport, for the accommodation of the inhabitants on both sides of the Bay, affording facilities for traveling at a moderate rate, in a direction where they have hitherto been both infrequent and uncertain."[10] Following trial runs across the bay, a few alterations were required to increase the vessel's speed "as to perform 50 miles in six hours (the average distance . . . each day)."[11]

By the mid-nineteenth century, as tourism became a factor in the economy of the bay area, the steamer *Statesman*, plying between Sag Harbor and Greenport, advertised "excursions for families on Wednesdays and Saturdays, through July and August."[12] The *Statesman* also offered a fare of $2.25 "from Sag Harbor to Brooklyn."[13] No, the jaunty little steamboat was not venturing out of the Peconic Bay estuary and traveling nearly a hundred miles to the other end of Long Island! Rather, the *Statesman* was meeting the train at Greenport and transporting vacationers across the bay. The steamboat even made an extra trip on Saturday to meet the 4 p.m. train from Brooklyn. The train was, of course, the Long Island Rail Road, which had reached Greenport in 1844.

The brainchild of Brooklyn businessmen who envisioned their new line, built though the flat center of the island, as a shortcut to Boston, the Long Island Rail Road (LIRR) was intended to be a major regional carrier. The swift five-hour rail journey to Greenport, combined with a steamboat trip across the Sound from the Greenport wharf to connect with an existing rail line from Stonington, Connecticut, to Boston, added up to a total of 11.5 hours, on average. This was quicker by far than the steamboat journey through Long Island Sound and around Point Judith, Rhode Island, where the currents almost guaranteed a bout of mal de mer. The trouble was that the backers of the Long Island Rail Road—the men who celebrated the line's opening on July 27, 1844, by toasting their success with multiple cases of champagne and a half case of brandy during a gala affair at the Greenport depot—failed to take the competition seriously.

Although they knew, full well, that from an engineering standpoint it was feasible to bridge the rivers flowing into Long Island Sound through Connecticut, thereby permitting the construction of a rail line along the mainland shore, they figured it would be decades before this would happen and in the meantime they would realize a handsome return on their investment. In a sense they were right. Considerable time would pass before a railroad paralleled the coast all the way to Boston, but in 1848 the New York, New Haven and Hartford Railroad completed a line from New York to New Haven. Since an inland line from New Haven to Boston, by way of Hartford and Springfield, Massachusetts, was already in place, travelers could now reach Boston without enduring the LIRR's steamboat trip between Greenport and Stonington, a voyage that was not too appealing in winter.

Following bankruptcy in the mid-nineteenth century, the Long Island Rail Road was reorganized. By the 1870s, having absorbed shorter lines running along the South Shore and up to Sag Harbor, the railroad's Montauk Division offered direct service to Hampton Bays, Southampton, Water Mill, Bridgehampton, and Sag Harbor. One delighted traveler was very pleased with the new timetable that took effect in June 1879. "Quicker trips and more trains will mark the conveniences offered for travel to the East End," he said, adding:

> The company have wisely retained the able and experienced conductors so familiar to those who go down to Greenport, or the Harbor. In the morning you find the veteran Ryan at his post, and in the afternoon, the energetic Hobson sees that you get through on time and in safety; while on the Sag Harbor branch the good looking Sweezy takes good care of his passengers.[14]

More than a century later some East Enders who made frequent trips from New York to the Hamptons felt the same way about their favorite drivers on the Hampton Jitney, the Hampton Express, the Hampton Ambassador, and the Hampton Luxury Liner. For decades the Sunrise Express offered similar service between the North Fork and New York City. When Sunrise was acquired by the Hampton Jitney in 2006, Dan Rattiner, editor of *Dan's Papers*, dubbed the North Fork "a Hamptons in training." Residents of the North Fork shuddered and hoped Dan was wrong, but the influx of new people over the course of the next few years proved otherwise. Although welcomed by many, the opening of a Bookhampton bookstore in the heart of Mattituck in 2012 was viewed by some as further evidence of the changes occurring on the North Fork. In spite of or, in some instances, because of these changes, people seeking second homes flocked to the North Fork because of its beauty, relative affordability, and proximity to New York City and its suburbs. Getting there might not have been half the fun on a Friday night in summer but even the detested Long Island Expressway, sometimes called the "big LIE" or "the world's longest parking lot," was more bearable thanks to the opening of the first stretch of the High Occupancy Vehicle (HOV) lane on the expressway in the mid-1990s. One hundred years earlier the extension of the railroad to East Hampton, Amagansett, and

Montauk had accomplished something similar in terms of speed and comfort for vacation-bound travelers.

For some tourists, however, getting there by boat rather than by rail was part of the vacation experience. It was slower but, in the days before air-conditioned railway cars, a journey by sea was sometimes preferable to endless hours on a hot train. As early as the 1830s New Yorkers could reach the South Fork by boat via New London, Connecticut. By this time, the cross-Sound connection between the East End and Connecticut was well established. In 1825 the packet sloop *Bee* was making three trips each week between Sag Harbor and New London. In 1831 the packet *Argonaut* linked Sag Harbor and New London "every day, wind and weather permitting."[15] An early advertisement for the boat touted its "elegant accommodations" and noted that "private sailing parties can be accommodated separately if desired."[16] In 1837 both the *Bee* and *Argonaut* crossed the Sound daily with one boat leaving New London at 8 a.m. and the other departing from Sag Harbor at the same time. Three years earlier the *Maria* linked Sag Harbor with Norwich, Saybrook, and New London.

One of the *Maria*'s competitors, the steamboat *General Jackson*, advertised a special fare of $3 for passengers from Sag Harbor to New York via New London in 1833. In 1837 the "new and elegant steamboat *Clifton*" charged $2 for the trip to New York.[17] This vessel departed from Sag Harbor three mornings per week, depositing its New York–bound passengers at Saybrook, where they boarded the *Cleopatra* for the remainder of their journey. During the 1838 summer season the steamboat *Clifton* departed from Sag Harbor three afternoons per week at 3 p.m., "intersecting the Steamboat *Bunker-Hill* at Lyme, which will arrive at New York early the next morning."[18] In 1853 the "new, fast and splendid steamer *Island Belle*" collected passengers at Sag Harbor and Greenport, taking them to Saybrook to connect with the New York–bound "Steam Palaces" *City of Hartford* and *Granite State*.[19]

On the eve of the Civil War the *Massachusetts* provided service to New York from Sag Harbor, Greenport, and Orient as did the

*Cataline*, which advertised that "new staterooms have been added, and many alterations made to insure comfort and safety."[20] Another ad for this boat noted that "should the weather prove too stormy to leave Sag Harbor on Mondays and Thursdays, she will leave (weather permitting) on Tuesdays and Fridays next succeeding her regular days"; in 1863 the "new and spacious steamer *Sunshine*" linked Sag Harbor and Greenport with New London and Hartford.[21]

Following the Civil War the *Artisan* made stops in Sag Harbor, Orient, Greenport, New Suffolk, and New York. The boat's captain was George C. Gibbs, whose fledgling steamship enterprise was financed by capital from Greenport and Sag Harbor businessmen. No sooner had Gibbs embarked upon his new venture than a group of mostly Greenport men financed a rival company that soon began running the *Edward Everett*. Yet another player entered the competition in the early 1870s when the Atlantic Mail Steamship Company, which ran vessels between New York and Bermuda, began offering service to the East End. The source of funding for the new operation may have been the Long Island Rail Road, which was understandably eager to run the homegrown East End steamboat lines out of business. The bankruptcy of Atlantic Mail during the panic of 1873 was followed by the creation of the Montauk and New York Steamboat Company, with George Gibbs as captain of the *W. W. Coit*. The Long Island Rail Road soon began running a chartered steamer to the East End in a futile attempt to drive the new company out of business. The end result was that the Gibbs operation had a grand new steamboat, the *Shelter Island*, built to its specifications. This totally state-of-the-art iron-hulled ship went into service in 1886, the year that the Montauk and New York Steamboat Company became the Montauk Steamboat Company. Captain Gibbs served as CEO of the company until his retirement eight years later. During his tenure the *Montauk*, identical in almost every respect to the *Shelter Island*, was placed in service. In 1896 the well-appointed steel-hulled *Shinnecock* made its inaugural voyage. At 238 feet the vessel was considerably larger than either the *Shelter Island* or the *Montauk*, which were both 185 feet according to the company's 1898 brochure.

This beautifully illustrated booklet described the various landing places on the East End, starting with the Orient harbor wharf in a community characterized as "cool and delightful."[22] Shelter Island's Manhanset House Hotel was the second stop; Greenport came next. Then, like Shelter Island's North Ferry, *Niantic*, which in the 1890s linked Greenport with both Manhanset and Shelter Island Heights, or the steamer *Endeavor* employed on an Orient/Manhanset House/ Shelter Island Heights/Greenport route in the nineties, the Montauk Steamboat Company's boats crossed to Shelter Island again. The vessels stopped at the Heights and from there crossed the bay to South-old, "a pleasant old fishing village" that attracted numerous visitors.[23] After leaving Southold the boats headed for their last East End stop at Sag Harbor, "whence readiest access is had" to the "fashionable" Hamptons.[24]

It wasn't only the destinations that were fashionable. The boats themselves were very elegant. The *Montauk* featured mostly outside staterooms "assuring perfect ventilation and fine outlook" while the *Shinnecock* had "a superb dining saloon . . . with seatings for more than 100 guests at once."[25] Following dinner the dining saloon became a smoking room and café, but travelers were assured that "none of the smoke can possibly penetrate" to other parts of the vessel.[26] On the main deck there was a "commodious and elegantly furnished ladies' cabin" and throughout the boat one found electric lights and bells.[27] Moreover, everything was designed "to assure the utmost comfort, safety and luxury."[28] The beautiful appointments of its vessels might have been sufficient reason for another company to buy out the Montauk line. But in 1899, when the Long Island Rail Road purchased the Montauk Steamboat Company, what it had in mind was creation of a monopoly rather than continuing to run majestic steamboats. The railroad remained in the steamboat business only until 1915. By then competition from automobiles and from its own vastly improved rail service resulting from the completion, in 1910, of an East River tunnel, which permitted LIRR trains to run directly into Manhattan, had made the Montauk Steamboat Company a drain on the railroad's resources or so the railroad claimed.

## Camp Meetings: Preaching, Praying, and Playing

The demise of the Montauk Steamboat Company occurred at the end of an era that had witnessed the first wave of tourism on the East End. Enhanced transportation, along with the popularization of the region by nineteenth-century artists, enabled countless numbers of people to discover the area's charms. But there was another factor that helped light the spark of tourism: religious revivals, known as camp meetings. Going back to the 1830s the steamboat *Clifton* advertised that it would "leave Norwich . . . and New-London . . . via. Lyme, leaving there on the arrival of the *Bunker-Hill* from New York, and the *Cleopatra* from Hartford, and touching at Saybrook, Oysterpond Point, Greenport and Sag-Harbor, and will arrive at the Camp Ground, between 6 and 7 o'clock next morning."[29] The *Clifton*'s destination was Jamesport. It was there that the boat disgorged a throng of newcomers, some of whom would become so enamored of the area that they would return again and again.

Residents of the sleepy North Fork may have shaken their heads incredulously as they viewed the masses disembarking but, along with these "invaders," many locals attended the camp meetings. Historically, the inhabitants of this area were an extremely observant people. From the time the first settlers arrived in the 1600s, religion played an important role in the lives of North Fork natives. Despite the consolidation of some congregations and the repurposing of houses of worship in the early twenty-first century, even today, on any given Sunday morning, houses of worship, including Roman Catholic churches established by Polish and Irish immigrants of the nineteenth century, are often filled. Standing room only is not uncommon in summer as is gridlock on Main Road, where most of the churches are located, from East Marion through Aquebogue. For some curious reason, year-round Sunday morning traffic jams in the parking lots of churches are replicated, immediately after services, in the lots of the area's handful of supermarkets. Some shoppers pick up the Sunday paper while others, presumably those who peruse newspapers online, purchase a few items forgotten on previous visits earlier in the week. Then they hurry home to change their clothes, in most instances replacing their Sunday best with something more comfortable.

Aside from tourists and second homeowners, who think nothing of showing up for church in casual attire, local people dress up on Sunday and they exhibit respect and reverence in other ways as well. Crosses, for example, are an extremely popular article of jewelry. This religious symbol has even been replicated by the Candyman shop in Orient as part of its Easter merchandise. The fact notwithstanding that the Candyman purveys some of the finest chocolate available anywhere, some visitors to the shop may find it a little disconcerting to see a sacred religious symbol alongside the ubiquitous chocolate bunnies and ducks, but one can just imagine what attendees at camp meetings in the 1800s would have thought.

The first of these gatherings took place in Jamesport in September 1835. In attendance were people from Connecticut, the Hamptons, and every hamlet on the North Fork. Methodist societies from these places supplied prayer tents, which were set up by volunteers. Other volunteers secured provisions for the weeklong gathering and coordinated transportation. In addition to the large steamboat ferrying the devout from Connecticut, "many sail vessels of various sizes were plying between Jamesport and the other landings on Peconic Bay."[30] After renting the site of the camp meeting for several years, the Methodists purchased property in South Jamesport and built a church in the new campground. Financial problems led to the sale of most of the property but not the church. "After that three camp-meetings were held at Sag Harbor; three were held in Wiggins Grove, Greenport, one or two at Southold, and then another at Greenport."[31] In 1862 a leafy grove in Southold's South Harbor area was chosen as the site of the camp meeting. Six years later it was Greenport's turn. Southold farmer and fisherman Gilder Conklin noted in his diary that he traveled by train to the Greenport gathering. Others arrived by boat.

In the 1870s the meetings were again held in their original location after the Methodist churches of Suffolk County "conceived the idea of buying back the old Jamesport campground."[32] Following the 1870 gathering, the Sag Harbor *Corrector* observed: "The Long

Island District Camp Meeting for N.Y. East Conference, has just closed its session, upon Peconic Bay. And no better spot for such a purpose could be found."[33] People came from as far away as New York City and Brooklyn, then a separate municipality. One Brooklynite was delighted with his trip to Greenport on the steamer *Eastern City*. For him it was "an escape from the city's gridiron of roasting days."[34] The meeting itself was "very precious. Able preaching; crowded prayer meetings; sterling exhortations; no extravagance; the best of order and no police."[35] The Brooklyn gentleman was so pleased with the meeting that he urged people to "go to Jamesport another year, if real good is the object, social, spiritual or sanitary. Go to break from the 'ruts'—to bathe in pelucid Peconic Bay—to sail row or fish upon its waters."[36] He also pointed out that cottage lots were selling rapidly at $25 each. Initially, however, many people who attended the meetings dwelled in tents but those who built cottages tended to spend considerably more time in Jamesport, both before and after the annual camp meetings.

A number of cottagers were Brooklynites lured by their ministers to the shores of Peconic Bay for the summer. Ruth Marsland Demarest, who spent childhood summers in Jamesport, revealed that her parents learned of the campgrounds through their minister. "We were anxious to find a nice place where there would be congenial people, to spend the summer," she said, adding that the minister "said that Jamesport had no mosquitoes, had a beautiful bay to swim in with no jelly fish, and in fact it was paradise!"[37] Frequent rain, general dampness, and mold galore marred the family's first summer in Jamesport in 1907 to the point that they packed up early and went back to Brooklyn; but after investigating other vacation possibilities, they returned to the campgrounds the following year, bought a lot for $50, had a $350 cottage erected, and lived happily ever after there during the summer. In 2010 a similar cottage, erected in 1900 and completely restored and updated, with a new kitchen, central air conditioning, and 1,250 square feet of living space on two floors, was on the market for $440,000. With only two bedrooms, one up and one down, and one bath, accommodating overnight guests posed a challenge. In the early twentieth century, if a cottage became too crowded, overflow guests stayed at the dormitory built by the Epworth League, which, together with other Methodist groups, operated Fresh Air vacation homes for city children. Two of the homes were located on Peconic Bay Boulevard. The homes continued functioning until the 1950s "when the land was sold and the buildings torn down."[38] Private homes and a marina "were built on former Methodist land between the Camp Grounds and the bay."[39]

Early in the century, when the camp meetings flourished from mid-June until the end of September, residents and visitors alike enjoyed an array of sports including tennis, baseball, croquet, and "the moonlight sails . . . on the beautiful bay."[40] For one week each year, however, leisure pursuits were abandoned as thousands of people descended upon the campgrounds located "on the highest ground in Jamesport and, consequently swept by the Atlantic and Peconic Bay breezes" for the annual camp meeting.[41] Devout Methodists, people seeking meaning, and the merely curious gathered in the beautiful oak grove whose trees were mowed down by the hurricane of 1938. Ministers from near and far preached and conducted prayer meetings. In 1878 a prizefighter turned preacher, Howell "Horrible" Gardiner, "the first who in the history of this country has stepped from the prize ring into the church . . . gave a stirring exhortation."[42] Following sermons of this type, it was not unusual for hundreds of people to come forward to affirm their conversion.

## Shelter Island: From Praying to Playing

Shelter Island camp meetings, which began in 1872, also featured outstanding preaching. Methodist ministers from Brooklyn, New York City, Long Island, and New England addressed not only fellow Methodists but members of other Protestant denominations who attended the August gatherings. For the most part, the preachers were eloquent and their delivery was traditional but in 1876 a former Sing Sing inmate and Irish immigrant, the Reverend Jeremiah McCauley, livened things up. In all truth, revivalist-style preaching was not needed to pack in the crowds, for as early as 1873, only the second year of the Shelter Island meetings, throngs arrived from points west and north for the ten-day gathering. Methodists from Connecticut and Massachusetts, who had previously gone to the Martha's Vineyard camp meeting "so well and favorably known," found it more convenient to board steamboats for Shelter Island.[43] Some Brooklynites were invited to Shelter Island by their ministers.

One Brooklyn couple headed to Shelter Island after receiving a letter from their pastor, who described the island as "an Eden" and declared that if he lived another thousand years, he "would be willing to spend them all here."[44] Since many of her friends were vacationing in Europe, something her husband had rejected as too costly, the woman was not initially thrilled about visiting a place barely two hours away, but once there she loved the scenery and was intrigued by the idea of building a ten-room cottage for under $2,000. Cottages and other improvements were part of the ambitious plans of the Shelter Island Grove and Camp-meeting Association, which, in 1872, purchased three hundred acres. Naming the place Prospect Grove, the association set out to improve the property "with both a religious and a worldly object in view."[45] The Brooklyn Methodists who purchased the land wanted to create a camp meeting similar to the one on Martha's Vineyard and lease or sell property and cottages to "respectable families desiring to spend the summer in a pleasant country not too far from New York."[46]

Among the attractions of Shelter Island were "the views . . . of the winding shores of the innumerable little bays and inlets made by the irregular shape of the island."[47] Thanks to an agreement the Methodists reached with the town, the unsightly and odoriferous menhaden processing plants in the vicinity had been removed. With this obstacle out of the way the Methodists felt confident about improving their property. Just a few months prior to the 1873 meeting, the association had begun construction of a hotel, the Prospect House. Designed to accommodate 150 guests, the Prospect, which lacked a bar and billiard room, was "an anomaly among Summer hotels."[48] Before long a billiard room and bowling alley were added despite the objections of some visitors, but guests desiring liquid refreshments stronger than lemonade had to go across the bay to Greenport.

Temperance would not triumph on Shelter Island forever, nor would the Methodists. The camp meetings ceased and, while the Prospect Chapel continued to flourish as the Union Chapel in the Grove, the camp meeting association was succeeded by the Shelter Island Heights Association. All the while the Prospect House continued to flourish. The hotel's beautifully illustrated brochure for the 1898 season touted not only its own assets but those of the island itself, pointing out:

> Shelter Island is attractive from its very unlikeness to every other haunt by the sea. Instead of low, flat, weary wastes running back from the shore, it presents in many places a long curving strip of white, pebbled beach bordered by cozy cottages, or by rows of bathing pavilions, backed and shielded by bluffs rising hundreds of feet in height, topped with shrubbery and forest trees, wild as the most devout lover of nature could desire—yet held so firmly in hand that every nook is a bower of beauty, and every outlook a new picture.[49]

The brochure also stressed the fact that Shelter Island was a very healthy place, noting:

> Government medical statistics class it as one of the most healthful townships in the United States, not a single death having occurred amongst summer visitors, from diseases contracted upon the island, during its twenty years' history as a Summer Resort. The Heights, which include the boat landings, have an abundant supply of soft, pure water, and a perfect system of sewerage, every house in the place being connected with the same.[50]

In keeping with its emphasis on health, the Prospect House offered hot medicinal saltwater baths "in a large handsome pavilion at the foot of the lawn."[51] Guests were also assured that the hotel, which had been expanded to accommodate three hundred people, had "perfect sanitary appointments."[52] As if this weren't enough to lure prospective visitors, there were cool, newly furnished guest rooms, each with its own bath.

The Prospect House Annex, connected by awnings to the main building, was described as "a favorite abode of those who desire quiet and seclusion rather than the bustle and merriment of a large company of pleasure-seekers."[53] Of course, if Annex guests became bored it was only a short stroll to the "fine large ballroom with polished hardwood floor" and the "luxurious parlors."[54] Guests wishing to venture beyond the hotel grounds could rent horses and carriages. With the dawn of the automobile age, the New Prospect Hotel still offered horseback riding but its advertising paid more attention to nautical activities, pointing out: "Sail and motor boats are rented for short or season periods at moderate rates. Gardiner's Bay, Peconic Bay, Southold Bay, Shelter Island Sound and Noyac Bay are all adjacent and from the New Prospect their waters afford a panoramic view of rare charm."[55] Pleasant excursions from the New Prospect ended abruptly at the beginning of the 1942 season when fire destroyed the place. Twenty years earlier, in August 1922, when the resort was operating under the name Poggatticut Hotel, there had been another blaze, which left the building standing but severely damaged by the tons of water used to fight the fire.

Shelter Island's other grand hotel, the Manhanset, also experienced untimely fires. In comparison with the Prospect House of the nineteenth century, the Manhanset was pricier and widely regarded as more elegant or perhaps stuffier and less fun. No matter, the Manhanset, complete with a chapel, which was an afterthought intended to attract the devout who otherwise might have opted for the Prospect House, was a huge success right from the get-go. Built in 1874 by Boston investors who acquired 200 acres on Locust Point, bordered on one side by Greenport Harbor and on the other by Dering Harbor, the hotel accommodated 350 guests. Those desiring ultimate privacy could stay in a cottage on the grounds. "Suites of rooms for families" were available in the hotel's annex.[56] The Manhanset's brochure for the 1891 season, which ran from June 25 to September 15, described the "hotel proper" as a "model of architectural beauty," adding: "It contains many large, handsomely furnished, light . . . perfectly ventilated rooms from which are had charming views of marine and rural loveliness."[57]

The hotel's 1896 brochure mentioned the availability of steam heat to take off the chill on damp days and it assured prospective guests that the sanitary facilities and drinking water were excellent. All of this was very reassuring to people who were considering bringing their families to the Manhanset, which, from a marketing standpoint, positioned itself as an upscale family resort. One wonders how child-friendly the hotel was, however, because in the 1896 brochure the management noted: "The 'Manhanset' may justly be styled a paradise for children, yet the spaces are so extensive and alluring as to give promise that the hotel will not be made—as it is complained some hotels are—the other thing for their seniors."[58]

The behavior of young guests at the Manhanset was just about the last thing on anyone's mind on August 13, 1896, when fire broke out at the hotel. Ironically the Manhanset's 1896 brochure claimed that "precautions against fire are extraordinarily complete and extensive."[59] Despite the availability of steam pumps, abundant water, and hoses, the fire, which originated shortly before 8 a.m. in the hotel's laundry, where large stoves overheated "the thin wood partition which ran across the laundry," spread at breathtaking speed."[60] Fanned by a breeze, the flames leapt from the laundry facility to the hotel itself. The huge kitchen was almost immediately engulfed in flames and unfortunately the pump kept on hand for exactly this sort of problem was stored beneath the kitchen and could not be accessed.

Realizing they lacked the ability to fight the fire, the hotel management summoned help from Greenport by firing a cannon. Within minutes Greenport firefighters and their equipment were transported across the bay. Some of the Greenport men had a narrow escape when a chimney crashed through a roof where they had been fighting the flames only seconds before. Observers, who had gathered to watch the fire, sensed what was about to happen and shouted to the firefighters to come down. Other bystanders made their yachts available.

"The steam yacht *Freelance*, owned by Frederick A. Schermerhorn did good work in fighting the fire," the *New York Times* noted.[61] "It tied up to the pier and the powerful pumps threw two heavy streams on the flames."[62] Despite the valiant efforts of many people, including the Manhanset's own fire brigade, which had attempted to contain the blaze at the outset, the fire raged through the afternoon, destroying the oldest section of the complex and rendering the still-standing annex uninhabitable. Incredibly, in the fall of 1896 live coals were still found beneath the debris of the once-glamorous Manhanset.

Undaunted, the hotel's owners started rebuilding and by the summer of 1897 an even bigger Manhanset, accommodating 600 guests in the main building, annex, and cottages, opened. A letter preserved in the archives of the Shelter Island Historical Society reveals that a vacation at the new Manhanset was not inexpensive. For a Georgia family of three adults, three children, and one maid, the grand total was nearly $500 per week for "all good rooms in good locations."[63] A decade after the new Manhanset opened, the financial panic of 1907 presaged the beginning of the end for the hotel. The Manhanset Improvement Corporation filed for bankruptcy and a new manager took over but, before the place could be turned around, another tragic fire broke out.

Occurring as it did at the start of the 1910 season, this conflagration was the Manhanset's death knell. Perhaps symbolic of the end of an era in the bay area was the toppling of the Manhanset's great tower, which cascaded down the bluff and plunged into the water. A young eyewitness described watching the hotel burn, "all night long, until the big tower fell out into the bay with a great big crash and a hiss."[64] In the aftermath of the fire, what was left of the resort was sold at auction. The bank that acquired the property then transferred it to a corporation established by occupants of the Manhanset's cottages. The new entity erected a clubhouse containing dining facilities, lounges, and a game room. In time, the former Manhanset Club became a private residence. The clubhouse and the hotel cottages formed the nucleus of the Village of Dering Harbor, the state's tiniest incorporated village.

## Hotels Great and Small: Riverhead and the North Fork

More enduring than the grand resorts on Shelter Island were some of the smaller hotels on both sides of Peconic Bay. Among them was the Hallock House in Flanders, a Peconic Bay community described by the *Brooklyn Daily Eagle* as "a pretty and healthy little resort."[65] In Jamesport, another hamlet in the Town of Riverhead, the Riverside House, the Sunnyside House, the Bay Side Hotel (later known as the Bayview), the Great Peconic Bay House, and the Miamogue Hotel welcomed weary visitors from the city. The original Miamogue dated from the 1830s. Its successor, which was destroyed by fire a century later, could accommodate 125 guests. An advertisement for the "new and handsomely appointed house . . . situated in the beautiful village of South Jamesport, within a few feet of Peconic Bay," enumerated the hotel's amenities, noting:

> Every comfort desired in a country home is supplied here—meals, the best, rooms commodious, and newly furnished throughout. Hot and cold water are supplied throughout the house. Bath rooms and electric bells are among Miamogue's equipments, and a gas plant situated upon the premises furnishes modern lighting facilities that cannot be surpassed. A perfect system of drainage insures against disease, and the toilet accommodations in every respect are equal to those of any metropolitan hotel.[66]

And if all of this were not enough to lure visitors, the ad pointed out that the "climate is free from malaria and healthful in every respect, and the refreshing breeze from the bay produces an equable temperature that is at once a surprise and delight to visitors."[67]

By the early 1890s Jamesport was such a hot destination that the hotels and boarding houses were turning people away. A tourism promotion booklet published by the Long Island Rail Road in 1893 acknowledged the demand for accommodations in Jamesport and concluded: "The popularity of the place is easily understood. It stands at the head of Peconic Bay. . . . The boating in Peconic Bay is regarded . . . as even superior to that in the Great South Bay. . . . There is much life and gaiety at Jamesport and those who go there once are apt to become permanent visitors."[68]

With the competition for accommodations in Jamesport, it was only natural that nearby communities would reap the benefit of overflow guests. A Long Island Rail Road tourism booklet of 1897 described one such place, the "modest village of Mattituck, with its charming water vistas, its good taverns and . . . sound old farm houses . . . another comfortable place that is in present favor, and increasing in popularity all the time."[69] Although many tourists found the Mattituck House, the Fairyland House, the Shady Point House, as well as the community's handful of boarding houses perfectly fine, the truly discriminating visitor to the North Fork preferred a long peninsula extending into the bay from Cutchogue.

Known as Nassau Point, this spit of land was slated for resort development, as Peconic Park, in the 1880s. An elaborate brochure depicting a grand turreted hotel was produced and rather than linking the proposed development with the North Fork, to which Nassau Point is geographically attached, the publication noted that East Hampton was "but twelve miles from Peconic Park."[70] The booklet speculated about the possibility of direct boat service between Canoe Place on the South Fork and Peconic Park. Instead of taking the train to Peconic, visitors might avoid the North Fork altogether by traveling to Canoe Place on the southside rail line and boarding a small steamer to Peconic Park. Once there they could enjoy "some of the prettiest and most perfect inland sailing that can be had anywhere in this country."[71] According to the brochure, the bay bottom was "clean sand and pebble and the water . . . so clear that unless it be too much ruffled on the surface, one can look down through it and see the bed at two or three fathoms deep."[72] As for the climate, it was "equable and the season is long. The distribution of land and water is said to resemble that of the Bahamas."[73]

Its elaborate brochure notwithstanding, the Peconic Park project was stillborn. Several decades would pass before Nassau Point was developed and when it was, private homes rather than a large resort dominated the peninsula formerly known as Little Hog Neck. In the early twentieth century a baronial home, built in the nineteenth century by an English family named Wilson, was transformed into a hotel and club but the mansion was reduced to smoldering ruins by a 1928 fire. A decade earlier Brooklyn investors had acquired Nassau Point and over time, beginning in the twenties, spacious country homes were built on the peninsula.

For those who could not aspire to home ownership on Nassau Point, there were at least affordable hotels where one could have an economical summer vacation. MacNish's Hotel in New Suffolk was just such a place. An early ad for this establishment noted that "the village of New Suffolk is beautifully situated on a rising ground, commanding an extensive view of Peconic Bay and the adjacent villages."[74] The Southold Hotel, which was replaced in the 1920s by the Southold Savings Bank building, had an intown location but guests were transported less than a mile to swim in the bay at Founders Landing. Opened in the 1830s the hotel was updated in the 1870s with the addition of new parlors, a kitchen, and elaborate chandeliers. The Eagle House, a five-minute walk to Peconic Bay, began welcoming guests in 1860 and by the 1890s the Paumonok Inn was accommodating visitors to Southold.

Farther east on the North Fork, Greenport was a popular destination. In the 1870s its Peconic and Wyandank Houses, "situated on the Peconic Bay," advertised that "families stopping at these Houses enjoy all the quietude of private life, together with the convenience, advantages and attention of First Class Hotels."[75] The Sterlington Hotel, the Clarke House, Pipe's Neck House, and the Booth House were also located in Greenport.

East of Greenport the most celebrated hotel was the Orient Point Inn overlooking Long Island Sound and Gardiner's Bay. The Mount Pleasant House was also on the north side but, given the narrowness of the peninsula, the bay was not that far distant (see fig. 9). Closer to the bay was the Village House, which has been preserved as part of the Oysterponds Historical Society's museum village. "Splendid beach and scenery" was the motto of this popular inn.[76] One hundred and sixty citizens of Worcester, Massachusetts, who chartered the *W. W. Coit* for a weeklong cruise in August 1868, evidently agreed because the souvenir book of their journey said, of Orient, "The scenery in this place is rather romantic."[77] Describing the nautical geography of the area, the book stated: "A little to the left is Gardiner's Bay and Gardiner's Island, one of the most splendid and safe harbors to be found."[78] The waterfront was the asset the Bay House Hotel and Cottages near the Orient wharf emphasized in its advertising (see fig. 8). "The Bay House itself, faces directly on beautiful Orient Harbor, a part of Peconic Bay—clustered closely around the Bay House are our 10 wonderful cottages (they are really houses!)," declared an early-twentieth-century brochure.[79] Prospective visitors were informed that "our entire atmosphere is informal so you may 'feel at home' in your most comfortable clothes!"[80] That is still the case on the laid-back North Fork where tourists and second homeowners head not to be seen but rather to enjoy the simple pleasures of the area without worrying about what to wear. In the early-twenty-first-century North Fork, chic equals jeans or shorts and a T-shirt, and frankly a lot of people prefer it that way. It's sort of a perverse Ralph Lauren look without the logo.

8. Bay House postcard, Orient. Courtesy of Oysterponds Historical Society.

9. Mt. Pleasant House, Orient. Courtesy of Oysterponds Historical Society.

## Southampton: Natives and Newcomers

On the other side of Peconic Bay, in the eternally fashionable Hamptons, casual sportswear, with designer labels, constitutes daywear but when the sun goes down, people often don something dressier, all of which means toting along more luggage if you're a weekend guest at the home of the rich and famous or the merely rich. In most second homes the closet space is sufficiently adequate to permit the second homeowners to have an entire country wardrobe on tap. It wasn't too different in the nineteenth century when wealthy families began building homes in Southampton and East Hampton. Trunkloads of clothing, much of it rather stiff, accompanied the newcomers, who provided plenty of work for laundresses and maids. The fashionable set, composed, in the 1870s, of a New York physician and his socially prominent patients, gravitated toward the ocean in Southampton; but decades before the Hamptons rivaled Newport as a summer destination some of the town's other assets were noted by visitors. "An air of antiquity and simplicity pervades this entire village," observed one vacationer who spent the summer of 1860 there.[81]

Twenty-five years later a writer described Southampton as "an altogether charming place," but admitted that not all of the locals agreed.[82] As more people discovered the place, the pace of life quickened. Some of the natives objected to "all these carriages going up and down the street," but the writer thought that they "ought to find a certain consolation in the fact that land has advanced to $1500 per acre."[83] There were locals who took the money and ran, if not completely out of town, at least away from the mighty Atlantic. Underscoring the fact that Southampton natives and wealthy newcomers from New York were worlds apart, the *New York Times* explained that while the New Yorkers were bathing in the ocean, "the permanent Southamptonites are splashing informally at North Sea, on the other side of the isthmus."[84]

In the 1920s, prior to the stock market crash of October 1929, oceanfront estates cost between $500,000 and $2,000,000 but on the bay side shacks could be purchased for under $500. Not all waterfront property was created equal, however; views or no views, land on or near Peconic Bay was clearly less valuable, but for natives the bay was a convenient playground. Local residents, who rented their homes to summer people, retreated to North Sea and dwelled in second homes known as camps.

Elsewhere along the north shore of Southampton township, prime property on Little Peconic Bay was acquired, in the 1880s, by the Noyac Cottage Association, which erected a clubhouse and hotel and offered lots "only to such persons as desire to secure a summer home, all of whose moral, as well as physical surrounds, are healthful and pure."[85] The lots ranged in size from 50 by 100 feet to one acre. An interesting feature of the proposed community was the use of the hotel for meal preparation. Cottage owners could elect to dine there or be served at home, thus giving "women an equal chance with the men to get vacation rest and recreation, dispensing, as it does, with the necessity of cooking . . . at home, and the presence and expense of servants" to assist with the task.[86] The family laundry was to be done in a central facility, thereby eliminating another laborious task. Potential buyers were also assured of the "absence of mosquitoes and like pests" and they were told that "the view is extensive, and the scenery diversified and charming to a high degree."[87] Taking an oblique swat at the increasingly fashionable south side of town, the prospectus declared: "The site selected for this enterprise is the most charming and picturesque spot anywhere to be found on the beautiful shores of Long Island, and is not excelled by any location on the Atlantic Coast."[88] Aiming more directly at real estate south of the highway, the prospectus stated: "The surroundings will not grow monotonous and stale as when one has only an expanse of ocean to look upon from day to day."[89]

During the 1880s, when the Noyac Cottage Association was luring people to Peconic Bay, the Long Island Improvement Company purchased property at Shinnecock Hills. An English-style inn was erected on ten acres in 1887 and the remainder was sold to such prominent individuals as Austin Corbin, president of the Long Island Rail Road, and art patron Samuel L. Parrish. Cottages soon rose amid the hills, which the Long Island Rail Road described in one of its tourism booklets as "delightful to all for their peculiar charms."[90] Describing the area, the booklet said, "At this point Peconic Bay is on one hand and Shinnecock Bay is on the other, both at our feet, deep, blue and calm, and gleaming in the sunlight."[91]

Not far from Noyac, another vacation spot some distance from the ocean proved very attractive to visitors. It was the old whaling village of Sag Harbor, which began welcoming tourists even before the whaling era ended. An 1848 advertisement for the Mansion House touted the fact that the building was "entirely new," could accommodate sixty guests, and was centrally located on Main Street.[92] No mere commercial hotel, the Mansion House featured rooms that were "well ventilated, handsomely furnished, and conveniently arranged for families."[93] Although the hotel had "conveyances to the Ocean, on the south side of the Island, always at hand," its ad placed greater emphasis on excursions to the nearby bay.[94] Prospective guests were informed that a "good bathing house, belonging to the establishment, well-calculated for seabathing, is appropriated to the use of those who patronize the house."[95]

The Mansion House was not the only Main Street hotel catering to tourists. Other establishments, namely the Bay Side House, the Sea Breeze Cottages, and the Ross Cottage, were also welcoming guests. The Nassau House, which was refurbished in 1848, was still going strong a half-century later as was the American Hotel, a très chic destination in the early twenty-first century. Flattering articles by travel writers as far away as San Francisco have lured a steady stream of upscale visitors to the sturdy red brick building on Main Street. Where sailors and, later, Victorian-era tourists once enjoyed repose, now well-heeled and fashionably clad guests rest their weary heads on fluffy pillows, enjoying the freshest fruit and other breakfast treats on the hotel's sidewalk veranda.

Farther to the west, on the south side of the bay, other hotels endured though none as long as the American. One of them was the Union Hotel at Good Ground, as Hampton Bays was originally known. For people journeying between Riverhead and Southampton an ad for the Union noted the superiority of the road "passing through Good Ground . . . by way of this Establishment."[96] Good Ground was also the home of the Clifton, described by the *New York Times* as "comfortable," and the legendary Canoe Place Inn, which had been welcoming visitors since the eighteenth century.[97] Fire destroyed the historic building in 1921 but it was rebuilt. A few years earlier, during World War I, the Hampton Pines Hotel, located on Peconic Bay in Red Creek, served as a rehabilitation facility for children stricken with polio. In the 1930s the property became the site of a Girl Scout camp. To the west, the Brewster House, originally a farm homestead, was enlarged and transformed into a boarding house in the 1880s. From the 1920s through the early 1960s it functioned as a hotel. In 2010 restoration of the building, which had been partially destroyed by fire in the 1980s, was a goal of the Flanders Historical Society, but funding the massive job was a real challenge. The Town of Southampton was approached about purchasing the structure through the Community Preservation Fund but a commitment was not forthcoming.

## East Hampton

As Southampton matured as a summer resort, the neighboring Town of East Hampton also evolved as a warm-weather recreational mecca. Writing for the *Brooklyn Advance* in 1879, a gentleman who had been spending his summers in East Hampton since Civil War days declared, in amazement, that "the number of visitors at East Hampton this Summer has been unusually large, numbering between four and five hundred in all; and the scene on the beach at the hour for bathing was brilliant and exciting."[98] The beach was, of course, on the Atlantic but hinting at other lovely places, the writer said: "To any or all in search of a charming, healthy, quiet resting-place, I most heartily recommend the east end of Long Island, particularly East Hampton and vicinity."[99] Those who did choose East Hampton as their vacation destination stayed, initially, at boarding houses, Gardiner's Hotel, or rented cottages that shrewd locals erected to generate additional income. By the 1870s some of the summer visitors were occupying grand cottages built to their own specifications.

In a community that was becoming more dependent upon tourist dollars, there was no room for anything visitors might find repulsive. For that reason, in 1874 the East Hampton Board of Health made it a misdemeanor, punishable by fine or imprisonment, to "spread or deposit in any way, any fish within eighty rods" of a house, whether or not it was inhabited."[100] In East Hampton, as elsewhere on the East End, neither menhaden processing plants nor the application of fish fertilizer to farms and gardens was compatible with tourism.

In the 1890s, when direct rail service to East Hampton began, the number of visitors increased dramatically. Decrying the fact that "Southampton is too crowded and fashionable," a writer for the *New York Times* magazine section in 1898 expressed the fear that East Hampton, "a model of quiet and picturesqueness," might soon be overwhelmed.[101] "The railway now gives access to thousands, whereas in former years only hundreds cared to brave the tiresome six miles of dust to and from Bridgehampton station," observed the *Times*.[102] The newspaper also commented on the community's lack of pretension.

"Many of the children are allowed the supreme happiness of running barefoot the greater part of the day," noted the *Times*, "and simplicity in costume is still the unwritten but accepted law for ladies."[103] Perhaps sensing that things were about to change, however, the *Times* journalist asked: "How long will East Hampton retain this sensible and wholesome attitude? It is hard to say."[104]

## Montauk: The Beginning and the End

One part of East Hampton town that remained unassuming right through the twentieth century was Montauk. Near the end of the first decade of the twenty-first century, however, two developments shattered the tranquility of this very special place. First, young Hamptonites discovered its night spots, a number of which had been transformed into something resembling Soho by the sea; and second, the home of the disgraced financier Bernard Madoff, architect of the biggest Ponzi scheme in American history, was seized by the federal government and subsequently sold. Neither of these developments is likely to deter visitors seeking sunshine, sand, and salty air. Crossing the Napeague strip, where the mosquitoes were sometimes so "thick" that "a driver could not see the color of the horse he drove," one enters a remote and beautiful place.[105] It's no wonder that developer Carl Fisher, who had transformed Miami Beach into a major resort, set his sights on Montauk in the 1920s, hoping to make it the Miami of the North. Fisher proceeded to construct a skyscraper office building in downtown Montauk, the imposing Montauk Manor, a yacht club, a marina, and various other improvements. Before Fisher came along, Montauk was a rather deserted place. Vacationers seeking a real adventure boarded with the keeper of Montauk Light or with the Osborn family, who lived, at various times, in both the historic First and Second houses. A register of guests kept by Florine Osborn from 1863 to 1871 listed visitors from Brooklyn, Rhode Island, Throgs Neck, and various spots in the Hamptons.

In 1879, when Brooklyn businessman Arthur Benson acquired the property of the Montaukett Indians and relocated the remnants of the tribe to East Hampton, he engaged the architectural firm of McKim, Mead and White to build seven cottages, a clubhouse, and outbuildings. For a fleeting moment toward the end of the nineteenth century there was speculation that Montauk would evolve as a quieter alternative to Newport. Austin Corbin, president of the Long Island Rail Road, who, together with partners, acquired Montauk following Benson's death, had other ideas. He proposed turning Montauk into a free port and major steamship terminal for transatlantic commerce between the United States and the United Kingdom. His untimely death, in a runaway horse accident, pretty much ended that dream though it was revived from time to time in the early twentieth century. Carl Fisher's vision of Montauk as "the Miami of the North" was more enduring, but the Great Depression and World War II constituted significant pauses in Montauk's development as a resort. Even after the war ended the *New York Herald Tribune* lamented the fact that "Montauk Point is known better abroad than at home."[106] Maybe so, but at least among American fishermen, especially those in the New York and New England areas, Montauk was very well known.

Montauk did not emerge as a world-famous fishing mecca until the mid-twentieth century, but adventurous sportsmen found their way there in the nineteenth century. In 1858 the sloop *Flying Cloud* shuttled fishermen between two spots on the North Fork, New Suffolk and Greenport, and Napeague and Montauk. The boat's newspaper advertisements, which made clear that there was "no room for children" on board, "held out the possibility of catching seven-pound bluefish or searching for "beach plums."[107] The latter activity was presumably for female guests, who were assured that there were "accommodations for ladies or gentlemen each side of the sloop's hold—a fluffed bed of straw is provided."[108] That was the extent of the amenities because passengers were told to "provide themselves with Blankets or Quilts, to make themselves comfortable—and they are advised to furnish their own provisions. Salt for fish will be furnished on board."[109] By the 1930s, when the charter boat industry developed, fishermen and women could expect a little bit more in the way of creature comforts. Describing the beginnings of this important business, the *East Hampton Star* pointed out that this new recreational venture was jump-started by "the dredging of Lake Montauk . . . to Block Island Sound" and the opening of the Montauk Yacht Club.[110]

Although many of the charter boats headed for the depths of the Atlantic, the Long Island Rail Road's Salt Water Fishing brochure for 1934 announced the debut of "a new recreation beach and pier" in Montauk that was ideal for family outings.[111] While a father could enjoy a day on a charter or open boat, "for the wife and children who may not want to fish, there is a bath house and an opportunity for a good swim in the pure waters of Ford Pond Bay."[112] Another option, in the 1930s, was for the family to enjoy a "rail-water" cruise from Montauk through Gardiner's Bay and Long Island Sound to New London.[113] Excursionists were assured that they would be back in Montauk in time for the return trip to the city. A similar guarantee was offered for the $1.50 round trip to Greenport with its "excellent facilities for the bather."[114] Not surprisingly, the railroad urged people to take the train because it was "cheaper, quicker, more comfortable."[115]

### The Ones That Got Away and Some That Didn't

The LIRR's advertising campaign was especially effective in persuading die-hard fishermen to jump aboard the train. Tens of thousands of people traveled on the line's popular fish trains, which ran from March through the beginning of November. In 1937 alone, the railroad's ninety-nine fish trains carried 33,950 passengers. The trains featured ice cars to keep the fishermen's catch "fresh and firm."[116] Besides depositing anglers in Montauk, the railroad also ran low-cost "Fisherman's Specials" to Canoe Place, where boats were waiting to take the sportsmen out on Peconic Bay. Anglers who made the trip were assured that Peconic Bay was the first place weakfish appeared in the north following their annual migration from Florida. In addition to the prospect of returning home with a good catch, fishermen were reminded of the health benefits of a day on the water. "Fill your lungs with the invigorating tang of the sea," they were told.[117] One Depression-era LIRR brochure even included a physician's prescription for a fishing trip "instead of pills and painful regulation of diet" in "this period of business competition and worry."[118]

During an earlier financial downturn, the Panic of 1893, which lasted for four years and was the worst depression in the nation's history prior to the cataclysm of the 1930s, fishing had also been quite popular. The *New York Times* reported in 1895 that occupants of summer cottages were enjoying "much sport . . . fishing for snappers and small bluefish in Peconic Bay."[119] A few years later the *Brooklyn Daily Eagle* stated that "crabbing is a great sport at Town Creek in Southold."[120] Rosalind Case Newell, a Southold native, was especially fond of another type of shellfish, Peconic Bay scallops. "There is nothing more delicious than the small, sweet bay scallop, fried or in a milk stew," she wrote.[121] Describing fishing trips in nearby waters, Newell said:

> My father used to take me fishing on Peconic Bay in one of those first gasoline-engined open boats called a "launch". . . . One summer morning we caught enough to fill a large net which Papa kept hanging over the side to keep the fish alive. It became so heavy that the drawstring in the bottom broke and off swam all our fish! I was ready to cry but Papa comforted me by saying that we'd catch plenty more. And we did! In later years the Bay has been a Mecca for hundreds of ardent fishermen from western Long Island and the city, and a mention of Peconic Bay wherever we go brings a gleam of recognition and a pleased, "Oh, I've been out fishing from New Suffolk!"[122]

Like Rosalind Case Newell and her father, most anglers who tried their luck in the Peconic Bay estuary did so from boats. But in the mid-twentieth century, Arthur Godfrey, a radio and television personality in the early days of the latter medium, landed his seaplane in Gardiner's Bay to go fishing. He did it often enough that his Grumman amphibian attracted less attention than one might think, except perhaps from the fish and other denizens of the deep.

One of the most unusual inhabitants of the estuary was a 600-pound turtle caught in Peconic Bay in 1859. Comparing this creature to a 400-pound turtle caught off Islip in the summer of 1860, the

Sag Harbor *Corrector* declared, "His turtleship, big as he is, does not come up to his prototype caught in the waters of Peconic Bay."[123] In addition to its superior weight of 600 pounds, the Peconic Bay turtle was reported to be six feet, nine inches long. The *Corrector* did not give the location where the turtle was found, but one suspects that throughout the estuary bathers became more cautious, just as they did in August 2011 when an eight-foot bull shark, one of the three most dangerous species, was caught in a fish trap in Orient harbor and released. Back in 1859, the season was really over when the turtle surfaced, but the water temperature of the bay is sometimes warm enough for swimming well into October. Indeed, it is often said that fall is the best season in this area because of sun-filled days, with low humidity, crisp nights, and splendid fishing and swimming.

### Taking a Dip and Setting Sail

In the late nineteenth century, when bathers were encumbered by considerably more attire than today's Speedos and teeny bikinis, taking a dip in the waters of the estuary was a favorite recreational pastime. Southampton's Rose's Grove, located at North Sea, was an especially popular spot for swimming. In the 1890s this well-known day resort attracted visitors from both sides of the bay. Excursion boats from Greenport deposited North Fork natives and tourists at Rose's Grove for a day of picnicking and swimming. On Shelter Island, taking a dip was so popular that the *New York Times* reported, in August 1895, that the number of bathers had increased so much that it had "become difficult for the bathhouse keepers to find accommodations for all who wish to bathe at the popular morning hour."[124] Describing the situation on Shelter Island, the paper declared: "The still water of the bay affords much better opportunity for swimming than does the surf"; for that reason people who spent the summer on the island were likely to master the technique of swimming.[125] Especially intriguing to the *Times* reporter were "the older men who can be seen daily swimming out in the bay, diving off the floats, and evidently enjoying the waters as much as they ever did in their youth."[126] The swimming ability of some of the young ladies vacationing on Shelter Island was also noted in the press. In an era when most women who ventured into the water merely took a quick dip, there were girls who actually swam and were very good at it.

Some members of the fair sex vacationing on Shelter Island were also adept at handling boats. During special races sponsored by the Shelter Island Yacht Club, the *New York Times* noted, "all the boats must be steered by ladies."[127] Even women who did not compete were enamored of boats. Describing Shelter Island, where the New York Yacht Club established a station at the Manhanset to accommodate its members sailing between New York and Newport and to host visiting clubs, as "the yachtsmen's paradise," the normally staid *New York Times* waxed poetic when referring to the magnificent yachts moored in Dering Harbor "resting upon the water like great white seabirds after a long flight."[128] At night the yachts were "aglow with twinkling lights . . . mermaids waving star-tipped wands."[129] As for the women who gazed upon this scene, the *Times* concluded that they were "all charming, or they wouldn't be at Shelter Island."[130] With tongue in cheek, the *Times* warned bachelors about Shelter Island's female beauties, saying that the bachelor visiting Shelter Island feels "lost" initially surrounded by "a rosebud garden of girls" but he quickly realizes that he is fortunate to have "landed upon Shelter Island's hospitable shores."[131]

Steam yachts and sailing vessels literally paraded around those shores practically every afternoon, completing their circumnavigation in approximately three hours. Sag Harbor was also a popular place for boating. In the 1890s the demand for yacht charters from Sag Harbor frequently outstripped the supply of available vessels. Throughout the estuary system residents and visitors alike gravitated to the water, and why not? A turn-of-the-century Long Island Rail Road tourism brochure sang the praises of the waterway, declaring: "The bay itself is a beautiful body of salt water, on whose placid bosom all manner of pleasure craft may be seen during the warm months, bearing happy groups of care-free folk. They sail or row over the blue waters in landlocked security from the rollers of the open sea."[132]

Six decades later the bay was still luring yachtsmen, including the members of East Hampton's Devon Yacht Club. The Devon is located on a beautiful stretch of coast where, even at the start of the Labor Day weekend, at the end of the twentieth century, the only swimmer was an athletic senior citizen clad in a short wetsuit to afford warmth during her lengthy water aerobics and long, leisurely swim. The club was described in the 1960s as an organization whose members "have had a whale of a lot of fun with relatively small boats."[133] Small boats were also very much in evidence in Orient. Recalling the early days of the Orient Yacht Club in the 1930s, club member Anne MacKay said, "Sailing and racing was the focus at that time, the social aspect took over when the boats declined in the 1960s."[134] For Anne MacKay "the best part of the Yacht Club . . . was the annual beach party . . . when after eating, everyone sang for hours, old songs, college songs, traditional songs, etc."[135] Mildred Younie Cobb has similar memories of happy summers spent in Orient. "I remember the sailing parties, which I was allowed to be on when a late teenager," she said, adding:

They would sail to Greenport sometime, and go ashore for ice cream. . . . We used to sing all the old songs. We also used to sail to Bug Light, tie up the boat and climb up on the rocks. The owner and his wife would invite us into the house. He would play the fiddle and we would dance, although there was very little room there.[136]

Sailing, singing, and dancing filled countless happy hours for some of the lucky people who either lived or vacationed on the East End. Cycling was also a popular pastime and, once again, women were enthusiastic participants. "The bicycling craze is raging worse than ever, especially among the young women," the *New York Times* stated in 1895, adding that, to be thoroughly modern, women "must learn to manage a wheel."[137] To promote ridership by cyclists, the LIRR published a promotional booklet titled "Cyclists' Paradise" in 1897. The publication pointed out that "from Riverhead to Orient Point or the end of the north fluke, the road is always first class."[138] Describing biking conditions from "Good Ground to Canoe Place, at the beginning of the Shinnecock Hills," the booklet observed: "Here a narrow stretch of land, most peculiar in formation, separates Great Peconic Bay from Shinnecock Bay. . . . The road runs for some four miles through the woods and is very sandy; there is, however, a good edge path, which will soon be changed to a cycle path."[139]

Fast-forwarding a hundred years to the twenty-first century, when cycling is again a craze, it is truly déjà vu at the Mattituck station when cyclists and their equipment detrain for weekend biking tours along ever-expanding designated cycling routes on the "north fluke." The bike path flanking Routes 48 and 25, with scenic detours along back roads, is clogged with helmet-clad riders on sunny weekend days, particularly in fall and spring; on the south side of the bay cyclists are somewhat less visible, certainly along busy Montauk Highway, but head north or south of the highway in Southampton and East Hampton and there they are, enjoying, in some spots, the same views that their predecessors gazed upon a century ago. To a certain extent, this holds true for golfers as well. Although the surrounding areas have undergone considerable development, many of the original views have been preserved.

Golf emerged as a popular sport in the 1890s when enthusiasts were chasing little white balls at Southampton's Shinnecock Hills Golf Club and at the Shelter Island Golf Club, where "an old farmhouse" was "transposed into comfortable quarters" as a clubhouse.[140] On the eve of World War I *Southampton Magazine* positively swooned over the new clubhouse of the National Golf Links of America "high up on Sebonac bluffs, overlooking the broad, blue waters of Peconic bay," where the golfer stepping up to the tee of the "next-to-last-hole . . . is on a high elevation with the sail-dotted blue waters of Great Peconic bay spread out before him."[141] Expanding upon its verbal portrait of the club, the magazine said:

> From the broad cool piazza, superb views can be had of Peconic
> bay with its distant shores brilliant in the morning sun or dimmed
> by mists arising from the nearer waters, the high sand cliffs of Red
> Creek and Robbin's Island, the dark dense wooded shores of Cow

Neck point, with its long sand spit reaching . . . almost to our feet, Island Creek, and West Neck point and Millstone Brook shore each with its own distinctive individuality and each so different from each other.[142]

To accommodate members arriving by yacht, the club constructed a huge dock, thereby becoming "as accessible by water as by land, which is true of few other golf clubs anywhere in the world."[143] On the opposite shore of Peconic Bay, the North Fork Country Club, on the south or bay side of Route 25 in Cutchogue, emerged as a mecca for golfers on the eve of World War I. In the early twenty-first century Laurel Links in Mattituck and the Long Island National Golf Course in the Northville area of Riverhead were attracting golfers.

If the clock were turned back to the nineteenth century, the popular sporting activity on the North Fork was not golf but horse racing at the track at the Riverhead fairgrounds and at Fleet's track in Cutchogue. Reporting on an 1867 contest that attracted 300 spectators to what was known locally as the "Cutchogue Pleasure Grounds," the Sag Harbor *Corrector* noted that all of the East End towns were represented by "admirers of equine speed and beauty."[144] Perhaps the most famous East End horse, the trotter Rarus, born in 1867 on a Southold farm that evolved into the full-fledged Conklin horse-breeding enterprise, not unlike the Barker and Entenmann Jamesport equine businesses in the 1980s, won contests as far away as California.

Fast-paced horses weren't the only speedy animals racing through the bay area. In 1894 New Jersey's Monmouth County Hunt Club established temporary quarters at the Peconic Country Club in Southampton's Shinnecock Hills to hunt "boar and wild fox several times a week" during the month of September.[145] "Hunting, handicap golf matches, boating parties, numerous hops, and dinner parties will make September a gay month," the *New York Times* observed.[146] With the exception of boar and fox hunts, other sporting activities, as varied as duck hunting and baseball, were available on both sides of the bay. Hotels and clubs offered a dizzying array of recreational opportunities, some as tame as "card parties" and "fancy dress hops."[147] Other popular events were clambakes, especially those that included a boat excursion on Gardiner's Bay to the Dinah's Rock picnic grounds on the east side of Shelter Island. In addition to a sumptuous repast, guests were usually treated to music, especially if one of Shelter Island's resort hotels sponsored the outing. The hotels dispatched their own orchestras to serenade the diners as they gorged themselves on the delicacies of land and sea. Music was such an integral part of resort life at the Manhanset that, when the hotel's new wing was completed in 1893, four musicians from Bernstein's band, the resident orchestra, were dispatched to its tower on clear nights to "make moonshining music which floats down like vapor from the pinnacle to the piazza, puzzling the guests to imagine whence it came."[148] In the daytime "the view from the top of this tower," which was accessed by an Otis elevator, "has a range from Sag Harbor across Peconic Bay to the Shinnecock Hills."[149] Ah, the gay nineties, when the music seemed to go on forever! Unfortunately, all good things come to an end, including delightful summer vacations. The affluent guests privileged to stay at the great resorts of the nineteenth century enjoyed genteel pastimes in elegant surroundings, but this way of celebrating summer did not endure.

## At Play in the Twentieth and Twenty-First Centuries

In the late twentieth century a handful of entrepreneurs, including the daughter of household guru Martha Stewart, refurbished various types of lodgings, adding cachet where none had existed before. On the North Fork and Shelter Island, investors created trendy European-style resorts while in Sag Harbor, the aforementioned American Hotel, a genuinely historic building, was meticulously refurbished. In comparison with the well-heeled guests registering at the East End's "in" hotels in the 1980s and, even more so, the 1990s, vacationers flocking to the forks or Shelter Island for most of the twentieth century did not possess unlimited travel budgets. For them, a weekend at a motel or at one of the bed-and-breakfast establishments that began springing up toward the end of the century, or a day trip, constituted time away from the ordinary routine.

As the population of the greater New York area grew, the State of New York, Suffolk County, and the municipalities in the bay area recognized the need to set aside parkland where John Q. Public and Joan Citizen could enjoy the great outdoors. A 1929 bill introduced in the New York State legislature called for "providing for the control and management of common beaches and other common land in the village of Orient."[150] Over the objections of many Orient residents who signed a petition protesting the state's plans, Orient State Park was created. State property was also acquired in Montauk for Hither Hills State Park, Montauk Point State Park, Montauk Downs State Park, and Camp Hero State Park. Suffolk County, too, set aside property for the Theodore Roosevelt County Park in Montauk and Cedar Point County Park in East Hampton and also established Meschutt Beach County Park in Hampton Bays and Shinnecock East County Park in Southampton. On both forks municipalities created parks but, as with county facilities, residency requirements prevail. Although nonresidents are allowed in, provided they pay higher usage fees, in reality these facilities are not completely public. This also holds true for camping programs operated by county and municipal governments.

Throughout the Peconic Bay area there have been numerous summer camps, private as well as quasi-public. Administered by scouting and other youth organizations as well as religious and fraternal groups, the camps provided a badly needed respite from urban life earlier in the twentieth century. On the eve of World War II, first dozens and then hundreds of city boys attended a "Big Brother" camp established by Anthony Drexel Duke at Jessup's Neck, Southampton. After working at a New Hampshire camp for several summers while attending St. Paul's School, Duke, along with two other students, who supervised the same twenty children for three summers, "decided freshman year in college, that we'd take those kids that we'd worked with for 3 years and have a tent camp out here in Peconic Bay. And we decided to do it."[151] From 1954 until 2006 Anthony Drexel Duke's Boys and Girls Harbor Camp on Three Mile Harbor in East Hampton flourished. After the camp closed, Suffolk County and the Town of East Hampton jointly funded its acquisition with the intention of preserving the land. Decades before open space preservation became an important goal, another property that remained largely open by virtue of the way it was utilized was Fireplace Lodge Camp in the East Hampton hamlet of The Springs. It was there that Ozzie Nelson, later a famous bandleader and costar of the popular 1950s television program *Ozzie and Harriet,* and his brother Al were counselors in 1926 and 1927. Ozzie had a close call during his second summer when he attempted to swim from the camp to Gardiner's Island. Although challenged by a storm-tossed sea for a half hour, the Rutgers University swimming team member made it in under three hours. Even if the weather had been calm this still would have been quite an accomplishment because of the strong currents in the area.

In the prosperous 1920s camps such as the one where Ozzie Nelson was employed attracted a full complement of well-to-do students whose parents were eager for them to enjoy healthful outdoor recreation in beautiful surroundings. Adults, too, sought this type of opportunity and developers were eager to provide it. A *Long Island Real Estate Review* from 1906 proclaimed that "Long Island may, with truth, be regarded as the health resort of the future."[152] A year later the Shinnecock Hills and Peconic Bay Realty Company published a booklet promoting what it termed "the last high-grade summer resort tract left so near to New York City where a realization of an ideal summer colony can be obtained."[153] Prospective buyers were told that the property was "unique" because "every plot has a full water view. Many overlook both Peconic Bay and Shinnecock Bay and the ocean beyond."[154] The realty company's ambitious plans did not materialize. A portion of its property was sold to the National Golf Club and the remainder was sold, at auction, in the 1920s.

The Great Depression and World War II slowed the influx of people into the bay area but pleasure seekers arrived in record numbers during the second half of the twentieth century. Some people also left. Mrs. Charles Hamilton Sabin, the remarried widow of Dwight Davis, adviser to President Franklin D. Roosevelt, and tennis enthusiast for whom the Davis Cup is named, decided to part with a magnificent

Southampton bayfront mansion built in 1919. The house, surrounding acreage, and a 1.5-mile stretch of Great Peconic Bay beach were acquired by the International Brotherhood of Electrical Workers following World War II. The union utilized the estate, known as Bayberry Land, as a convalescent facility for members and as a summer camp for children. At the end of the twentieth century the union decided to sell the place, which borders the National Golf Club. When a representative of Manhattan developer Donald Trump photographed the property from the air, rumors about an exclusive residential enclave, with golf course, began to circulate. In the end it was not Trump but Michael Pascucci, the owner of Channel 55, who bought Bayberry for $45 million; in August 2001 he announced plans for homes, an organic golf course, and a nature preserve on the 307 acres. Five years later, after the mansion had been demolished, the new Sebonack Golf Club, complete with fifteen four-bedroom cottages for members' use, opened. The club's $650,000 initiation fee made it the most expensive golf club in the Hamptons.

At the time the Sebonack Golf Club opened, the economy was robust. Flush with stock market gains or profits from other investments, people were willing to indulge themselves. Membership in an exclusive club was the reward for a fortunate few while for many others it was a vacation home. The demand for new residences precipitated a building boom throughout the East End. Even on remote Shelter Island enormous new homes went up in the blink of an eye, causing one *New York Times* article to be headlined, "Shelter Island: Paradise Lost."[155] As for the North Fork, in 1998 a *Washington Post* reporter, who, with her husband and children, spent several summers in the "Un-Hamptons," described "the sheer beauty of the place," noting:

> The flowers here are more brilliant, the sky bluer, the air cleaner. The locals claim that the North Fork actually gets better weather than its flashy cousins on the southern side of Peconic Bay, the Hamptons. And—like the Hamptons—the area is blessed with some of the most fertile soil ever to find its way to a coastline. Nowhere else are the corn and tomatoes this sweet.[156]

Given all of this, can you blame people for beating a path to the North Fork? By 2013, when *Dan's Papers* featured a North Fork landmark, the Modern Snack Bar, on its cover, and a lengthy *New York Times* travel section article bearing the title "Looking for the Hamptons? Go the Other Way" oozed enthusiasm for the north side of Peconic Bay, the once sleepy region was positively trendy.[157] But, whether North Fork or South Fork, avid fishermen, windsurfers, jet skiers, swimmers, or just plain old beach bums, people are naturally drawn to the sea. With its spectacular beaches, calm boating waters, and bountiful harvest for recreational fishermen, Peconic Bay is being rediscovered as an aquatic playground. Provided the waters remain clean and contiguous upland areas retain a semblance of rural ambience, more and more people will come to this very special place where paint boxes and prayers launched the tourist industry in the 1800s and, like the artists and camp meeting participants of long ago, they will play, on and on.

# 4

# At War

## Down to the Sea in Subs

The genial host and his world-famous guest were no strangers to conflict. One produced weapons of destruction; the other had recently witnessed the ravages of war in Cuba. The guest, seventy-seven-year-old Clara Barton, founder of the American Red Cross, took her host, John Holland, designer and builder of submarines, to task for manufacturing lethal weapons. He, on the other hand, viewed the stealth craft produced at the Holland Company, the New Suffolk firm he had established, as deterrents to conflict. Despite this difference of opinion, Miss Barton and Mr. Holland seemed to have gotten on famously when she, along with other distinguished guests, visited New Suffolk on Sunday, July 23, 1899, a day when the weather was anything but auspicious. Despite the mist and oppressive humidity, the weather did nothing to dampen the enthusiasm of the A-list invitees who included Miss Barton's brother Stephen, an official of the American Red Cross; Frank Leavitt of Sag Harbor's Bliss Torpedo Company and various members of his family; several attorneys, including E. B. Frost, counsel for the Holland Company; and assorted army and navy brass.

Once on board the Holland Company's yacht *Gleam*, guests were accorded VIP treatment, including "a finely prepared luncheon."[1] The repast was followed by special tours of the company's prototypical submarine, known simply as the "Holland boat."[2] A sudden and unusually severe thunderstorm stirred up the normally calm waters of the bay to such an extent that the planned demonstration of the sub was canceled, but when Mother Nature relented, the guests were able to board the sub. The military men and those from the Bliss Torpedo Company "went aboard first and made a lengthy examination."[3] When they completed their tour, to the surprise of some male skeptics who believed a woman's presence on board meant bad luck, female guests were invited to inspect the sub. According to the weekly newspaper the *Corrector* (Sag Harbor):

> The remainder of the party then took a look below, and contrary to previous custom some of the ladies were allowed on board. Miss Barton was one of this number and her advanced years did not hinder her from walking along the narrow superstructure and crawling down the narrow kettle like hole that affords the only entrance to the strange craft.[4]

Later that afternoon, when the *Gleam* set sail for Sag Harbor, she was escorted by the sub for part of the trip. Although the submarine did not completely vanish under the waters of Peconic Bay, "there was but little of her visible and she looked like a boat that had turned turtle, and at a distance might easily be taken for a tide rip."[5]

John Holland remained on board the *Gleam* until all of his guests were safely deposited at Sag Harbor or Greenport. The *Corrector* noted, "He and his attorney, Mr. Frost, proved genial hosts and made the day a delightful one for all."[6] What the *Corrector* did not report was that Frost was the real power at the Holland Company, following its acquisition by the Electric Boat Company. The financial problems leading to John Holland's loss of control would haunt him until his death in 1914. Ironically, Holland's distinguished guest Clara Barton, who, like Holland, had been a highly respected teacher before pursuing other interests, would, in a few short years, be pushed aside by new leadership at the American Red Cross. Miss Barton's autocratic management style proved to be her undoing; but in John Holland's case it was lack of capital and plain old bad luck, especially when it came to timing.

At first glance, Holland seemed to have everything going for him. This curious and creative man, known as the "father of the submarine," stood out even in the small Irish fishing village where he was born in 1840. During the ensuing decade the potato blight struck, resulting in disease, starvation, and mass emigration from the Emerald Isle. Like others who lived through this horrific period, the Hollands blamed not only Mother Nature but England, as well, for not alleviating the suffering of the Irish. Given his family's feelings toward England, it was perhaps fitting that John Holland received initial funding from Irish revolutionaries for the submarines he began building following his emigration in 1873.

Michael Holland, John's brother, who had emigrated before him, was committed to the cause of Irish independence, and it was he who acted as the liaison between the American branch of the Fenians, the Irish Republican brotherhood, and the inventor of a device the organization hoped to use against the English. With the financial assistance of the Fenians, John Holland not only built but also demonstrated a working model of a sub before going on to create an underwater craft powered by gasoline. During a trial run on the Passaic River in New Jersey in the spring of 1878, the vessel went to the bottom. Raised and altered somewhat, the sub performed well a month later. But Holland was eager to build an improved craft and to protect his first successful full-sized model from being seen by competitors (or, for that matter, British spies), so he dismantled the engine and sank the sub in the Passaic River. Three years later, a new sub, known unofficially as the *Fenian Ram*, was put through its paces in the Narrows separating New York's upper and lower harbors. Holland subsequently built a smaller model of the *Fenian Ram*, which his Irish revolutionary supporters claimed as their property after deciding to withdraw all financial support for Holland's experiments. This vessel went to the bottom of Long Island Sound not far from the Whitestone Bridge during an unsuccessful attempt by the Fenians to tow what they considered *their* sub. The loss of the model notwithstanding, "the Fenian Ram was to underwater technology what the Wright brothers' first airplane was to aviation—the first of its kind and a portent of the shape of things to come."[7]

For John Holland, there was no time to mourn the loss of the model. He had other things to do, chief among them entering the

U.S. Navy's design contest for a submarine torpedo craft. While preparing for the competition, Holland established the Holland Torpedo Boat Company. Attorney Elihu B. Frost was the intermediary who found the venture capital the inventor needed. Ironically, the new company's initial contract from the navy was for a sub powered by steam that was inferior to Holland-designed craft. The vessel was completed in 1897 but required modification. Early in 1898 the *Holland*, a gasoline-propelled submarine, was proudly launched by the inventor. Soon thereafter, naval officials viewed trial runs of the new vessel. Although the officials were not enthusiastic, Assistant Secretary of the Navy Theodore Roosevelt urged the navy to buy the *Holland* and, following additional trials, in 1899 the inventor's company received a contract for two submarines. That same year saw the absorption of the company by the Electric-Dynamic Company of Philadelphia. John Holland functioned as manager of the enterprise, but "what control he had in the company's operations had been eroded by the complex and bureaucratic corporate organization, as well as his own lack of capital."[8]

The inventor may have been short on cash, but when the company relocated to New Suffolk in May 1899, North Fork residents who supplied food and shelter to the growing number of Holland employees profited. Charles Morris, superintending engineer, who had been dispatched to the North Fork to find a new location for the company, went first to Greenport and then concluded that the Goldsmith and Tuthill boatyard in New Suffolk was ideal for a submarine base. The bulkheading and the breakwaters there, combined with the easy access to Little Peconic Bay, made it a natural choice. Moreover, in the quiet waters of the bay, subs could be put through their paces without the sort of interference encountered during earlier trials in New York Harbor. Reporting on trials conducted toward the end of July, the *Brooklyn Daily Eagle* said they "were a decided success. . . . On her first trial the boat was submerged and run for one mile, coming to the surface for rapid observations and again disappearing."[9]

But it was not all smooth sailing for the company in New Suffolk. In October 1899 "the crew of the Holland submarine had a narrow escape when a leaking gas tank filled the boat with fumes," according to Southold's *Long Island Traveler*, which noted:

> The submarine came to her dock after a trial run apparently all right. Some old salts on the pier became alarmed when nobody appeared on deck and went to open the hatch. The six men of the crew were discovered to be unconscious but were soon revived.[10]

Less than a month later, the *Long Island Traveler* proclaimed:

> The final and official trial of the Holland sub-marine torpedo boat over the course in Little Peconic Bay . . . was entirely successful. . . . The Holland dove at the head of the course and ran submerged one mile, then rose and fired the first Whitehead torpedo. . . . The torpedo sped on its course like a fish, going along the surface of the water and leaving a white streak of foam as it sped on the errand of supposed destruction, true to the mark, some 800 yards distant. Amazement was exhibited by everyone who witnessed the marvelous achievement and scarcely had ten seconds elapsed from the time when the turret appeared and the torpedo was fired, when the Holland was again out of sight beneath the waves and making a circuit, returned to the starting point.[11]

Although John Holland joined naval officials on the bay for the all-important November tests, he was not permitted to captain the sub during the trials. By this time he had been shunted aside by attorney Frost and Isaac Rice, chief executive officer of the conglomerate that had absorbed the Holland Company. Holland was, nevertheless, a witness before the House Committee on Naval Affairs. His testimony helped pave the way for passage of an appropriation for the purchase of five Holland-type subs. Russia, Japan, and Great Britain also bought Holland subs. Although contracts for the building of the vessels were fulfilled at shipyards in Baltimore and San Francisco, submarines launched on the East Coast were outfitted and tested in Peconic Bay, where the company created an enclosed area for trials. One by one, the *Fulton*, the *Adder*, and the *Moccasin* were put through grueling tests, but not under the watchful eye of John Holland, who was rumored to be experimenting with personal flying machines. In the spring of 1904, when representatives of the Japanese government journeyed from Washington, D.C., to New Suffolk to tour what, in reality, was the world's first submarine base, the *Fulton* was the sole vessel remaining, and, ironically, it was the *Fulton* that had almost gone to a watery grave in Peconic Bay a few years earlier. "The submarine boat *Fulton* sank in the Holland Co.'s basin Tuesday morning through one hatch being carelessly left open," according to the *Long Island Traveler*.[12] Offering additional details, the newspaper noted:

> The stern of the boat was hoisted up that some work might be done on the bottom and this tipped the bow down so deep that the water rushed in through an open hatch. The machinist, John Wilson, who was in her, rushed out through the conning tower. The boat was raised Wednesday morning.[13]

In 1905, the New Suffolk base was closed by the conglomerate that had absorbed the Holland Company.

Interestingly, John Holland, who resigned from the company in 1904, continued to experiment with submarines and even derived some income from this activity. After selling plans for two subs to Japan, which intended to use such craft during the Russo-Japanese War of 1904-1905, Holland was honored by the Japanese government. Conferral of the Order of the Rising Sun brought no new business from abroad, however, because foreign patents Holland had secured earlier had been sold by the company that had absorbed his business, and resulting legal issues proved a stumbling block to customers and investors alike. Although Holland won a protracted court case involving the contention of the Electric Boat Company, Electric-Dynamic's successor, that any patents secured by Holland during his entire life were the property of the company, the inventor could not muster sufficient financial support to build a prototype of a new, faster submarine. John Holland died in August 1914, the very month World War I began. Submarines of the type the inventor had envisioned would play a critical role in that conflict, but it would not be the first time underwater craft were utilized in warfare.

## Independence: Round One

Nearly a century and a half earlier, during the American Revolution, a one-man propeller-driven sub, invented across the Sound in Connecticut by Yale graduate David Bushnell, attempted, without success, to blow up British ships in New York Harbor. Tested at Old Saybrook, Bushnell's *Turtle* was placed on a sailing vessel for the trip down Long Island Sound. This occurred at the very time Long Islanders were fleeing across the Sound to patriot-controlled Connecticut to escape British domination of the island in the aftermath of the American defeat at Brooklyn Heights in August 1776. The unwelcome occupation forces built forts in Hampton Bays and Sag Harbor; dispatched troops to both sides of Peconic Bay; anchored nearly two dozen ships between Cherry Point on Gardiner's Island and Orient Point; and exacted tribute in the form of cattle, produce, grain, and other necessities. Shelter Island and Gardiner's Island were raided by enemy forces who freely took what they wanted. Thousands of cattle and sheep pastured at Montauk were prevented from falling into British hands only because Captain John Hurlburt organized a special force to remove the animals. Yet for many people, the situation was so intolerable that they seized the first opportunity to flee to the mainland. Not wasting a minute, South Fork residents flocked to Sag Harbor in mid-September 1776 to embark for Connecticut. In time, many refugees sought permission to return to the island to collect belongings left behind or to take elderly relatives to the mainland. Some Long Islanders who fled to the safety of Connecticut during the Revolution returned to harass the island's occupying force and its Tory supporters.

Jumping into small, easily maneuverable boats of the type carried by "mother" ships engaged in ocean whaling, these whaleboat warriors turned up on the island throughout the war. One of their more successful expeditions, commanded by Colonel "Return" Jonathan Meigs, so-called because he promised to return to marry a particularly lovely young woman, was launched from Guilford, Connecticut, in May 1777. Helped by Elnathan Jennings, a Southampton native who had fled to the mainland and joined the Fifth Connecticut Regiment, Meigs planned an attack on Sag Harbor, where the British had a major garrison and supply depot. With General George Washington's approval, thirteen whaleboats carrying more than a hundred volunteers crossed the Sound under the protection of two sloops. This armada landed at Hashamomuck Beach in Southold. Leaving three dozen or so men there in anticipation of the return trip to the mainland at the conclusion of the mission, Meigs and the others "carried the boats on their backs over the sandy point, embarking again on the Peconic Bay."[14] The patriot whaleboatmen had actually transported their boats across King's Highway (today's Route 48) and launched them in Hashamomuck Pond. From there, it was on to Mill Creek and Southold Bay. Once past Paradise Point, Southold, they crossed the bay and probably spent some time on Jessup's Neck, Southampton (now the Morton National Wildlife Refuge), resting up until nightfall. Then it was on to Sag Harbor.

Guided by Jennings, who was thoroughly familiar with the place, they quickly seized the British guardhouse, a former school building where Jennings had attended classes. After taking prisoners at the guardhouse and the nearby barracks, they captured a real prize, the British commanding officer, at a tavern on the site of today's American Hotel. Following this triumph, it was on to the British fort on the hill where the Old Burying Ground was located. A half-dozen British troops were slain and fifty-three were taken prisoner there. At Long Wharf, the American raiders rounded up additional prisoners, burned a dozen enemy ships, and destroyed foodstuffs. From there, the Americans, with ninety prisoners in tow, retraced their route across the bay to the North Fork and from there to Connecticut.

In February 1779, a trio of American ships seized a British privateer at a Sag Harbor wharf, but the arrival of additional British vessels and the stranding of the lead American vessel on the Middle Ground brought the mission to a premature end. Happily, the crew from the stranded vessel made it to one of the other American ships, which "immediately left the bay."[15] In November 1781, a number of Americans "being ashore at Sag Harbor . . . were betrayed and taken prisoners."[16] Two vessels belonging to the Americans were nearly set on fire, but the sudden appearance of a sloop from Stonington, Connecticut, saved the boats.

Across the bay in Southold, the Americans had scored a minor victory over the British a few years earlier in December 1777. Enemy troops were preparing to load wood on a ship when they learned of the arrival of patriot forces. "Hastening to their ship they were overtaken," according to Southold historian Wayland Jefferson, "and in a running fight the British forces lost seven prisoners and the rest of the little group were either killed or wounded."[17]

Despite valiant American attempts to thwart the enemy, Long Island was under British domination throughout the war and for some time thereafter, the occupying force remaining in place until late 1783, when news of the Treaty of Paris ending the war reached the New World. Thus, for seven long years, the island, including the Peconic Bay area, was subjected to all kinds of assaults. Early in 1778, for example, more than a hundred Tories from upisland "came down to Southold, Oyster Pond, etc., and robbed the honest inhabitants of a large amount in clothing, money, grain, cattle, etc."[18] One poor victim had to give up 120 pounds to the invaders. In May 1779 Southold resident David Gardiner forfeited forty pounds to a robber and the Widow Case and her son were forced to surrender household goods and personal items. These victims were fortunate, however, in that their property was recovered. Scarcely a month after this incident, the Americans scored a minor victory when a party of whaleboatmen from Connecticut landed at Mattituck and removed supplies from a vessel driven ashore during a storm. A group of Southold men "brought wagons from the east end of the Island" and stripped the boat "of her sails, rigging, etc., which they carried off, and have no doubt sent across the Sound."[19]

On Shelter Island, former resident patriot Moses Sawyer, who had fled to Connecticut, returned in 1778 to seize grain from William Nicoll's farm. Since William Nicoll had not signed a pro-independence resolution, Sawyer assumed he was a loyalist and, according to Shelter Island historian Helen Otis Lamont: "The raid would then have been a punitive expedition on a supposedly Loyalist estate, in reprisal for enemy depredations on Shelter Island."[20] In September 1781, patriots again targeted Shelter Island. After landing in Southampton, where they killed some sheep, forty men in two whaleboats proceeded to the island. There "they ransacked the house of Nicoll Havens, Esq. . . . took 2 fowling-pieces, a silver-hilted sword, silver-mounted hanger, some tea, etc."[21] Then it was on to the home of Captain James Havens, where they grabbed "a watch-coat, fowling-piece, etc."[22] After that they proceeded to the home of Widow Payne, where they insulted the occupants and, after threatening to burn the house down, took silver, clothing, and guns. From there they crossed the bay to Southold, "disarmed the people on their way up to the settlement, and fired at some unarmed people, entered the house of David Gardiner . . . with fixed bayonets, took goods and family articles."[23] Having been repeatedly victimized, poor Gardiner was in the process of fleeing to Connecticut at the time, but had not gotten away fast enough.

Like Gardiner, other Southold residents fared poorly. "On their way down to the shore," the invaders "beat with a gun-breech Mr. and Mrs. L'Hommedieu, an aged couple, threatened to burn Widow Moore's house, because armed men had assembled there to resist them, flashed a gun at John Vail, aged 60."[24] The real heroine of this episode was Charity L'Hommedieu, wife of the celebrated scientific farmer and statesman Ezra L'Hommedieu, who had left his home at Town Harbor on the bay to serve first in the New York Provincial Congress and then in the Second Continental Congress. When a British soldier thrust a sword toward her husband, Mrs. L'Hommedieu interposed herself between the two men and suffered a broken arm in the process.

Whaleboat raids were not always this dramatic, nor did they necessarily produce triumphant results for the invaders. At Canoe Place, Hampton Bays, in April 1781 a whaleboatman from New Haven "was taken by surprise . . . by a party . . . who lay in ambush for him."[25]

Nearly a year after the formal British surrender at Yorktown in 1781, there was another landing at Canoe Place. The men who had crossed from the mainland scooped up cash, clothing, and tea from people living within two miles of the landing spot. The next day, when the locals found the invaders calmly sitting on the sand dividing the loot, they opened fire, killing one of them, wounding two, and capturing five. Earlier in the war, after the British had erected earthworks at Canoe Place, the Squires family, whose home was nearby, fled to the swamps and forests of Red Creek Island in Great Peconic Bay.

The beautiful but isolated Red Creek area, across the bay from Jamesport on the North Fork, was also the hiding place of Francis and John Fournier. This father-and-son team from Southold had volunteered for military service at the start of hostilities in the New York area and were captured at Brooklyn Heights in August 1776 and incarcerated on one of the fetid British prison ships moored off Brooklyn. The men escaped by slipping "over the side one night" and after obtaining "a small sailboat . . . laid a course towards the Sound."[26] The Fourniers eventually got to Southold "only to find that news of their flight had preceded them and certain Tories were watching for them. Thus warned, they sailed into Peconic Bay and settled at Red Creek and spent the rest of the war period in hiding."[27]

Ordinary people did extraordinary things during the war. In East Hampton, women, as well as men, bravely confronted the British. Jane Conkling Sherrill held off British soldiers searching private homes for deserters by threatening them with a fire shovel. Betsy Huntting, while residing in Montauk's Third House with her family, scared off enemy troops by hurling boiling water at them. Ax-wielding Amy Miller managed to deter soldiers bent on stealing her fowl and, in the process, elicited praise from one of them, who said, "She would make a good soldier."[28] In Southampton, Mrs. John Hurlburt personally confronted General Erskine after her horse was stolen by British soldiers under his command. Whether it was the woman's pleas, her determination, Erskine's reputation for being a much more reasonable man than the ill-tempered Major Charles Cochrane, who had administrative jurisdiction over Sag Harbor and Bridgehampton, or a combination of these factors, the horse was promptly returned.

On the other side of Peconic Bay, female inhabitants of Oysterponds or Orient disposed of the contents of whiskey barrels in a local inn to prevent the usual sort of mayhem that resulted when soldiers imbibed. In Mattituck, Major John Corwin's wife stood up to British soldiers intent on using the Corwin wheat field as a cafeteria for their horses. Reaching for her husband's gun, she threatened to shoot the first horse to set foot in the field. Almost instantaneously the troops beat a hasty retreat.

Another East End woman, the wife of Abraham Gardiner, might have played a significant, albeit behind-the-scenes role during the war had she imparted highly sensitive information to American Major John Davis, who in 1775 commanded a group of several dozen militiamen attempting to rid the waters around Gardiner's Island of British ships. Although Mrs. Gardiner paid a visit to Major Davis to inquire about her son, Dr. Nathaniel Gardiner, she neglected to tell him what she had heard about an American general's plans to turn over certain forts to the British. The general was Benedict Arnold, whose liaison in the British Army was the dapper Major John Andre. For a time, Andre stayed in the East Hampton residence of Abraham Gardiner. Also in the house, hidden away, was Dr. Nathaniel Gardiner, on leave from the Continental Army to pay a visit to his father. Although he seems to have known Dr. Gardiner was there, Andre chose to ignore his presence, thus enabling the patriot physician to conclude his mission and head back, unharmed, to his unit. The Gardiners, like other bay area families, walked a fine line during the Revolutionary War. Patriots to the core, they nevertheless took the required oath of allegiance to the Crown. Only a week after the British victory at Brooklyn Heights in the summer of 1776, Colonel Abraham Gardiner was singled out for the unenviable task of administering the oath to the inhabitants of Southampton and East Hampton. He could have refused, of course, with deadly consequences; but, thinking it wiser to do what he had been told, he acquiesced. According to Ilse O'Sullivan in *East Hampton and the American Revolution*:

Rather than a disloyal act, Colonel Gardiner's administering of the oath, must be considered one of friendship and concern for his fellow townsmen. . . . . The harsh incidents visited on the western part of the Island had great effect on Colonel Gardiner. Should the East Hampton people refuse to take the oath, he reckoned Rebels they would be and imprisonment and the laying waste or confiscation of property . . . would be their inevitable lot.[29]

The oath notwithstanding, the East End did suffer under British domination and not even the property of the Gardiners was spared. Enemy soldiers used the manor house on Gardiner's Island as barracks. The house of the manor's superintendent became a British hospital. Offshore, in late 1780 and 1781, were ten enemy ships standing guard in anticipation of an encounter with vessels dispatched by America's ally, France, from Newport, Rhode Island. One of those British vessels, the *Culloden*, a large ship with a crew of 650, was wrecked in a northeaster in January 178. Valuable supplies were salvaged by the crew before they set fire to the ship, and what was left of the vessel was driven ashore on the west side of the Lake Montauk jetty.

Although the official end of the Revolutionary War came at Yorktown nine months after the *Culloden* went to its watery grave, the conflict endured on Long Island, not only because of the continued British presence, which lasted through 1783, but also because in the aftermath of the war New York State imposed a special tax of 37,000 pounds on the island "as compensation to other parts of the state for "not having been in condition to take an active part in the war."[30] If that weren't enough to cause rancor throughout the island, in the Peconic Bay area, the acts of attainder stripping loyalists of property and political rights certainly were.

Divided by adherence to opposing sides during the war, Southold's Wickham family was still split in the postwar period. Whereas Thomas Wickham had been a patriot, Parker Wickham was accused of being a loyalist and was deprived of considerable land, including Robins Island, long known as the "jewel of the Peconics." In the late twentieth century, Parker Wickham's descendants attempted, unsuccessfully, to have the attainder reversed in order to reclaim Robins Island and save it from development. Parker Wickham, in their view, was simply not guilty as charged. Another Southold man, Colonel Phineas Fanning, "who had cast his lot with the Tories," was "a buffer between the Whigs and Tories," according to historian Wayland Jefferson.[31] Loyalist though he was, Fanning, unlike Parker Wickham, was not stripped of his property. In general, the immediate aftermath of the war was a most difficult time in the bay area. Compared to New York City, where the evacuation of British troops in November 1783 was marked by celebration, on Long Island, "the situation . . . was a tragedy. . . . And while New York suffered beyond the fate of any other City, yet Long Island suffered more than any other rural district, save, perhaps, the Valley of the Mohawk."[32] With the divisiveness of the war years carrying over into the postwar period, the healing process in the bay area was a long one complicated by the outbreak, within a generation, of yet another war with the former mother country.

## Independence: Round Two

Although blessedly brief in comparison with the earlier conflict, the War of 1812 impacted the East End and its inhabitants, none more so than Joshua Penny, who dwelled in a house at Three Mile Harbor, East Hampton. In Penny's day, the homestead, which was later moved to a spot on Three Mile Harbor Road near the marina, was at the water's edge. It was here in August 1812 that Penny received a surprise visit from men serving aboard the *Ramilies*, the flagship of the British fleet blockading America's eastern seaboard. The sailors had been sent to this quiet spot with its lovely view of Gardiner's Bay by their commander, Sir Thomas Hardy, who had recently learned, from a paid informer, that Joshua Penny had attempted to blow up the *Ramilies* off Montauk. Approaching the British ship in a wooden submarine, Penny intended to attach explosives to the vessel, but was compelled to flee when the British took to longboats and started closing in on him. Earlier in the war when the *Ramilies* was off New London, another failed attempt to destroy it had been made by a sub.

To head off future attacks, Sir Thomas Hardy placed a hundred or so American war prisoners on the vessel and promptly notified New London's mayor and the governor of Connecticut that these men, as well as Hardy and his crew, would go down with the ship should the Americans blow it up.

British threats did not faze Joshua Penny because he had spent much of his youth defying the Crown. Indentured at age fourteen to a physician in his hometown of Southold, Penny was released from his contract within a year and, like countless young North Forkers ever since, he promptly headed for New York, but not for long. Instead of seeking his fortune in the metropolis in the heady days of the mid-1780s when Americans, fresh from their victory in the Revolutionary War, envisioned a rosy future, Penny shipped out to sea on a vessel bound for Guadalupe. The vast oceans, not Peconic Bay, would be his aquatic environment for the next three years. He was back in Southold for a visit during his eighteenth year and became reacquainted with friends who tried to persuade him to remain in Southold, but "they were disappointed; my fondness for the sea was undiminished."[33]

Penny may have regretted not remaining at home, because when he returned to sea on an American merchantman, he was impressed by the British. While their ship was in the West Indies, Penny and three other sailors were taken aboard a British warship and forced to serve in His Majesty's navy. Intimidated, flogged, and poorly fed, Penny suffered bouts of illness, but was determined to regain his freedom. Following several reassignments, he found himself in Cape Town, South Africa, where he was recaptured after he jumped overboard and tried to reach a merchant ship. Beaten senseless for this escape attempt, the young sailor ended up in a British hospital from which he made a successful bid for freedom. His home for more than a year was the top of Table Mountain, which looms above Cape Town Harbor. "At last I reached the summit, and selected a spot, in view of the Western Ocean for my residence. I occupied a cavern which secured me from storms, near a good spring of water," he explained in his autobiography.[34] Upon its publication in 1815 the book became a runaway bestseller in large part because of its thrilling tales of battles with Bushmen, experiences in Santo Domingo during the uprising against the French, and even lighthearted moments such as the Fourth of July when Penny convinced his British captain to provide American sailors with wine and brandy to toast their nation's independence. For some readers, the most intriguing part of the story was the author's survival on a diet of small game and plants during his sojourn on Table Mountain before eventually boarding a merchant ship departing from Cape Town.

After a series of further adventures on various ships, he landed in New England in 1808 and immediately made his way across the Sound, where he fractured his knee when "a violent thunder storm drove us on shore at Oyster Pond Point, where the lighter, by a surge, was suddenly thrown on me," he lamented.[35] Penny spent a quiet summer recuperating, but after his marriage in December, he went to sea again, "either coasting or going to the West Indies."[36] He and his wife may also have been lighthouse keepers on Cedar Island in Peconic Bay at the start of the War of 1812. Joshua himself was forced to bid farewell to this area following the *Ramilies* incident. Snatched from his home at Three Mile Harbor by Sir Thomas Hardy's men, Penny was imprisoned on the *Ramilies*. As Penny was being taken away, his wife followed him "to the door and shrieked; upon which a sergeant of marines struck her with the breech of a gun, the point of which he thrust at her left breast, with so much violence, that she is unwell from that cause to the present time," Penny reported in his memoirs.[37] While Mrs. Penny nursed her wounds at home, her husband was transferred from the *Ramilies* to a prison in Halifax, Nova Scotia, after turning down a payment of $3,000 and a promise of immediate release for the return of the torpedo. During the nine months prior to his release, Penny learned, from other prisoners, that a neighbor had been paid $1,000 for supplying Sir Thomas Hardy with information about the attempt to destroy the *Ramilies*. The actual sum was probably no more than $200, but the disgusted victim frequently proclaimed that "a Tory had sold a Penny for $1,000."[38]

As for Penny's sub, toward the end of the war, in the autumn of 1814, the tranquility of a Southold church service was interrupted by artillery fire from British ships off Arshmomoque Beach in Southold.

The British targeted this spot in 1814 because Joshua Penny's submarine had been driven ashore by gale-force winds. In the midst of the cannon fire, Noah Terry, an Orient man who happened upon the scene before alarmed male churchgoers arrived, jumped atop the torpedo boat and defiantly waved his hat while shouting at the British. He soon took cover, however, along with the worshippers as the enemy finished off the torpedo boat and then sacked the artillery-damaged home of Deacon Abraham Mulford. The deacon's young slave, Sambo, together with other property, including a beautiful silk dress, which was one of Mrs. Mulford's prized possessions, were carted off but everything was returned after the deacon, under a truce flag, rowed to the British ships and pled his case.

Elsewhere along the Sound Shore of the East End and several miles from Great Peconic Bay in Jamesport, skirmishes occurred at Northville in 1814 after troops were landed from the British ship *Sylph*. An American vessel, the *Nathan Hale*, was captured, but British troops who hit the beach at Penny's Landing were sent packing by the local militia. To the delight of East End residents, the *Sylph* ran aground off the South Shore near Shinnecock Point in 1815.

As far as *major* military action was concerned during the War of 1812, Sag Harbor, which had both a fort to protect Shelter Island Bay and a Union Street arsenal containing artillery pieces, ammunition, and other supplies for the fort, took a direct hit from the British in July 1813. Accounts of the attack varied but some stated that the British captured several vessels in the harbor and torched one ship before coming ashore under cover of darkness. They were said to have been in the process of burning a vessel that had been tied up at the wharf when shots rang out from the fort, causing them to flee. The enemy was quickly repulsed by the Fourth Regiment of the New York State Artillery stationed at the fort. Sag Harbor also had a maritime force, the U.S. Sea Fencibles, that patrolled area waters. "Both units performed admirably, driving the British invaders from the port on the one occasion they chose to attack it."[39] Thirteen months after the attack on Sag Harbor, Congressman Ebenezer Sage of Suffolk County detailed the suffering of the local people:

Women who have seen better days are obligated to wash for and billet soldiers, to share with them their rations; no happy countenances among us but the children for want of reflection and soldiers made happy by whiskey; but for our clam beds and fish many would go supperless to bed.[40]

Other bay area residents also had terrifying experiences during the war. Toward the end of her very long life, Orient resident Jemima Terry Latham recounted, in an interview with the *Brooklyn Daily Eagle*, how, as a child during the War of 1812, she was startled by the appearance of British ships in Gardiner's Bay. Ten years old at the time, Jemima was on a strawberry-picking expedition. She headed home immediately to alert her parents, who quickly gathered up their valuables and buried them on the property. Jemima herself was put in the garret of the family home until the danger passed. Years later, she noted that the British frequently came ashore at Orient to buy foodstuffs for which they paid local farmers. Jemima also recalled how North Fork men, who typically went to Montauk to fish in the fall, stayed home in 1813, but still fared well when an unprecedented number of mackerel arrived in the bay. According to Jemima, "When the water receded the mackerel were left on the flats in vast quantities. The whole village went to the flats and got a supply of the fish. This was considered a remarkable providence."[41]

That same year, Orient fishermen were issued a strong warning not to get too close to British ships. This came in the wake of the imprisonment of American Captain Eliphalet Beebe and the burning of his ship *Jupiter* "at the entrance to Hallock Bay."[42] Artifacts from the *Jupiter* were discovered "near the Long Beach shoal, opposite Peter's Neck Point."[43] Captain Thacher Paget of His Majesty's Ship *Superb* formally apologized for the destruction of the *Jupiter*, but nevertheless he wanted Americans to stay far away from British vessels.

Although British ships were ominously visible off the East End and sometimes landed troops for purposes other than grocery shopping, actual encounters with Americans were few and quite unexpected. Historian Henry Hazelton recounted the story of British officers who disembarked from their ships and "went ashore at Gardiner's Island."[44] According to Hazelton, "Mrs. Penny, the wife of Captain Penny, who kept the light at the harbor, saw them going to the island. As soon as they were out of sight she informed the militia by signal and Decatur and others went to the island and captured every one of them."[45]

On another occasion, Americans who managed to reach Gardiner's Island, after evading the British blockade of Commodore Stephen Decatur's fleet in New London, were surprised by an enemy landing force. The Americans were spirited away to an inglorious imprisonment in Connecticut. Meanwhile, on Gardiner's Island, the lord of the manor would have suffered the same fate had his quick-thinking wife not sent him to his room, where she arranged bottles of medicine on a night table and took maximum advantage of both his customary frail appearance and the green décor of the room, right down to the bedhangings, to convey the impression that the lord was a very sick man. The British presumably did not want a famous hostage who would surely die before he could be of any use to them so they asked for his eldest son. Happily, the boy was in school, off-island, and was not taken prisoner.

Some men imprisoned during the War of 1812 were held by their own forces pending the outcome of military trials. Such was the case in January 1815. The very month the war ended with General Andrew Jackson's victory at New Orleans, a court-martial took place in Sag Harbor for a soldier charged with "absenting himself from camp without leave."[46] The accused pled guilty "whereupon the court decided that he be deprived of ten days rations of whiskey and be put on fatigue duty in cleaning out the post and, in close confinement, until tomorrow morning guard relieve then to be discharged with a reprimand by the officer on guard."[47]

## That Splendid Little War

Military trials, dishonorable discharges, and the ever-present possibility of enemy attack all began to recede from the consciousness of bay area residents during the long interval between nineteenth century wars. Following the War of 1812, eight decades would pass before the Peconic Bay area would be overrun by soldiers. When large numbers of men in uniform were again seen on the East End they would not be members of a hostile force but, rather, Americans fresh from triumphs in the tropics during the Spanish-American War. In 1898 East End residents feared the sudden appearance of the Spanish fleet en route to attack New York City. The arrival of U.S. naval vessels in Peconic Bay only served to heighten apprehension. Fortunately, the conflict known as "that splendid little war" because of its brevity and the bravado of some members of the armed forces, most notably Long Island's own Colonel Theodore Roosevelt, ended before a nineteenth-century Spanish armada disturbed the tranquility of the bay area the way the British presence offshore had done so earlier in the century.

In the immediate aftermath of the Spanish-American War 28,000 troops were repatriated, but instead of being mustered out and sent to their respective homes, they were brought to Camp Wikoff at Montauk. Fearful that the troops would spread tropical diseases among the general population, Congress was reluctant to allow the boys back into the country. But Theodore Roosevelt came up with a compromise, namely to quarantine the soldiers in one of the most isolated parts of Eastern America. Amazingly, "in less than thirty days was raised a camp of thirty thousand soldiers."[48]

Transporting returning soldiers to this remote location was no easy task because Montauk's dock was not strong enough to withstand the pounding of thousands of feet, and its T-shaped front made docking difficult. Consequently, it was impractical to transport all of the returning soldiers directly to Montauk. Instead, many went from Cuba to Florida, where they boarded trains for New Jersey. They were then ferried across New York Harbor and up the East River to the Long Island Rail Road depot in Long Island City for the last leg of the journey. So many trains headed for Montauk that they became backed up at Amagansett, forcing already weary soldiers to walk the rest of the way to Camp Wikoff.

Living in a tent city stretching from Fort Pond to Lake Montauk and down to the Atlantic, the men, many of whom were ill, received visits from members of the Women's National War Relief Association. One of the female volunteers at Camp Wikoff was Emily Roebling, who had assisted her husband behind the scenes during the construction of the Brooklyn Bridge after he nearly succumbed to caisson disease (the bends) and could not fulfill all of his duties as chief engineer of the project. At Montauk, Mrs. Roebling supervised the construction of field hospitals and tent platforms designed to raise the men's makeshift living quarters above the damp sand. Another volunteer, Miss Reubena Hyde Walworth, a recent Vassar graduate who served as a nurse at Montauk, died of typhoid fever and "was buried wrapped in an American flag" and "had a military funeral."[49]

## The Great War

As Miss Walworth was being laid to rest, the United States was preparing for the next war, World War I (or the "Great War," as it was known before the outbreak of World War II), by testing torpedoes in Noyac Bay. This area of the Peconics was selected for weapons trials by the E. W. Bliss Company in 1891 because of its protected waters, depth, and lack of strong currents. The actual manufacturing of the weapons was done in Brooklyn. Following careful inspection of each torpedo it was dismantled and sent, in sections, either on the Long Island Rail Road or by boat to Long Wharf, Sag Harbor, where the Bliss Company had erected a building "covering powerful air compressors, and there the torpedo was charged for trial."[50] After that, the weapon was tested on a course, marked by buoys, approximately five miles from Long Wharf. Initially the range was under 800 yards, but on the eve of America's entry into World War I, it had "increased to twenty times that distance."[51] Local baymen were not exactly thrilled by this intrusion but managed to come to terms with it, according to the *Brooklyn Daily Eagle*, which observed that "the skeptical baymen no longer sneer at the efforts of the men off on the bays who are trying to make undersea weapons run straight courses."[52]

Between the early 1890s and the teens of the twentieth century, the torpedoes manufactured by the Bliss Company became more sophisticated. The Whitehead torpedo, with a range of 800 yards, was superseded by a weapon invented by Frank W. Leavitt, one of the principals in the Bliss Company. As the size of the weapons increased, the company required larger vessels. The tugboat *Agnes* was succeeded by the gunboat *Sarah Thorpe*, which, in turn, was replaced by the gunbarge *Eliphalet Bliss*. In 1902 an eighteen-and-a-half-foot-long, two-thousand-pound prototype of the Leavitt torpedo, still in the experimental stage, exploded on board the *Sarah Thorpe*, sending "bits of the steel case of the cylinder flying in all directions with terrific force."[53] A machinist lost his right arm in the accident.

The unfortunate victim, John Walden, a family man with a wife and seven children back in Brooklyn, had incredible stamina. After being wounded, he calmly strolled to a chair, asked his coworkers to remove his coat, and then gave them a quick course in first aid as he told them how to stop the bleeding. In an effort to obtain medical treatment, the steam launch *Stella* deposited a man at Short Beach. He biked to Sag Harbor at top speed only to discover that two of the town's doctors were away. Two other Sag Harbor physicians, along with an East Hampton doctor who happened to be in Sag Harbor at the time, rushed to the aid of the injured man. After amputating the lower part of the victim's arm, the doctors discovered tiny pieces of steel beneath the skin in the upper part of the arm and decided to amputate everything below the shoulder. Anesthetized for two hours, the unfortunate Walden "stood the operation wonderfully well."[54] When this shipboard surgery had been completed, the *Sarah Thorpe* headed to Long Wharf and poor Walden was carried to his lodgings at the American Hotel. That night he "rested easily. . . . He has the best of medical and surgical attendance and two trained nurses are with him to watch and minister to his wants both night and day."[55] (See fig. 10.)

The Leavitt torpedo that had nearly claimed Walden's life was eventually perfected, and once it was in full production, the Bliss Company acquired a scow barge and two speedy launches for use in testing the weapon. The 120-by-40-foot steel barge served as a gun platform where torpedoes slated for testing were charged with

10. Montauk Steamboat at Long Wharf, Sag Harbor, L.I. Courtesy of Suffolk County Historical Society, Riverhead, N.Y.

compressed air rather than a live charge. Torpedoes shot from the barge, which was secured by four anchors, each weighing a ton, traveled under Noyac Bay at the staggering speed of forty-five miles per hour. The torpedoes were supposed to float until they were retrieved by the power launches, but they did not always behave predictably. They occasionally hit the small boats manned by workers whose job was to record the time the weapon flew by the spot where the workers were stationed. When that happened, the fast launches raced to save the Bliss employees who had been thrown overboard. The fast launches, which were equipped with grappling hooks, were also dispatched to pull up torpedoes that malfunctioned and plunged to the bottom of the bay. In time, as the range of its weapons increased, the Bliss Company began using Gardiner's Bay for testing. More expansive than the landlocked Noyac Bay, Gardiner's Bay filled the bill.

No matter where in the vast Peconic Bay estuary system it was conducting trials, the Bliss Company was justifiably proud of what it was doing and was eager to show off a bit. For that reason, distinguished guests, including Thomas Alva Edison and various high-ranking domestic and foreign military personnel, were invited aboard the company's ship *Emblame* to view torpedo testing under the watchful eyes of either the vessel's first captain, George Page, or its second, Thomas Corcoran, both of whom had operated menhaden boats. Demonstration cruises of this type faded into history following World War I. Once orders for its highly accurate product stopped pouring in from both the United States and the European allies, the company began to rethink the need for its Sag Harbor facility. In 1919 Bliss had seventy-five employees in the old whaling port, but it remained a presence in Eastern Long Island for only a half-dozen years after the war ended. More enduring than Bliss Torpedo was the Greenport Basin and Construction Company, which produced submarine chasers, coal barges, and distribution and torpedo boats during World War I. On the South Fork a naval aviation base was constructed in Montauk in 1917. Aerial surveillance of East End waters by seaplane and by the dirigibles manufactured in Montauk during the war was conducted by hundreds of men who dwelled in hastily constructed barracks at Fort Pond Bay.

## Pirates and Rumrunners

Following World War I, the Peconic Bay estuary, minus torpedo testing and trial runs for newly constructed military vessels, should have been a decidedly tranquil waterway, but that was not to be the case—because no sooner had the war ended than a new conflict began. This "war," characterized by daring shootouts, nighttime raids, and extremely fast boats, pitted rumrunners and bootleggers against federal authorities seeking to enforce the prohibition of alcoholic beverages. Mandated by the Eighteenth Amendment to the United States Constitution, the ban on booze took effect in January 1920. For the next thirteen years, until the amendment was repealed, Eastern Long Island waters, including Peconic Bay, were the scene of considerable illegal activity. The comings and goings of rumrunners, who transported liquor from boats offshore to various harbors on the East End, were akin to the smuggling done centuries earlier by both ordinary inhabitants of the Twin Forks and by notorious pirates.

In the late 1600s Captain William Kidd, a minister's son from Scotland and a respected merchant who lived quietly with his wife in Lower Manhattan, was a troublesome presence in Long Island waters. Piracy was so rampant in the New York colony waters at the time that the Crown established a company to outfit a large ship, the *Adventure Galley*, to stamp out illegal activities on the colony's waterways and seize any French ships. Preying upon the commerce of an enemy nation was legal, but grabbing the cargoes of innocent vessels, something that Kidd was accused of doing, was illegal. He was also charged with hastening the death of one of his crew members by clobbering the fellow with a bucket. Following a trial in a kangaroo court in London, where he had been taken after voluntarily surrendering to British authorities in Boston, Kidd was hanged in 1701. He may have been the scapegoat for highly placed men who had a financial stake in his seafaring activities.

Two years before his death, Captain Kidd had landed on Gardiner's Island. Knowing that he was in deep trouble, Kidd, who at the time was en route to Boston to explain his activities and plead for leniency, buried a considerable amount of loot on the island during his three- day stay. Despite the Gardiners' hospitality, which included a roast pig feast so enjoyed by the dear captain that he gave Mrs. Gardiner a beautiful piece of gold fabric, Kidd warned the lord that heads would roll should the buried treasure, consisting of diamonds, rubies, silver, gold dust, and other items, not be there when he returned for it. Acceding to the demand of New York royal governor Lord Bellomont, the treasure, minus one exquisite diamond, which supposedly was overlooked when Lord John Gardiner turned over the loot, was used as evidence against Kidd. The gem remaining with Gardiner was passed down in the family and was worn not only by women but, in the twentieth century, by the colorful Robert David Lion Gardiner, sixteenth lord of the manor, who, as mentioned previously, was still battling, until his death in 2004, with his niece, Alexandra Goelet, and her husband over the future of the island.

The legal jousting of the Goelets and the Gardiners seems inconsequential, except to the parties involved, compared with what happened on Gardiner's Island in 1728. After failing to heed the warning of a couple of Montauk Indian women who informed him of the presence of a large vessel just offshore, the aged John Gardiner was attacked by an international crew of pirates. His hands were slashed, most likely because these troublesome visitors, who tore through the manor house doing considerable damage, were disappointed to learn that the bulk of the lord's wealth was safely stashed away on his property in East Hampton. The pirates stayed around a few days, however, and helped themselves to most of the silver in the manor house. A sharp-eyed group, they overlooked only one tankard.

Joseph Bradish, reputedly the most vindictive pirate to visit the East End, intended to unload his ship *Adventure* on Gardiner's Island soon after he arrived in Sagaponack back in 1699. Local boat owners from Southampton and Southold on opposite sides of the bay were hired to do the job, which was actually undertaken off Block Island because of wind direction at the time. With the cargo safely trans-ferred to the smaller vessels, the *Adventure* was sunk. Bradish eventu-ally suffered the same fate as his contemporary, Captain Kidd. Colonel Henry Pierson, a Sagaponack resident and member of the New York Colonial Assembly, to whom Bradish had entrusted gemstones for safekeeping, was turned in by a neighbor, whereupon he relinquished the loot to British authorities, all the while protesting his innocence.

Pierson may not have been culpable, but East Enders of the 1920s who augmented their income by supplying thirsty New Yorkers with banned alcoholic beverages were knowingly breaking the law. In 2001 the History Channel produced a documentary highlighting the activi-ties of these entrepreneurs. It was filmed in and around Greenport and included Claudio's Restaurant, which, during Prohibition, stood on pilings, thus enabling boats transporting liquor to pull in right under the building. With the repeal of Prohibition, the entrepreneurs who supplied Claudio's and other watering holes were viewed more as rascals than as real criminals. Since the 1930s the general reaction has been to smile and shrug when told of the antics of bay area residents whose second jobs were revealed neither to the IRS nor to the cen-sus takers. Nevertheless, in the early twenty-first century some elderly

North Fork residents who, as teenage boys, had run afoul of the law by working for bootleggers or rumrunners were willing to talk about their lucrative part-time jobs, but not for publication. The same wariness was evident in the 1980s when a reporter for the *Suffolk Times* interviewed a man who had accumulated considerable wealth during a rumrunning career that spanned a decade and a half. Not wishing to see his name in print, this fellow used the nickname "Scoundrel" while being interviewed. "Scoundrel" confided to the *Suffolk Times* that he was only fifteen when he began "unloading launches on beaches on the Bay and Sound in and around Greenport."[56] Later he was aboard trawlers that met ships at such East End rendezvous spots as "the deepwater hole inside the ruins off Gardiner's Island."[57] Rough seas did not deter rumrunners. In fact, they preferred stormy nights because the Coast Guard, not expecting any activity in bad weather, was generally absent. Once the precious but illegal cargo was safely ashore, it was usually transported directly to New York City, but "if the heat was on" liquor was hidden in barns.[58] If the cache was too large, it was hidden in gullies under a blanket of hay.

Hiding alcohol from the authorities was a lucrative business. Baymen could make as much as $150 per night for hauling cases of alcohol while farmers received "$100 a day for storing liquor in their barns."[59] A retired Montauk charter boat captain, who freely admitted that he became involved in rumrunning as a teenager, said he spent what he earned quickly. Captains who transported liquor into Greenport and Montauk could earn as much as "400 a trip."[60]

Sometimes the action took place on dry land. In early October 1923, a very active year for rumrunning on the North Fork, there was "a desperate gun fight somewhere between Arshmomoque and Nassau Point between bootleggers and rum pirates."[61] A large sailing vessel named the *Clarence* was caught with hundreds of cases of liquor on board in the fall; more than two dozen cases were uncovered during a December raid at a Sandy Beach cottage. The year's most newsworthy Prohibition story involved the motorboat *Charlotte*. Acting on a tip, the Coast Guard was waiting for the vessel at the Orient Point dock in the wee hours of the morning on June 8.

The boat, its entire crew, and two hundred cases of scotch were seized by the authorities, but a funny thing happened on the way to Greenport. The crewmembers, who were being transported in a farm truck that had seen better days, systematically dumped the liquor onto the road from the back of the old vehicle. By the time they arrived in Greenport, every trace of evidence had vanished, thus undermining the government's case against the men.

The feds were doing so poorly that captains of rumrunning vessels soon brought their precious cargoes right into Greenport harbor. Toward the end of 1924, the score evened out a bit when the *Pacific* was seized in the harbor. That same year a Coast Guard base was established in Greenport. In 1925 the action shifted from sea to shore when a genuine shooting match took place on Route 25, the main road linking Greenport and Southold. Along this well-traveled route, Vinnie Higgins, a gang leader, created frequent roadblocks to halt caravans of vehicles transporting cases of liquor from the Greenport dock to New York City. The objective was to seize the valuable cargo, which Vinnie and his men could then dispose of at a huge profit. Sometimes things turned violent, which is what happened the night Vinnie and his boys confronted gun-toting "entrepreneurs" speeding toward the city. Unwilling to give up their valuable cargo, the men heading for New York pulled out their machine guns. Before long, a two-hour battle disturbed the quiet of the bay area. When it was over the Higgins gang left the scene with three hundred of the nearly four hundred cases belonging to their victims, a number of whom sustained bullet wounds. The Higgins gang was clearly triumphant.

In the aftermath of this incident, irate residents from Orient to Cutchogue formed the North Fork Law Enforcement Society to take back the area's main road from gun-toting hoodlums, but they had only limited success. Until Prohibition was repealed, the illicit activities of rumrunners and bootleggers disturbed the tranquility of the area as evidenced by the title of a December 1933 newspaper article: "Large Shipment of Smuggled Alcohol Seized Monday on Nassau Point."[62] The article revealed that the Coast Guard and federal agents "intercepted a truck loaded with alcohol."[63] The agents then proceeded to Mattituck, where they made the mistake of leaving their suspect and the truck outside Albin's restaurant while they went in for a bite. When they emerged from the restaurant, they discovered that the suspect had escaped. A panicked phone call to the Southold Town Police elicited the assistance of a local officer who helped with a search that resulted in the apprehension of the escaped bootlegger on Nassau Point. With egg on their faces, perhaps literally as well as figuratively following their repast in Mattituck, the feds, in true Marx Brothers comedy fashion, followed the truck tracks to a garage near the end of the fashionable peninsula long considered one of the best addresses on the North Fork. There they found not only the missing truck, with 200 cases of alcohol, but an additional cache of 190 cases in the garage. All told the liquor was worth $12,000. According to the newspaper: "It is said to be packed six gallons to the case, and the tax is said to be about $5 per gallon."[64] The paper also noted that, off-season, Nassau Point was an ideal location for hiding alcohol because of its "seclusion that would favor such traffic."[65]

Nassau Point, where farmers hid booze amid their cabbages, was not the only place that afforded a generally safe haven to rumrunners and bootleggers. Throughout the Peconic Bay area there are roads, some of which were nothing more than tiny lanes leading to the water, and in the dead of night all sorts of vehicles parked at the ends of these roads, awaiting the arrival of boats transporting alcohol. Some bay area communities, such as Sag Harbor, Northwest, and Green-port, were preferred transfer points where hastily offloaded booze was quickly sent on its way to New York City, but Shelter Island was considered safer for unloading. "Mashomack was a preferred drop-off point, since the woods grew close to the beach. The woods provide essential daytime cover from the high-jackers' reconnaissance planes that circled overhead."[66]

At times when the feds turned up the heat in Greenport, the liquor entrepreneurs made a beeline for one of the hidden coves of Shelter Island. Instead of leaving their precious cargo on boats or stashing it away on the island, some of these clever fellows had a better idea, namely to attach ropes and nets to the cases of alcohol and then gently

submerge them in shallow water. Although the location of the contraband was marked with small white buoys, for various reasons the loot
was not always reclaimed. Decades later anglers occasionally brought
up well-aged beverages to accompany a good fish dinner. Whether
the liquid gold is safe and potable is another question. Bottles fetched
from the briny deep are more likely to remain unopened, adorning a
shelf and pointed to with pride by owners, some of whom consider
their treasures as the next best thing to Captain Kidd's haul!

More than two centuries after Kidd frequented these waters, the
Coast Guard scored a major victory in the war against rumrunning.
One fine May day in 1926 a Coast Guard boat patrolling Gardiner's
Bay near Cherry Harbor and Cartwright Shoals happened upon the
*Helen G. McLean*, a schooner from Nova Scotia, at the entrance to
Three Mile Harbor. The sailing vessel was a real beehive of activity with motorboats and an oyster boat coming up alongside and
offloading cargo. Before long the oyster boat headed for Three Mile
Harbor and one of the motorboats was en route to Sag Harbor. The
quick-thinking commander of the Coast Guard vessel put three crew-
men ashore at Three Mile Harbor to grab the oyster boat. A couple
of men were dispatched to the schooner while the Coast Guard vessel
proceeded to Sag Harbor, intercepting the hunted motorboat after
firing one shot at her. Meanwhile the oyster boat, with its 500 cases
of booze, was seized when it came ashore at Three Mile Harbor. So
successful was this operation that Coast Guardsman W. W. Woods,
who masterminded it on the spur of the moment, received a medal
for his efforts.

They could have used a good man like Woods in Montauk. Strategically situated on Rum Row, an area of the Atlantic stretching from
New England to South Jersey, the waters off Montauk were a favorite
spot for transferring cases of liquor to smaller boats that would take it
ashore. With so much of this nefarious activity occurring, there were
occasional mishaps. In December 1922, for example, the *Madonna V*
foundered and ended up on Napeague Beach. When the ship's cargo
began washing ashore, local people, including at least one self-pro-
claimed teetotaler, rushed to the beach to salvage the precious goods,

the teetotaler protesting all the while that the liquor might come in handy for medicinal purposes! Another South Fork resident, who acquired sauternes unloaded from the *Madonna V* before the vessel hit the beach, was still enjoying the wine in the 1960s. The man told a reporter for the *East Hampton Star*, "It's as good as ever."[67] Although this amiable wine connoisseur toted along an unopened bottle of *Madonna V* sauterne to the *Star* office and thereby revealed his identity, he did not want his name to appear in print. The editor obliged.

There were other men, as well, who sought anonymity because of their activities in and around Montauk during Prohibition. Some had participated in "floating operations," so-called because liquor and wine were placed in orange crates and floated from the offloading ship to a nearby shore. Boot-clad men waded into the water to retrieve the crates and transfer them to waiting vehicles. Others hid the liquid contraband in all sorts of places, including Third House. In 1925 liquor valued at $200,000 was dug up behind the historic building following a gun battle between rival bootleggers. Five years later a British schooner, carrying a cargo estimated to be worth a cool million, was seized in Fort Pond Bay. According to journalist and historian Jeanette Edwards Rattray: "It is probable that far more 'pirate gold' was handled off the beaches here during the prohibition era than ever was in the days of Captain Kidd and Joseph Bradish."[68]

Whether in Montauk or elsewhere on the East End, people who were benefiting financially by slaking the thirst of New Yorkers in the twenties and early thirties probably hated to see Prohibition end. Whether they were offloading the goods from boats, transferring it to motor vehicles or providing temporary hiding places, East Enders were accumulating additional income. For some, however, the good times did not last very long. A Sag Harbor bootlegger, for example, was put out of business after his neighbors complained to authorities, who then raided the bootlegger's home, where multiple gallons of "alleged illegal intoxicants and mash were seized by the raiding party."[69] The brewmeister was also taken into custody and transported all the way to Riverhead for arraignment, because neither Sag Harbor nor Bridgehampton magistrates were available the day the raid occurred.

Medical doctors were also hard to find during Prohibition, especially when called upon to respond to queries about binding the gunshot wounds of rumrunners and bootleggers. Physicians on both forks, as well as hospital personnel in Riverhead, Southampton, and Greenport, were quizzed in November 1932 after one of three men aboard a motorboat was felled by Coast Guard fire. Their boat had been deliberately run aground at Cedar Beach, Southold, an ideal place for rumrunning boats with shallow bottoms. The liquor was loaded onto trucks right on a boardwalk that ran along the beach. The men on the receiving end of Coast Guard fire in the late fall of 1932 did not have the luxury of motorized transport, neither for their liquor nor for themselves. They escaped on foot. The injured man limped off into the brush despite the severity of his wound, as evidenced by the amount of blood on a coat left behind on the beach. Although his fate remains a mystery, the beached boat, heavily laden with liquor, was seized by the Coast Guard.

Within a year of the Cedar Beach incident, the Eighteenth Amendment was repealed, in part thanks to the efforts of Pauline Sabin of Southampton, who had previously supported Prohibition. Troubled by the crime, corruption, and impact it was having on youth, Sabin established the Women's Organization for National Prohibition Reform to lobby for repeal. Following repeal, alcohol flowed freely once again, and ever since East Enders have had no excuse for being thirsty, especially today, given the proliferation of wineries, craft beer breweries, and specialized liquor distilling.

## The Genius and the Genie in the Bottle

Of history-making events in the Peconic Bay area, ranked on a scale of one to ten, one could argue, at least for the time being, that the proliferation of wineries and other establishments producing alcoholic beverages amounts to no more than a three. What happened on the shores of Peconic Bay a scant five years after the repeal of Prohibition was a ten-plus in terms of its global, let alone regional, impact. The chief actor in this historical drama was the amiable physicist Albert

Einstein, who spent two delightful summers on the North Fork. Although he tried his best to get away from it all, Einstein was very much a celebrity and the locals were thrilled to catch a glimpse of him if only for a fleeting moment. Of course, the North Fork being the sort of place it is, the populace was rather nonchalant, or tried to be, in the presence of the great man.

The Webb family of Greenport, out for a drive on Nassau Point, where Einstein was staying in 1938, had piled three generations into the car and headed west to Cutchogue in the early evening of June 17. After exploring various roads on the fashionable peninsula, they parked at a dead end "on the southerly shore of the stretch of land that stretches westerly from Nassau Point cove towards Fleets Neck but is separated at the western end by a small creek. . . . The . . . motor had hardly been turned off when three figures came into view walking along the shore," recounted one member of this happy group, adding:

> As they crossed . . . in front of us . . . I immediately said "and do you know who it is?" None other than Professor Einstein, the very personage we had previously been talking about. He was in company with two girls who I would judge to be about thirty or thirty-five years of age. He walked between them with his hands clasped behind his back and his long grayish tresses of hair flowing in the wind like a young girl's. It was about 8:15 and Una suggested that having seen our "personage" and the children becoming very restless, we should be starting homeward. But I immediately refused and insisted upon waiting until they came back down along the shore. The "personage" with his two lady companions at last . . . began to retrace their steps towards us. To better enable myself to address them, I stepped out of the car and walked a few steps in their direction. As they came closer, I greeted him questionably, "How do you do Professor? I am Mr. Webb from Greenport and would like to ask you some questions."[70]

One of the questions concerned a professor at Princeton, but while acknowledging that he had heard of the man, Einstein did not recollect ever having met him. Another query dealt with electricity. "My mother would like to know if you would give her a definition of electricity in one sentence?" said Mr. Webb, to which Einstein "answered with a broad smile, 'That is impossible-in two pages!'"[71] The great man was less interested in conversation than he was in the Webb children. "He looked admirably at first one child and then the other and with a throaty chuckle said 'Lovely!!' The children certainly took his eye," according to their father.[72] Shortly thereafter, when Einstein and his companions were about to depart, Webb "realized that I must obtain his autograph."[73] After asking one of the ladies accompanying Einstein "if she thought he would consent," he obliged when the request was made, in German, by the young woman.[74] In an attempt to head off future requests, however, "she with a worried expression, said, 'please do not tell anyone about this?'"[75]

Despite his understandable desire to hide from adult autograph hounds, Einstein genuinely enjoyed spending time with children, including a six-year-old who passed happy moments with the world-renowned scientist, throwing stones in the water from a bluff at Old Cove, as Einstein munched on chocolate chip cookies made by the child's mother. When his fourteen-foot catboat *Tinif,* which means "junk" in Yiddish, was capsized by a strong breeze, it was young people who rescued Einstein. The teenage boys who came to the scientist's aid on more than one occasion established their own ad hoc yacht club not far from the physicist's home and invited Einstein to become a member. He declined but gave the boys a donation. One of those lads, Robert Fisher, awarded Einstein an "A" for effort when it came to sailing, but something less in terms of his actual performance. "He wasn't a natural sailor," according to Fisher.[76] "It didn't come easy for him. I remember reminding him innumerable times that you should duck when you are going about so the boom wouldn't hit him."[77]

Einstein would have been wiser to leave the sailing to someone else and concentrate on his violin playing, something he did very well, according to David Rothman, who shared pleasant evenings playing duets with the physicist. The two became acquainted after Einstein's daughter strolled into Rothman's Department Store on Route 25 in the heart of Southold to buy a tool to sharpen a sculptor's chisel. Rothman actually stocked this unusual item, and he presented it to Margot Einstein Wibtelar as a gift because of his admiration for Einstein. Not only had Rothman read all of the physicist's writings, but he even knew who Margot was from pictures that appeared in the press. Once he realized that Einstein was residing on the North Fork for the summer, Rothman was anxious to get a firsthand look at the great man. He didn't have to wait long, for the very next day Einstein arrived in Southold to purchase what, in his heavily accented English, sounded like "sundials" but actually turned out to be sandals. It took David Rothman a little while to grasp what Einstein actually wanted, but once he did, a pair of $1.50 open-toed shoes was quickly produced.

While the sale was being rung up, Einstein was listening intently to the classical music playing in the background. Rothman also observed him "conducting" the Mozart symphony, at which point he engaged Einstein in a conversation about his interest in music. When each man learned the other was an amateur violinist, Einstein invited Rothman to his home for the first of many musical evenings. Einstein also visited the Rothman residence, and he accompanied Rothman to a meeting held at the Southold Fire Hall to raise funds for Christian refugees fleeing the Nazis. In advance of the gathering, which attracted several hundred people, Rothman told the organizers that they could announce that Einstein was in the audience but that, under no circumstances, should they call upon him to speak. Disregarding these ground rules, the minister in charge of the meeting did indeed ask the illustrious guest to say a few words. Einstein complied, but was exceedingly brief as he urged the large Christian audience to organize the way Jews like himself had done.

Precisely because he was fully cognizant of the Nazis' potential for unspeakable evil, Albert Einstein was open to recommendations made by fellow scientists in the summer of 1939. On July 30 of that year, Eugene P. Wigner, a Hungarian-born professor of physics at Princeton University, and his countryman, Leo Szilard, a faculty member at Columbia University, journeyed to the shore of Peconic Bay in search of Einstein. Not knowing exactly where he was staying and confused by the island's Indian names, they ended up in Patchogue rather than

Cutchogue, but they quickly regrouped and, with the help of a young lad whom they encountered once they reached the North Fork, they eventually made it to Einstein's rented home on Old Cove Road. The scene that greeted them when they arrived was vintage Einstein, for the noted scientist, informally clad in old pants, which were rolled up to resemble clamdiggers, and an undershirt, was catching the breeze on the screened porch. After greetings were exchanged, the uninvited guests proceeded to enlist Einstein in their mission to convince the administration of President Franklin D. Roosevelt of the need to commence work on an atomic weapon. German scientists had smashed the atom the year before and, while physicists in the United States had quickly followed suit, in America there were no plans for weapons development. Einstein wasn't sure there should be such development; in fact, he questioned whether the energy of the atom could be harnessed for this purpose.

Despite his skepticism, Einstein and his fellow scientists sat at a table on the porch of his vacation home and discussed the possibility that Germany might attempt to gain control of the high-grade uranium found in the Belgian Congo. Then they decided to draft a letter explaining their concerns to the Belgian government and to send this communiqué, together with a cover letter, to the U.S. Department of State. After further consideration, the trio decided to take a different tack, and what resulted was Einstein's historic letter that convinced a reluctant President Roosevelt to pursue the development of an atomic weapon. Urging the administration "to speed up the experimental work, which is at present being carried on within the limits of the budgets of University laboratories," Einstein was very concerned that the United States had "only very poor ores of uranium in moderate quantities."[78] He pointed out there was "some good ore in Canada and the former Czechoslovakia," which, in 1938, had been dominated by Germany.[79] "I understand," he said, "that Germany has actually stopped the sale of uranium from the Czechoslovakian mines which she had taken over. That she should have taken such early action might perhaps be understood on the ground that the son of German Under-Secretary of State . . . is attached to the Kaiser-Wilhelm-Institut in

Berlin where some of the American work on uranium is now being repeated."[80] The letter, which was hand-carried to President Roosevelt by his friend Alexander Sachs, an officer of the Lehman Corporation, was dated August 2, 1939. That Wednesday Szilard and Wigner, with another Hungarian physicist, Professor Edward Teller of George Washington University, in tow, visited Einstein at his vacation retreat to finalize the communiqué. The rest, as they say, is history.

One cannot help but wonder whether the history of World War II, the postwar atomic age, and the Cold War would have been different if Einstein had not gone along with his scientific colleagues. He did have misgivings about his participation in the genesis of the nuclear age. Writing to a longtime friend and fellow German physicist, Max von Laue, only a month before his death, he said: "Because of the danger that Hitler might be the first to have the bomb, I signed a letter to the President which had been drafted by Szilard. Had I known that that fear was not justified, I no more than Szilard, would have participated in opening this Pandora's box."[81]

In history there are so many cases of "what if—?" This is surely a most significant one. Aside from speculating about what might have happened or not happened had Einstein turned down Szilard and Wigner, one is also struck by the thought that Einstein could have easily perished in the waters of Peconic Bay on at least two occasions. When the *Tinif* capsized, fate intervened in the form of a fifteen-year-old boy who plucked the great scientist from the sea. As a nonswimmer, Einstein probably had no business being out there on his own, certainly not without proper flotation devices. Nearly sixty at the time and somewhat overweight, he was seen flailing about by his rescuer. Would his heart have given out or would the death certificate have read "death by drowning"? The bay could have claimed Einstein's life on yet another occasion when he set out from Nassau Point at nine o'clock one morning to sail to David Rothman's Southold home. It was the summer of 1939 and, by this time, Einstein and Rothman had become great friends, enjoying quiet musical interludes as well as discussions of politics and science. Einstein took pleasure in explaining complex scientific theories, in layman's terms, to his bright and eager "pupil" David Rothman. Nearly twenty years younger than the world-renowned physicist, Rothman revered Einstein. The friendship that matured along the shores of Peconic Bay deepened Rothman's esteem for the scientist and on that summer's day in 1939 Rothman was absolutely panic-stricken. Nine hours after his departure from Nassau Point, David Rothman's friend, confidant, mentor, and fellow musician was missing. It was almost dark when a disoriented Einstein turned up on a Southold beach. The news that his friend was safe came by way of a New York City police officer, who was acquainted with Rothman. Describing Einstein as a "wild-looking guy" badly in need of "a haircut—some helluva looking looney," the officer proceeded to tell Rothman, during a telephone conversation, that Einstein was "down here on the beach wanting to know where you live."[82] A relieved David Rothman was out of the house in a flash as he went to claim his friend.

Interestingly, the police officer's reaction to the great physicist was not atypical of North Forkers, whether natives, newcomers, or those who chose to vacation in an area that remained conservative through the final decade of the twentieth century. Given the area's casual lifestyle, unique individuals like Einstein were able to enjoy the rural ambience of the bay area without feeling uncomfortable. In fact, Einstein concluded that his two summers on Nassau Point were the most enjoyable of his life and, when compelled to choose the Adirondacks over the North Fork in the summer of 1940 because of his daughter's health, he expressed profound regret.

**World War II**

By the time Einstein headed for the mountains of upstate New York, the war in Europe had been raging for nearly a year. During World War II, East Enders, who had survived the lean years of the Great Depression by fishing, farming, cobbling together odd jobs, and working on New Deal construction projects, saw jobs open up in the defense industry. In Sag Harbor the Grumman Corporation, which for several years prior to the war was manufacturing parts for the company's seaplanes in a multibuilding plant, began turning out parts for warplanes. As soon as they rolled off the assembly line, these crucial components of the Grumman F4F Wildcat and other military aircraft were sent to the company's plants in Bethpage and Calverton. Airplane components were manufactured at Grumman's Sag Harbor facility right through the Korean War. On the opposite side of Peconic Bay, the Greenport Basin and Construction Company, which expanded its facilities by the addition of three cavernous metal buildings erected during the first and second years of American involvement in World War II, turned out camouflage destroyers and minesweepers. Once production of the YMS class minesweeper was fully under way, the plant turned out one vessel every two weeks, on average, more than any other shipyard in the United States.

Before it slid into the Peconic Bay estuary system, each ship was properly christened. Sometimes it was members of the Brigham family, owners of the company, who did the honors, but from time to time entertainers such as singer Lily Pons journeyed to the shores of the bay to break bottles of bubbly as part of the launching ceremony. The *Bowline*, the Greenport Basin and Construction Company's inhouse publication, reported in May 1943 that "a more beautiful rendition of the Star Spangled Banner has never been heard in Greenport than the one given by the . . . very lovely Lily Pons."[83] According to the *Bowline:* "Every ounce of Lily Pons' 104 pounds in weight and all of the leverage of her five feet, two inch height went into her roundhouse swing that broke a bottle of champagne across the bow of the wooden minesweeper and sent it down the ways into Peconic Bay."[84]

A year earlier there had been even more fanfare when Kate Smith, a popular singer and radio personality, arrived at the Greenport Basin and Construction Company in a five-car convoy with a Suffolk County police escort. "Kate Smith Launch Big Success, Songbird Given Royal Reception," was the headline in the *Bowline*.[85] The publication reported that plans to broadcast the popular entertainer's radio program from Greenport had to be scrapped because telephone lines could not replicate the sound quality required for radio. Kate did her regular show in Manhattan and then set out for Greenport for the 6 p.m. launch. Greeted by an enthusiastic crowd of 2,500 people who lined the streets, Kate Smith was surrounded by a guard of honor from Greenport Basin and Construction's yard police and a color guard. On a subsequent radio broadcast, she described her experience in Greenport as "truly an inspiring and thrilling occasion. The Village of Greenport itself is old, serene and beautiful," she declared.[86]

While skilled workers toiled away on shore building ships like the one Kate Smith christened, off shore ships were on the lookout for enemy submarines. In 1943 a German submarine actually landed four saboteurs at Amagansett. Although the men were subsequently captured in New York City, the United States remained extremely vigilant. It was no easy task. Lacking enough military vessels to mount a traditional antisubmarine campaign early in the war, the navy utilized sailboats, yachts, and motorboats to venture up to two hundred miles off the coast to search for subs in the North Atlantic. This makeshift fleet, known as the Picket Patrol, was staffed primarily by young men who had been classified 4-F or physically unfit for regular military duty, although there were some volunteers who joined the Picket Patrol because age and/or educational prerequisites proved to be stumbling blocks in their quest for commissions. The attraction of the Picket Patrol was that one did not need a commission to command a boat. Operating out of a half-dozen East Coast ports, of which Greenport was one, the Picket Patrol spotted German submarines but there were no armed clashes with enemy vessels. For the *Edlu II*, a yacht put at the disposal of the government by its owner, Rudolph Schaefer of Schaefer Beer, however, there was a close call in September 1942 off Montauk. The yacht encountered a German submarine on the surface and approached it with machine guns at the ready, depth charges not yet having been distributed to the Picket Patrol. Before anything happened, however, the sub disappeared into the depths of the Atlantic. When the *Edlu II* made its maiden voyage as part of the Picket Patrol three months prior to this incident, it lacked not only guns but also sonar, which became standard a bit later. On this trial run the *Edlu II* used a radio to stay in touch with the base in Greenport. Two reports per day were required even if no enemy subs were spotted. If subs were detected, shipping convoys taking supplies and men to Europe were warned about the danger and combat vessels were notified to attack. In all, 33 boats and 350 men composed Greenport's Picket Patrol unit. Though not impressive in numbers, both the equipment and the personnel made an important contribution to national security during the early days of World War II.

Military camps and forts on the East End were other vital components of the country's security. On Plum Island, Fort Terry, which had been built in 1897, was a lookout post watching for German aircraft and submarines. In Montauk Carl Fisher's once-lavish Montauk Manor and skyscraper office building were transformed into barracks. The navy replaced the civilian settlement at Fort Pond with a seaplane hangar, housing, and docks while the army installed four sixteen-inch guns at Camp Hero, which is now a state park. An unfinished fort that the government had started building at Gardiner's Island lighthouse during the Spanish-American War was used for bombing practice in World War II. In 2013 federal officials doing a bird count at this spot, which is known locally as "the Ruins," came upon an unexploded bomb. The Suffolk County bomb squad detonated the device in an operation that involved marine units from East Hampton, Riverhead, and Southold as well as the county marine unit's new vessel built to respond to chemical, biological, and nuclear incidents, whether accidental or acts of terrorism.

## Toward the Millennium

In the late twentieth century, the eerie remains of one relic of World War II, the decommissioned Camp Hero, conjured up images of secret time-altering experiments known as the Montauk Project. True believers in the Montauk Project may not have any problem envisioning Princess Diana, John Fitzgerald Kennedy, and others freeze-framed somewhere in time and space to be set in motion again the way images on a DVD begin to move at the push of a button. This is the sort of thing author Peter Moon, in a series of books on the Montauk Project, says was discovered accidentally during mind-control experiments conducted at Camp Hero. According to Moon, "The Montauk Project obtained a superior understanding of how the mind functions and achieved the sinister potential for mind control. A full report was made to Congress who in turn ordered the project to be disbanded."[87] Instead of being curtailed, however, the research proceeded. "Private concerns that helped to develop the project did not follow the dictate of Congress and sought to seduce the military with the idea that this technology could be used in warfare to control enemy minds," Moon asserted.[88] A well-financed group proceeded with the creation of "a new research facility at Camp Hero," which already had "a huge radar antenna that emitted a frequency of approximately 400–425 Megahertz. Coincidentally this is the same band used to enter the consciousness of the human mind."[89] Research involving people and animals took place at Camp Hero from the late 1960s through the early 1980s, according to Peter Moon, culminating in a "time portal" that was "fully functioning."[90] Moon was one of the people featured in producer Christopher P. Garetano's film *The Montauk Chronicles*, which was premiered at Gurney's Inn. The film was slated for release in 2014.

Just as time travel captivates the imagination, so, too, do UFOs. In the summer of 1991 the East End was abuzz with reports of mysterious lights in the sky and other unusual happenings, and some people were convinced that all of this had to be extraterrestrial. The *Suffolk Times*, in an article headlined "What Was It—UFO Spotted in Peconic," declared that a mysterious object had been seen in the sky near Pindar Vineyards at dusk on a Friday evening in early August.[91] A New York City businessman and the driver transporting him to his North Fork residence reported seeing something unusual about 8:30 p.m. And they weren't the only witnesses. According to the newspaper four teenagers living on a nearby farm "were terrified by the appearance of the enormous object that seemed to them 'three or four times as big as a house' as it flew over them flying off without a sound."[92] One of them described it as a disc framed in lights, some of which appeared to be red.

A purported visit by a delegation of East End police officers to the United Kingdom to inspect crop circles allegedly created by UFOs generated new rumors. To some residents of both forks all of this was quite amusing. Other people, on the East End and elsewhere, took it seriously. The latter group included members of the Long Island UFO Network, an organization headed by John Ford. After years of attempting to generate public interest through a newsletter and lectures, illustrated with slides and videotapes, given at public libraries and museums, Ford, a retired court officer, was arrested in 1996 for allegedly plotting to murder Suffolk County officials by spiking their toothpaste with radium. Deemed mentally unfit to stand trial, the retired court officer was institutionalized in what his supporters claimed was a plot to silence him.

For years prior to his arrest, John Ford had accused Brookhaven National Laboratory in Yaphank of hiding the bodies of aliens whose UFO had crash landed on Long Island. Few took this seriously. Of far greater significance was the fact that Brookhaven Lab and the vast military-industrial complex served as the engine of Long Island's economy for nearly forty years after World War II.

While the strong defense industry of the Cold War era provided good jobs, another type of highly remunerative work, drug smuggling, proved to be an irresistible lure for some. Like the rumrunners of old, people bringing in cocaine, marijuana, and other illicit drugs found the Peconic Bay estuary to be an ideal place to ply their trade. According to Richard Holborrow, a special agent in charge of the federal Drug Enforcement Agency's Long Island district office, there were four factors that made the East End perfect for drug smuggling. One was "seasonal waterfront home rentals" occupied by people who were less cognizant of their surroundings.[93] Another was "relative desolation" along "undeveloped shorelines and creekfronts."[94] A third factor was "deep water," facilitating the transfer of cargo from large trawlers to small boats.[95] Finally, "proximity to New York City" was an important reason drug smugglers set up shop in the Peconic Bay estuary system.[96] Of course, not everything got through to the city. Twenty tons of marijuana aboard the *Ricardo*, a South American trawler, were seized by federal agents in July 1982. When the ship's illegal cargo, valued at $30 million, was unloaded at Greenport, village police chief Robert Walden compared drug smuggling to rumrunning. "It's like the good old days except for a few differences. There's a lot more money, different people and different substances—much more dangerous," he said.[97]

The world as a whole was a much more dangerous place by the 1980s, but the United Nations (UN) was striving to make it less so. In recognition of the international peacekeeping organization's fortieth anniversary in 1985, the Town of Southold declared September UN Month and sponsored an impressive array of activities, including lectures, a peace vigil, ecumenical church services, school essay contests, a bus trip to UN headquarters, and a ten-kilometer walk to raise funds for UNICEF, the UN's International Children's Emergency Fund. The idea for all of this originated with Greenport resident Jack Kamalko, who told the *New York Times*: "People at the U.N. have been delighted to hear about the little town that could."[98]

The *Times* also quoted Southold town supervisor Francis J. Murphy. Referring to the New England origins of the community's seventeenth-century settlers, Murphy pointed out that the original settlers "had to fight for peace then" and current residents "know you have to do everything to hang on to it."[99]

That one had to work at maintaining peace was evident to Kofi Annan, the Greenport resident who served as secretary-general of the United Nations from 1997 until 2006. Born in Ghana, Annan received a Ford Foundation scholarship to finish his baccalaureate studies at Macalester College in St. Paul, Minnesota. His intention was to return to Africa, but when a corporate position he had accepted back home was not forthcoming, he stayed in the United States and went to work at the United Nations. If one were to speculate about the factors shaping the future secretary-general as he advanced at the UN, what comes to mind are the blue UN flags flown at Macalester, the school's emphasis on international studies, and Annan's vacation retreat where he could contemplate global issues in the peaceful setting of the North Fork. Although he gave up his second home in Greenport because of the time constraints of his new position, Kofi Annan indicated, at the time, that he hoped to return to the bay area when he was no longer secretary-general. For a man of peace, especially one who, together with the organization he headed, was awarded the Nobel Peace Prize in 2001, coming back to a region that has seen its share of conflict for the past 200-plus years will be very welcome. In a sense, his return would mean that the region had come full circle—from the tranquil days of early settlement through conflicts from the American Revolution to the war against terrorism—and back again, one hopes, to a more harmonious period.

# 5

# At Peace

## The Day That Changed the World

No matter how much East Enders hoped for a more peaceful world reminiscent of the tranquility of the bay area in the late twentieth century, the approach of the new millennium engendered fear. Would computers crash? Would the economy be impacted by even a partial breakdown of global connectivity? Would terrorists mark the beginning of the new age by disrupting millennial celebrations? Happily, the new millennium was ushered in peacefully, and Americans went about their business after breathing a huge sigh of relief. On the first day of the first year of a new century and a new thousand-year period of history, people strolled the beaches, inhaling the invigorating salt- tinged air that envelops the East End year-round. In less than two years, however, many wondered aloud whether this great nation, whose early history had unfolded in this very place, would endure. When planes hijacked by terrorists crashed into the World Trade Center's twin towers on September 11, 2001, the world changed in a nanosecond. Suddenly, no place on earth was safe, not even the bay area to which some Manhattanites fled in the immediate aftermath of the tragedy.

As city dwellers enrolled their children in public and private schools on the East End, fear of additional terrorist attacks, of a different sort, became pervasive. Even before the anthrax incidents in the wake of 9-11, people wondered whether the weapon of choice would be a chemical or a lethal pathogen. Ironically, back in 1999, a reporter for an East End newspaper, recalling the earlier 1993 bombing at the World Trade Center, observed that lethal bugs "could arrive in the

U.S. tomorrow. A traveler could be infected, or a terrorist could attack the U.S. agricultural industry and cause more loss of life and damage than blowing up the World Trade Center."[1]

These observations were made in the waning days of the Clinton administration when the federal government proposed upgrading Plum Island from a biosafety level-three facility to a level-four facility for intensive research on pathogens likely to be used in agroterrorism. Given Iraq's use of biological weapons against enemy food supplies, the U.S. government viewed this sort of research as a top priority and was willing to spend $215 million upgrading facilities on Plum Island because, according to Floyd Horn, administrator of the Agricultural Research Service: "This is not about food per se; Americans would not go hungry if we were attacked. But such an attack, or even a credible threat, would severely disrupt America's economic and social infrastructure for weeks, if not months or years."[2] Dr. Alfonso Torres, deputy administrator of the Agriculture Department's Veterinary Services Division and a former Plum Island director, estimated the value of U.S. commodity exports at $140 billion annually, noting that the $14.5 million federal expenditure for Plum Island each year was "a small investment."[3]

Although it was hard to argue with the assertion that increased spending was needed to safeguard our agricultural resources from potential terrorist attacks, bay area residents did not warm to the idea of having a biosafety level-four facility in their midst. For decades there had been rumors about the real nature of the work on the 840-acre island off Orient Point. Established by the U.S. Army Chemical Corps, Plum Island was turned over to the Department of Agriculture in 1952. For the next four decades, the island was off-limits to visitors. In 1992 reporters were allowed in as part of the Animal Disease Laboratory's efforts to deal with safety questions. Speculation about the nature of the research conducted there persisted, however, and, despite the center's denials, rumors about biological and chemical warfare research continued to circulate. Even among those whose imaginations did not make the quantum leap from research on foreign animal diseases, which might threaten the American meat industry, to chemical and biological warfare studies, there was a certain wariness about the proposal to upgrade Plum Island. While stating unequivocally that safeguards were needed for the livestock industry, the *Suffolk Times* posed an important question concerning whether Plum Island was the right place for a level-four facility. "If there's an accident at the government's new level four animal disease research center," asked the paper in an editorial, "wouldn't it be easier to contain in, say, Ames, Iowa, than on Plum Island?"[4]

Nimbyism? Maybe, but many bay area residents concurred. In 2008, five years after Plum Island was transferred to the Department of Homeland Security, a public hearing on a draft environmental impact statement, dealing with a half-dozen sites in the United States being considered for a biosafety level-four facility, attracted more than a hundred people who turned out to oppose the selection of Plum Island for the new laboratory. The federal government ultimately chose a site in Kansas and proceeded to put up a "for sale" sign on all 840 acres of Plum Island. The U.S. General Services Administration, which had the job of disposing of the island, recommended selling it to investors and allowing them to erect hundreds of houses on the unique property. Donald Trump had a different idea, namely, to build a golf course. No matter who buys the island they will have to abide by local zoning enacted by the Town of Southold. In 2013 Southold created two zoning districts: the Plum Island Research District, encompassing the laboratory and surrounding 176 acres, which can be used for education or recreation, and a Plum Island Conservation District, where development will be prohibited. Residents of the nearby East End were pleased that the potential terrorist target, which is located within the Nuclear Evacuation Zone of another such target, the Millstone nuclear power plants in Waterford, Connecticut, would be less appealing to those who seek to do us harm.

### Millstone: Too Close for Comfort

As for Millstone, which, as the crow flies, is about two dozen miles from the East End, the vulnerability of nuclear-generating facilities became a matter of widespread public concern in the aftermath of 9-11, as it would once again following the 2011 Japanese nuclear catastrophe in the wake of a tsunami. A decade earlier, Americans were less concerned about the potential for storm damage to nuclear facilities. Back then terrorism was perceived as the danger. A month after the terrorist assaults on the World Trade Center and the Pentagon, the national news media descended upon eastern Connecticut for a closer look at Millstone. CNBC depicted the gentle waves of Long Island Sound lapping against the sandy shore in the vicinity of the nuclear power plants, while a reporter from upstate Hartford babbled about Connecticut residents' fear of a terrorist attack on Millstone in retaliation for the military offensive the United States launched, in October 2001, against Afghanistan. Town government officials appeared on camera to assert that, in the event of an incident, the people of Waterford would be evacuated to an inland community near Hartford. That was all well and good for the citizens of Waterford, but what about the folks a nautical stone's-throw away on Eastern Long Island? They weren't even mentioned in the CNBC report!

Yet, even before September 11, Long Islanders had good reason to be concerned about the aging nuclear facility on the other side of the Sound. A 1996 *Time* magazine cover story detailed serious safety violations at Millstone Three, whereupon Northeast Utilities, the plant's operator, temporarily mothballed the reactor. But not for long. In the summer of 1998 the Nuclear Regulatory Commission gave Northeast Utilities the green light to fire up Millstone Three despite the fact that a study undertaken for Congress had concluded that "a core meltdown at Millstone Three would have a devastating impact within a 20-mile radius, which could include 23,000 immediate deaths, 29,000 eventual cancer deaths as well as $174 billion in economic losses."[5]

The damage, of course, would not be limited to Connecticut, as Peter Maniscalco, the coordinator for Citizens for a Progressive Energy Policy, noted: "If an uncontrolled release of radiation at Millstone Three occurred while a northeast wind were blowing, that plume would be aimed at eastern Long Island. The farms, fisheries and wineries of the East End economy would be destroyed, instantly."[6]

In 1997 East End officials learned about the release of radioactive water into Long Island Sound from the press, rather than from the Nuclear Regulatory Commission (NRC). Is it any wonder, then, that they called for the NRC to create an evacuation plan for areas within a fifty-mile radius of the Millstone plants? Better still, in the opinion of many East Enders, who recalled the successful battle that prevented the Long Island Power Authority's Shoreham nuclear power plant from opening, was a complete shutdown of Millstone. This goal was articulated by speakers who addressed a Nuclear Regulatory Commission hearing at Riverhead Town Hall in the late winter of 1999. Members of the NRC sat and listened for nearly three hours but said very little. The meeting was interrupted by boos, shouts, and chants of the familiar refrain, "Shut It Down!"[7] The same sentiments were voiced by placard-carrying protesters marching back and forth outside Town Hall prior to the meeting. One protester's sign read, "Chernobyl Hamptons?"[8] The person carrying this placard joined approximately thirty other opponents of Millstone in chanting, "Decommission the NRC! They're in the pockets of the industry! Hell no, we won't glow!"[9]

Two months later East End opponents of Millstone took their protest across the Sound, where they joined with an anti-Millstone group from Connecticut in a demonstration outside the plant gates. In August the South Fork was the focal point of activity. Millstone opponents, including model and actress Christie Brinkley, flocked to East Hampton High School for a hearing on a proposed local referendum calling for the closing of Millstone until a fifty-mile-radius evacuation plan was in place. A petition supporting the referendum was circulated by STAR (Standing for Truth About Radiation) and that organization's program coordinator, Tina Guglielmo, explained that she had testified at a NRC meeting held, in Maryland, to discuss the fate of Millstone. "I told them I live 24 miles from Millstone and I'm on an island," said Ms. Guglielmo, adding, "The fact that we would all be trapped here is okay with them."[10] Ms. Guglielmo's daughter, Jennifer, expressed concern about the number of recent East Hampton High School graduates diagnosed with cancer and pointed to a possible connection with nuclear pollution from Millstone.

Reflecting the sentiments expressed at the meeting, the East Hampton Town Board voted to place the referendum on the ballot in the November 1999 election. A "close Millstone" proposition also appeared on the Southampton ballot. In the days prior to the election STAR took out full-page ads in local papers. Designed for maximum impact, these advertisements informed voters that in the event of a catastrophic meltdown at Millstone, 50,000 people might die. Readers were also told that Millstone had pled guilty to more than two dozen safety violations, among them permitting inexperienced personnel to operate the reactors. This was no exaggeration. In September 1999 Northeast Utilities pled guilty to federal charges of falsifying records and violating the Clean Water Act; the company was slapped with a $10 million fine.

Although the propositions passed with over 70 percent of the vote in both South Fork towns, opponents of Millstone could hardly rest on their laurels. More needed to be done, which is why the Coalition for a Nuclear Free East End, a group that included the Peconic Baykeeper, the North Fork Environmental Council, the South Fork Groundwater Task Force, the Group for the South Fork, STAR, and other organizations, recommended the creation of a nuclear-free zone within fifty miles of the bay area. Transportation and disposal of nuclear materials, as well as nuclear research, would be governed by local laws within the zone. Assemblyman Fred Thiele Jr. of Bridgehampton was an enthusiastic supporter of the plan. Its adoption, in his opinion, would underscore the fact that "the people of the Peconic Region are committed to a clean and healthy environment and opposed to rash and risky nuclear projects which jeopardize that healthy environment."[11] No matter how desirable local legislation aimed at *regulating* all things nuclear was, *closing* Millstone continued to be the overriding goal. Toward that end STAR joined with the Connecticut Coalition Against Millstone in the spring of 2000 to file environmental lawsuits against Northeast Utilities. Besides seeking a complete and final shutdown of the facility, the suits demanded reparations for the environmental damage done during the three decades of plant operation.

By early summer Northeast Utilities was in the process of divesting itself of Millstone Two and Three. When word got out that the likely buyer would be a British company, the Citizens Awareness Network of Connecticut dispatched costumed Revolutionary War–era soldiers on what was billed as a "Paul Revere Ride" to warn the citizens of Connecticut, Eastern Long Island, and Westchester County, where foreign buyers were considering the purchase of the Indian Point nuclear plants, about the dangers inherent in the sale of aging facilities to overseas companies. The Paul Revere brigade was welcomed with open arms at East Hampton's historic Hook Mill, where local opponents of Millstone joined them in a protest.

Later that summer, after the municipalities in the bay area had adopted a Nuclear Free Community Law drafted by Thiele, numerous local and environmental groups, organized as the Long Island Coalition Against Millstone, held a benefit in Montauk. With the recent mothballing of the last functioning nuclear reactor at Brookhaven National Laboratory (BNL), the island was truly nuclear free, but the Peconic Bay area was still threatened by the despised nuclear facility on the Connecticut shore. Attendees at the Montauk benefit were informed by Dr. Michio Kaku, an international critic of the nuclear industry, that Millstone would pose an even greater hazard if the NRC permitted a doubling of the capacity of the spent-fuel pool at plant number three. "You would have 10 full cores with no containment," Dr. Kaku told the partygoers.[12] If an accident occurred, the nuclear material released would be considerably in excess of what escaped from Chernobyl and it would drift across the Sound "descending on Long Island," according to Dr. Kaku.[13]

If this weren't enough to worry about, benefit guests had barely digested their hors d'oeuvres when they were hit with more bad news. It seems that Northeast Utilities wanted permission to relocate its radiological measuring devices at will and without public notification. Still reeling from the fact that the NRC had been allowing nuclear energy plants to do their own monitoring for two years, Long Island opponents of Millstone were livid. Alarmed by the incidence of thyroid cancer and radiation-related blood maladies near the plant, East Enders also wondered about the connection between exposure to radiation and breast cancer on their side of the Sound. The long-awaited cancer maps released by the New York State Health Department in 1999 did not include environmental data, but a study undertaken by Columbia University for the American Health Foundation, made public in 2000, appeared to let pesticides off the hook as a cause of breast cancer. Traces of banned pesticides in breast cancer patients and those in a control group were the same. Three years earlier, however, Robert Grimson, chairman of a Brookhaven National Laboratory (BNL) task force established to investigate any causal relationship between BNL and breast cancer, had cast a wary eye at the pesticide Temik, used to control potato beetles before being banned. Grimson theorized that Temik might be a factor in the high incidence of breast cancer on the Twin Forks. As for any links between BNL and breast cancer, preliminary findings by the task force Grimson headed exonerated the lab.

Until other studies are completed, the jury is still out on the causes of the breast cancer epidemic in the bay area but the gut feeling of many people is that Millstone just might be the culprit. The role nuclear radiation plays in the onset of other forms of cancer was the focus of the Tooth Fairy Project involving a study of thousands of baby teeth to determine the presence and quantity of the radioactive element strontium 90, a possible catalyst in the development of cancer. In the bay area STAR and the One in Nine Breast Cancer Coalition were leading proponents of the project.

## The Brown Tide

As if worrying about their own health wasn't enough, East Enders had to grapple with the well-being of the Peconic Bay estuary, which fell victim to the brown tide in the mid-1980s. The problem did not seem overly serious initially but, as the bay darkened to a tea-colored hue, people became alarmed. Some longed for the good old days when naturalist Julian Burroughs, writing in *Forest and Stream* magazine in 1911, described Three Mile Harbor as a pristine body of water.

"Never have I seen so many escallops, and it was fun to catch them," declared Burroughs, adding:

> Often they will come up to the surface and jump half out of the water, and even the biggest ones when disturbed will go zig-zag-ging along at a rate that makes one swing the net at a lively rate. The water is as clear as air, and the interesting life on the bottom, from big whelks to darting sand-colored flounder or flatfish, can be plainly seen.[14]

Twenty years later the estuary, at least at its western end, was anything but pristine. In 1931 the New York State Conservation Department prohibited the taking of shellfish from Flanders Bay and other areas close to the mouth of the Peconic River because of sewage pollution from Riverhead. In the mid-1950s the New York State Health Department targeted duck farms as a source of pollution. Duck raisers in the Flanders Bay and Peconic River area were required to install equipment to remove "all settleable solids from waters used by ducks" before it migrated to "natural waters."[15] In the mid-sixties the East Hampton Town Baymen's Association eyed pesticides used to control mosquitoes as the possible cause of low shellfish yields in Northwest Creek.

By the early 1980s concerns about pollution and its impact upon shellfish had receded. The *New York Times* characterized 1982 as "a dandy season for scallops."[16] According to the paper, "Northwest Harbor and Orient Harbor in Southold Town were the hot spots for scallops."[17] In addition to good yields totaling half a million pounds of bay scallops, baymen benefited from a new labeling program that identified Long Island scallops. A year later, however, labeling didn't help because scallops were scarce and smaller. A shellfish expert from the New York State Department of Environmental Conservation (DEC) felt there was no cause for alarm because, historically, lean years often followed good ones. Zeroing in on the cause of the disappointing yields, the DEC cited an increase in the number of starfish and other scallop predators; howling winter winds that tossed immature scallops into shallow water; and a diminution in the amount of plankton, the scallops' food supply. In 1985, the year bay waters turned brown, algae were identified as the culprit that, for all intents and purposes, obliterated the scallop population.

Given the commercial value of the Peconic Bay shellfish crop, this was hardly a little fish story to be relegated to the sports pages of East End papers. Recognizing the significance of a catastrophic development that threatened "the future of scalloping in the bay, one of the richest scalloping areas on the East Coast," the *New York Times* ran a front-page story about the problem.[18] The paper noted that the "400 to 600 full-time baymen who scallop the Peconic expect the worst season ever."[19] Highlighting the importance of the estuary's scallop crop, the paper said that approximately "a quarter of all bay scallops" in the United States came from Peconic Bay.[20] In 1984 the bay produced "278,532 pounds of scallop meat."[21] The total catch was "valued at $1.3 million."[22]

Experts were quick to point out that the height of the algal bloom coincided with the spawning of scallops, an extremely critical time. Only 30 to 40 boats, rather than the usual 300 to 400, could be seen on Peconic Bay on opening day of the 1985 scallop season. According to *National Fisherman*:

> The algal onslaught destroyed up to 90% of the Peconic's scallop crop. About the only scallops that survived are located in waters along the eastern periphery of the Peconic bay system, where there is oceanic flushing from Block Island Sound. Those areas include Orient Harbor on the tip of Long Island's North Fork. But even there, this year's crop is scant. More significantly, baymen have spotted no "bug" or seed, scallops.[23]

What was a poor bayman to do, especially in light of the previously discussed limitations on the taking of striped bass? With the decline of both the shellfish and finfish catches, baymen not only faced tough times financially but, as the *New York Times* put it, it was also a matter of a "culture at risk."[24]

While scientists studied the causes of the brown tide, shellfish reseeding programs were launched. The results in East Hampton were so satisfactory that by 1988 the delectable shellfish was back in sufficient quantity to warrant a shellfish season, "the first time in three years that baymen . . . will be able to bring in a catch."[25] Although baymen were not expecting to earn megabucks, throughout the East End, including Southold, which planned to place "into beds more than a million seed clams," even a shortened season was welcome.[26] On the eve of opening day in October the *New York Times* declared: "The baymen believe that this year's opening of a shellfishing season indicates that the East End's bad luck has bottomed out and that things will get better."[27]

A mere two months after the scallop season ended, the *Times* ran a front-page story bearing the headline, "Brown Tide Leaves Long Island Waters but Puzzle Remains."[28] Quoting Vito Menei, supervisor of the ecology office of the Suffolk County Health Services Department, who said that the disappearance of the brown tide was "very encouraging, but we're not sure whether the brown tide is gone forever or temporarily giving us a break," the newspaper pointed out that "at the height of the bloom in 1986, scientists found concentrations as high as 2.5 million cells per milliliter, 10 times the level at which scientists believe other marine life begins to suffer."[29] Why the threat declined three years later was anyone's guess. One theory proposed at the time was that the algae that turned the bays dark and nearly lifeless was a strange "ocean-going organism swept from the depths by a rogue current" transported to the coastal waters of Long Island.[30] Then, in 1989, a wet spring may have "altered environmental conditions in favor of the brown tide's predators," enabling algae-eating organisms to devour the pesky blooms before they damaged the bays.[31]

Things were definitely looking up in 1989 and 1990. But in the early summer of 1991 the brown tide algae reappeared in the Peconic Bay estuary system in alarming quantities: 2,000,000 cells per milliliter in Flanders Bay, Riverhead, West Neck Bay, and Shelter Island. In Northwest Harbor, East Hampton, the site of a scallop reseeding program, the count was 600,000 per milliliter. There was a scallop season in 1991 but yields were extremely low. The situation improved in 1992, worsened in 1993, and, to the relief of those baymen who had hung in there, the 1994 Peconic Bay scallop harvest was the "best in 9 years."[32] In an attempt to perpetuate this, environmentalists, who had succeeded in 1992 in having the Peconics designated a federal estuary, took on the Town of Riverhead. They were joined in this effort by public officials and East End celebrities. Pointing to nitrogen discharged from the municipality's sewage treatment plant as a possible factor in the brown tide, the Peconic Estuary Citizens Advisory Committee demanded that the plant clean up its act by upgrading the facility to tertiary treatment for all effluent. In the late nineties Riverhead proceeded to do just that at a cost of nearly $9 million. The town, nevertheless, was threatened with a whopping six-figure fine, in 1999, for a mishap resulting in the release of "over a quarter million gallons of improperly treated sewage into the Peconic River . . . and for allowing unacceptably high amounts of organic material to reach the Peconic estuary throughout 1999."[33]

Peconic Baykeeper Kevin McAllister, who began monitoring the estuary in 1997 under the auspices of Save the Peconic Bay and as part of the National Alliance of River, Sound, and Bay Keepers, sought intervener status in this case brought by the DEC but was rebuffed by the town. "Hey, Kevin, go jump in the bay," was "the less polite version" of Riverhead's reaction to McAllister's request, according to one North Fork newspaper.[34] Undaunted, McAllister persevered until a DEC administrative law judge in Stony Brook ruled that he could have "party status in the hearing," which meant that he "must approve any proposed settlement."[35] Riverhead appealed the ruling, whereupon the commissioner of the New York State Department of Environmental Conservation decided that McAllister, who served as Peconic Baykeeper from 1997 to 2014 (he was succeeded in 2015 by Brady J. Wilkins), when McAllister, along with Skip Tollefsen and Mike Bottini, founded Defend $H_2O$, a new advocacy organization, "should never have been granted interested party status . . . in the first place."[36] In the end, the DEC reached an agreement with Riverhead increasing the amount of allowable nitrogen released from the sewage treatment plant and reducing the fine to $22,000. The town also spent $8,000 on clam reseeding in East Creek, Aquebogue. Riverhead was not off the hook, however, despite implementation of upgrades at the plant in 2000. In 2009, after being ordered by the federal government to upgrade its sewage treatment plant again, the town was in the process of applying for a federal grant to underwrite part of the $18 million projected cost. Four years later the cost had risen to $20 million and Riverhead was attempting to secure funding from a Suffolk County reserve amassed by a quarter-percent sales tax for land preservation and water quality. In 2014 the Town Board voted to borrow $9 million to cover part of the cost of upgrading the plant. To accommodate development at EPCAL (Enterprise Park at Calverton), upgrading Riverhead's Calverton sewage treatment plant was a must. The work was facilitated by $5 million included in the 2014–2015 New York State budget. Nitrogen removal was part of the upgrade along with the redirection of effluent from the plant to avoid Peconic Bay. Farther east, going back to 2010, the Greenport sewage treatment plant was being upgraded.

Their cost notwithstanding, upgrades were welcome because, in addition to rendering less harmful the effluent flowing into the Peconic Bay estuary, they made the plant more acceptable to neighbors. That wasn't the case back in the 1970s, however, when a Shelter Island couple who had purchased a Victorian home facing Southold Bay sued the Shelter Island Heights Property Owners Corporation on the grounds that odors from a sewage treatment plant the corporation had built "at the foot of their property" permeated their home.[37] The corporation prevailed in court but, on appeal, the homeowners were awarded nearly a million dollars.

Sewage treatment plants weren't the only facilities accused of being unfriendly neighbors. The gigantic Brookhaven National Laboratory was suspected of polluting the Peconic River, whose headwaters are on the lab's sprawling campus. The lab was eyed suspiciously by Fish Unlimited, which, in 1996, sent the East Hampton Town Baymen's Association a copy of data contained in "BNL's 1994 Site Environmental Report which clearly states that high levels of Cesium-137 and Strontium-90 are found in fish of the Peconic River."[38] Fish

Unlimited's executive director, Bill Smith, told the Baymen's Association that he had contacted the author of the report "asking him if this were true; he replied 'absolutely.' Then when I asked him where the radioactivity was coming from he replied 'There's only one place it can come from, the reactors.'"[39] Smith went on to say:

> Obviously this is an alarming development. If the radioactivity is in the fish, it's in the sediments, plantlife, us, and most likely the Peconic Estuary. . . . There is a more than likely chance that the brown algae blooms we have all been forced to live with since 1985 come as a result of dumping activities by BNL and Grumman.[40]

In 1998 BNL published a report stating that chemical and radioactive matter in the Peconic River emanated from the sewage treatment plant at the lab. While admitting that fish found near the headwaters of the river could pose a hazard to human health, BNL concluded that the threat was nonexistent because fishing did not occur on lab property. This was not exactly reassuring to environmentalists in light of the fact that BNL had been on the federal government's Superfund list for remediation of pollution since 1989.

If that wasn't enough to give environmentalists gray hair, there was also the not so little matter of whether the Department of Energy would permit the lab's high-flux beam reactor, taken offline because of a tritium leak from its spent-fuel pool in 1996, to be restarted. In the fall of 1999 protesters blocked the entrance to BNL as part of an effort to persuade the Department of Energy to rethink plans to put the reactor back on line. One of the principal concerns of those who wanted the reactor mothballed forever was its location, in the Pine Barrens, astride the aquifer that supplies water for Long Islanders. The loss of potable water as a result of a reactor accident was a powerful argument, one the federal government could not ignore. A week before Thanksgiving in 1999 the Department of Energy announced that the reactor would remain offline permanently.

In the meantime, the Peconic Baykeeper and representatives from the New York State Department of Environmental Conservation, the

State Department of Health, and BNL began taking fish and sediment samples from the Peconic River to test for pollution. When BNL informed the press that only small amounts of plutonium were detected in sediment samples, incredulous environmentalists theorized that additional analysis of both sediments and fish might prove otherwise. Scientific investigation of samples taken from the river continued and, just to be on the safe side, the Suffolk County legislature, in February 2000, authorized the posting of signs on county-owned land adjacent to the river to let people know that contamination tests were being done. Five years later BNL announced that a major milestone had been reached in decontaminating the laboratory grounds. Contaminated buildings had been torn down, contaminated soil had been removed and sent by train to out-of-state disposal sites, and sediment had been removed from the Peconic River. Beyond the laboratory's sprawling grounds, tests were conducted at the site of a former plant in Calverton where the Grumman Corporation had manufactured weapons for the U.S. Navy. Concerned about drinking water in the area and the migration of volatile organic compounds to the Peconic River, the U.S. Navy undertook a study of methods that could be used to remediate these environmental problems. The study was completed in the spring of 2011 and the installation of pumps to filter contaminated groundwater was undertaken.

The open waters of the bay were also being subjected to ongoing testing in an attempt to find the cause or causes of the fluctuating brown tide. Although not comparable to those of the mid-1980s, there were threatening algae blooms in 1995 and, as with past infestations, precise origins remained elusive. In 1997 the British scientific journal *Global Change Biology* published an article dealing with brown tide research undertaken by scientists from BNL and the Suffolk County Department of Health. These investigators theorized that dry weather resulted in an increase in organic nitrogen in the water. Brown tide algae grow robust on organic nitrogen, found in fertilizer used on lawns and farms and in sewage. Organic nitrogen pushes out harmless algae that thrive on inorganic nitrogen; the latter is less abundant when rainfall diminishes and the flow of groundwater to the bay is substantially curtailed. Years ago duck farms provided an abundance of inorganic nitrogen for the bays. Farms and houses also produce inorganic nitrogen but it doesn't get to the bay for years, and drought conditions increase the time it takes to reach the estuary. To get a better handle on nitrogen, as well as dissolved oxygen and chlorophyll, in the bay, BNL, in 1998, placed computerized monitoring devices in several locations in the estuary.

Scientists from the Marine Sciences Research Center at the State University of New York at Stony Brook were also hard at work studying the bay. At the turn of the twenty-first century they made a most interesting discovery while doing research at Cornell University's marine laboratory at Cedar Beach in Southold. When they placed hard-shelled clams in tanks containing various types of nutrients, the water remained clear and largely free of brown tide cells; in tanks lacking clams the results were just the opposite. This discovery was made during the third year of an ambitious bay reseeding program for clams, scallops, and oysters.

After beginning life in the laboratory at Cedar Beach, the young shellfish in the Adopt a Bay Scallop Program were deposited in various creeks throughout the Peconic Bay estuary. Within Southold itself the SPAT (Southold Project in Aquaculture Training) program provided volunteers with instructions for monitoring oysters placed in plastic cages, which program participants then took to creeks or the open bay near their homes. SPAT, which was featured on CNN, was described by Cornell scientist Kim Tetrault as "the model for a community-based reseeding program."[41] In addition to the work being done by Cornell, a private aquaculture facility was established in Southold in the mid-nineties to produce seeds that are sold for municipal shellfish restocking projects in various parts of Long Island. By the second decade of the twenty-first century, when the East Hampton Town Shellfish Hatchery in Montauk was seeding oysters in South Fork waters, the significance of aquaculture was underscored by the selection of Karen Rivara, an aquaculture farmer, as president of the Long Island Farm Bureau. Like all farmers, those engaged in aquaculture are subject to the vagaries of nature, something that was evident from the mid-1990s through 2001 when, despite reseeding, yields were disappointing.

By early 2002, however, there was a ray of hope. Dr. Christopher Gobler, a professor of marine science at Southampton College, published a paper on his discovery that microscopic zooplankton consume brown tide cells more slowly than they devour other algae, thereby enabling the brown tide to multiply. Scientists who had done the Cedar Beach clam study took issue with the findings and further research was planned. In 2004 the Suffolk County legislature appropriated $1.7 million to be spent over three years to repopulate the Peconic Bay estuary with scallops. The program was described, at its inception, as the most ambitious undertaking of its kind in the United States.

Administered by Cornell Cooperative Extension, the program involved not only Cornell but also the State University of New York (SUNY) at Stony Brook and Long Island University (the latter had a campus on the South Fork until 2006, when it sold the property to SUNY). For the next four years, until budget cuts forced its closing, the renamed Stony Brook Southampton functioned as an outpost of Stony Brook's main campus.

The success of the scallop reseeding program was widely heralded. When the 2008–2009 scallop season opened, Dr. Chris Smith of Cornell Cooperative Extension could point with pride to the scallop rebound in Orient Harbor, the site of the world's largest scallop-spawning sanctuary. On the South Fork, Cornell Cooperative Extension, in conjunction with the Town of East Hampton, was moving ahead with plans to create sanctuaries in Napeague Harbor and Hand's Creek in the vicinity of Three Mile Harbor. While these initiatives boded well for the future, the 2008 annual report of the Peconic Baykeeper was far from optimistic. Noting that commercial scalloping could no longer be supported in the Peconic Bay estuary, the report expressed concern about the decline of eelgrass, which, along with other aquatic vegetation, was a key element in the survival of shellfish in wetlands.

Baykeeper Kevin McAllister urged the creation of a task force to formulate a plan for resolving the eelgrass issue and called for a reexamination of management plans for stormwater runoff. Given the very real concerns about the diminution of eelgrass, McAllister supported a Suffolk County program, approved in December 2008, to lease 600 acres of underwater property in Peconic and Gardiner's Bays to people engaged in shellfish farming. With the precedent for such a program having been established, shellfish farmers were eager to see the program expanded. So, too, was the baykeeper because as filter feeders shellfish actually cleanse the water, enabling light to penetrate, thereby encouraging the growth of eelgrass. As the first decade of the twenty-first century wound down, the 2009 scallop harvest got off to a great start with avocational and commercial fishermen easily reaching their daily allowable limits of ten bushels per person and twenty per boat, but bountiful harvests in Massachusetts kept a lid on prices. What was perhaps more important, however, was that the scallop population had rebounded. As a result, there was considerable optimism as the 2010 season began. Expecting a great harvest, more than the usual number of people took to the waters on November 1, opening day. Those who headed for Orient experienced low yields but the waters around Robins Island did not disappoint. Experienced baymen predicted that this part of the estuary would continue to be the season's hotspot but that yields would start dropping before the end of the year.

The situation was far from dire, however, thanks to the efforts that had been made to bring back the scallops. In recognition of this achievement, the North Fork Environmental Council, whose motto is "Save What's Left," had honored, as its environmentalist of the year, Suffolk County Executive Steve Levy, who spearheaded the program that provided $2 million for scallop restoration in Peconic Bay. Also honored were Dr. Chris Smith of Cornell Cooperative Extension and Dr. Stephen Tettelbach of Long Island University for their participation in the successful program. Pointing out that both men had "led the effort to restore healthy populations of bay scallops to local creeks and bays," North Fork Environmental Council President Ken Rubino praised the three honorees for "turning the nightmare of brown tides and vastly reduced scallop stocks into the realized dream of a rebirth of scallop viability that had helped baymen, fish market operators, restaurants and tourism."[42] Besides government funding to repopulate shellfish in the Peconic Bay estuary, an initiative financed by the Southold Baymen's Association was launched in Hallock Bay, Orient, with clams. In August 2011 researchers reported that the program had been extremely successful.

There was also an abundance of young scallops in Hallock Bay and thus reason to hope that the commercial harvest in the Peconic Bay estuary, estimated to be 100,000 pounds of scallops in 2010, up from 20,000 pounds in 2009, would exceed expectations. In November 2011, on opening day of the scallop season, however, the catch, while not meager, was smaller than the year before. Still, the increased harvests of recent years, according to *Baywatch 2011*, the annual report of the Peconic Baykeeper, "may indicate some recovery of the population."[43]

In 2012 scallops in Peconic Bay declined because of the rust tide, a phenomenon that had occurred periodically for a decade. Reduced nitrogen levels in ground and surface waters of Long Island were believed to be responsible for the severity of the blooms, which kill both finfish and shellfish. In response, the New York State legislature considered a bill requiring substitution of new nitrogen-reduction systems for existing septic systems located near sources of the public water supply and on the coasts.

### Open Space Preservation

Going forward, on both sides of the bay, there is a realization that controlling rust tide or brown tide, should it reappear, goes hand in hand with preserving the estuary's 100,000-acre watershed. Doing so is not easy given development pressures in recent decades. The combined efforts of several levels of government and private citizens and organizations will be needed to save threatened open space. In the past, Suffolk County's purchase of farmland development rights, beginning in the 1970s, was an important part of the initiative to preserve the rural landscape. So, too, were the efforts of nonprofit groups, such as the Nature Conservancy, the Peconic Land Trust, the North Fork Environmental Council, and the South Fork Land Foundation, an offshoot of the Group for the South Fork, which changed its name to Group for the East End in 2007 after expanding its work to the North Fork. When the South Fork Land Foundation was being organized in the mid-seventies, the Sunday *New York Times* reported that the foundation had received a donation consisting of "a vacant, 25 acre parcel near Northwest Creek," which East Hampton hoped to see included with 115 acres on Barcelona Neck, property the county proposed to acquire.[44]

Suffolk County did purchase part of Barcelona Neck, and New York State acquired other land there in 1992. The county land is a reserve as is a portion of the state property, with the remainder being a nine-hole golf course that was there when the state took over. Elsewhere in the Northwest Harbor area, the Town of East Hampton bought the 431-acre Grace Estate following a 1985 referendum on the $6.3 million purchase. Although some East Hampton residents contended that the town could ensure the preservation of much of the estate without spending a dime if it required clustering of the homes proposed for the property, *Newsday* editorialized about public access to the land. The paper pointed out that historically East Hampton residents had taken shellfish in the vicinity of the estate from one of the East Coast's "most productive bay scallop beds."[45] Ironically the brown tide problem surfaced soon thereafter, threatening those scallop beds. Nevertheless, a majority of East Hampton residents shared the paper's contention that the public's right to access the property, including the harbor, "could be restricted" if the purchase were not approved by a town referendum.[46] But East Hampton did step up to the plate and took title to the Grace Estate in 1986.

Two years later Suffolk County augmented Southampton's open space by purchasing Clam Island adjacent to the Morton National Wildlife Refuge, the first portion of which was set aside in the midfifties. In 1989, following protracted negotiations, the county bought the 1,641-acre Hampton Hills tract in Southampton. Since this was prime Pine Barrens land sitting atop the aquifer, the 300-plus homes planned for this environmentally sensitive property were viewed as a threat to Long Island's water supply. According to the counsel for the Group for the South Fork, the developers may have agreed to part with the property because "they faced tremendous obstacles, including . . . a public fiercely devoted to preserving the site, a determined county executive's office, and a sagging real estate market."[47]

Precisely because the Pine Barrens were so important for the island's drinking water, the Long Island Pine Barrens Society, in late 1989, filed suit in state supreme court against the towns of Riverhead, Southampton, and Brookhaven and the Suffolk Health Services Department, charging that they "failed to consider the cumulative environmental impact of 230 proposed subdivisions on the scrub pine forests, where most of the drinking water enters the ground."[48] A whopping 100,000 acres or 10 percent of all the land on Long Island was involved, and the construction projects halted by the suit were estimated to be worth a minimum of $11 billion. The Long Island Pine Barrens Protection Act, passed by the New York State legislature in 1993, designated half of the total acreage as a protected area. Although property owners in this region could develop land for which permits had been previously granted, they could also apply for transfer credits to increase density on building parcels beyond the protected core area. Not everyone was pleased with the transfer of development rights concept but an appellate judge, in 1999, rejected a claim by a developer who argued that the 1993 legislation had deprived him of his property rights.

While developers and preservationists were battling over the Pine Barrens, the Town of Southold played host to eight land use experts, four from across the pond in the United Kingdom and four from the United States. The task of the U.S./U.K. Countryside Stewardship Exchange Team was to "address the issues of sustainable economic development and countryside stewardship."[49] Following their July 1991 visit, they issued a report characterizing the North Fork as an area "of scenic beauty and rich resources, both natural and human, with a deep and meaningful history, truly one of America's great places."[50] The report went on to state:

Yet the North Fork is under threat of drastic change spreading east from the New York metropolitan area. Unfortunately, local controls are inadequate to cope with these changes. New directions and programs are needed now to change this situation for the benefit of the entire community.[51]

The task force made nearly a dozen recommendations relating to such issues as economic development, continuation of the town's tax abatement program for farms, and affordable housing. Concerning the environment, the task force report said: "Priority should be given to eliminating pollution in creeks and bays, identifying and eliminating non-point sources of pollution and solving the 'brown tide' problem in Peconic Bay."[52]

Although some of the recommendations were implemented, in 1997 a North Fork newspaper published an article about long-range planning in Southold and posed the question: "What happened to US/UK?"[53] That same year, however, town government pointed with pride to the acquisition of Fort Corchaug, a significant aboriginal site, while simultaneously contemplating other land purchases. A new source of funding for land preservation became available in 1998 when voters in the East End towns overwhelmingly approved a real estate transfer tax with the proceeds going to the Peconic Bay Region Community Preservation Fund for open space acquisition. Initially, many real estate brokers were opposed to the 2 percent tax on the amount of sales prices over $250,000 for developed property and $100,000 for undeveloped property on the South Fork; and over $150,000 for developed property and $75,000 for undeveloped land on the North Fork, where real estate values were lower. As real estate values on both forks climbed to new heights in the early 2000s, money kept pouring into the towns for land preservation. Then came the precipitous decline in real estate values and the cooling of the market. With fewer transactions and lower prices, the transfer tax funneled considerably less money into municipal coffers for the purchase of open space or development rights. Yet, as Bob DeLuca, president of the Group for the East End, noted: "On eastern Long Island, land protection is an investment in our region's economy and critical environmental infrastructure."[54] In 2013, as the real estate market rebounded, the Community Preservation Fund received $95 million from the transfer tax. This was a 42 percent increase over the year before and the second-highest amount since the inception of the fund.

East Hampton put some of its increased Community Preservation Fund money to good use restoring the historic Lester Farm, transforming it into the East Hampton Farm Museum. The museum depicts agrarian life on the South Fork in the 1900s, just as the Hallockville Museum Farm in Riverhead interprets the same period on the North Fork. In addition to open space acquisition and historic preservation, Community Preservation Fund proceeds can be used by towns to purchase coastal property thanks to a 2013 state law recognizing climate change and sea level rise as valid reasons for towns to use Community Preservation Fund money to purchase coastal property. In 2014 the Town of East Hampton proposed purchasing vacant lots surrounding Lake Montauk through the Community Preservation Fund. At the same time, the town was exploring the possibility of securing grant money from the U.S. Department of Agriculture's Natural Resources Conservation Service to purchase homes on the bay at Lazy Point in Amagansett. Elsewhere in Amagansett, the Town of East Hampton moved to preserve nineteen acres of farmland on Montauk Highway after plans to build a fifty-five-and-older community were abandoned. On the North Fork, in the spring of 2014, the last piece of the ninety-eight acres needed to complete the Peconic Land Trust's Agricultural Center, in the heart of Southold, was acquired by the trust through a land swap and purchase.

Going back to the 1990s, preserving farmland in the Town of Riverhead through the purchase of development rights was funded by a $2 million bond approved in 1996. The town also established a Transfer of Development Rights program for redirecting residential and industrial development to areas outside the town's agricultural core. The legislation creating these programs also recognized Riverhead "as a farming community as a matter of public policy" and created a Farmland Preservation Committee to undertake an inventory of farmland and recommend property for acquisition.[55] In 2001, as Riverhead worked to redo its master plan, the town contemplated limiting building to 15 percent of any given piece of farmland. During the next three years, Riverhead preserved 1,106 acres of open space and farmland and in 2004 the town board voted unanimously to authorize the bonding of an additional $2.5 million for preservation. To avoid what had happened in Riverhead, where, for a time, new subdivisions seemed to rise overnight in the 1990s and the first years of the new millennium, Southold considered upzoning farmland to five acres.

The Town of Southold had gotten serious about this issue when it commissioned Steve Jones, Suffolk County planning director, to study the impact of increased population upon water quality. In 1999 Jones informed the town board that under existing zoning laws Southold's population could triple to 63,000 inhabitants. Southold not only would be transformed from a rural community into a suburb in little more than a decade but also would be faced with a lack of potable water, traffic congestion, and environmental degradation. All of this could be avoided, in Jones's opinion, by expanding an existing development rights purchase program. Right off the bat, Jones recommended that owners of parcels that were acquired before the zoning law was amended (to require a minimum of two acres for building lots) be required to buy farmland development rights somewhere in town before being allowed to build on their subminimum lots. Anyone seeking a zoning change would also have to buy development rights. Although Jones wasn't exactly run out of town on a rail, his proposals evoked considerable opposition. Despite his assertion that a "number of farmers" had "already come forward, offering to sell their development rights to the town," some members of the agricultural community worried that the sale of development rights would reduce the value of their holdings and make it harder for them to obtain loans because of the reduced potential for residential development.[56]

An earlier recommendation made in 1992 by Dr. Lee Koppelman, Long Island regional planning director, would have required five-acre housing lots on farms atop the local aquifer. It, too, met with opposition as did a proposal to alter the zoning of more than three dozen parcels of land on Route 48, Southold's North Road, to prevent commercial development deemed incompatible with the rural character of the area. In the spring of 2001 Long Island Farm Bureau Executive Director Joseph Gergela proposed a novel solution to the Southold zoning controversies, namely the purchase of all property deemed necessary for the preservation of Southold as a rural community. According to Gergela, the town could borrow the estimated $25 million required "and pay for it with the revenue generated from the Community Preservation Fund (the 2% real estate transfer tax). It could be a no- or low-interest loan and it won't impact the taxpayers at all."[57]

Although town officials weren't sure they wanted to exceed Southold's $10 million bonded indebtedness for open space preservation, in 2002 they approved a moratorium on new subdivisions of ten or more dwellings and, when the ban was set to expire, it was extended until 2005. Looking ahead to a time when the moratorium would be lifted, and recognizing the growing need for workforce housing in a community where the price of starter homes had jumped from around $150,000 to approximately $400,000 in the previous six years, the Southold Town Board in 2004 unanimously approved legislation requiring developers to build one affordable home for every three houses sold at the market rate in future subdivisions of at least five homes. The percentage of affordable units was later reduced from twenty-five to twenty, and developers were given options that enabled them to fulfill the affordable housing requirement in other ways.

While Southold grappled with the problem of providing workforce housing while holding the line against suburbanization, on the other side of the estuary, quasi-suburban Southampton was making a valiant effort to slam the door on runaway growth by denying permission for the development of almost 300 acres in the Pine Barrens near Westhampton. Although a lawsuit by the developers resulted in a $14.2 million damage award, a sizable amount even for a wealthy community, an appeals court reversed the ruling in 1999. That same year Suffolk County made several significant land purchases in the core area of the Pine Barrens. The largest acquisition was a 144-acre parcel in Flanders.

As the new millennium dawned, the Town of Southampton was contemplating zoning changes to preserve its dwindling farmland. A Comprehensive Plan, adopted by the town in 1999, called for the preservation of up to 80 percent of farmland by creating a voluntary program that included stronger preservation guidelines to offset an expedited review process for subdivision applications. Some Southampton farmers balked at this idea, preferring instead a term easement whereby for a period of years a farmer would agree not to develop his land, thereby giving the town time to acquire the development rights to the property. If the town did not purchase the rights, the farmer would be able to develop it under zoning in place in the late nineties rather than any stricter zoning code.

In October 2001 the Southampton Town Board met to approve legislation embodying the proposal favored by the farmers and instituting transferable development rights. Supervisor Vincent Cannuscio did not attend the meeting. The previous July, Cannuscio had recommended a voter referendum on a $60 million bond sale to preserve farmland. Characterized by *Newsday* as "the most ambitious farmland preservation effort ever proposed by a Long Island town," the Southampton proposal called for the expenditure of almost as much money as the entire county had agreed to spend on open space and drinking water preservation the year before.[58] Considering the county's population of 1.2 million and the town's year-round population of a little under 50,000, the Town Board had second thoughts and voted against putting the proposal on the November ballot.

Meanwhile, East Hampton, with a year-round population of 20,000, was contemplating spending $1 million a year for twenty years to preserve farmland. The brainchild of town supervisor Jay Schneiderman, the plan, which was made public at the same time as Southampton's ambitious proposal, called for the town to subsidize 20 percent of the selling price of contiguous parcels homeowners wished to purchase and maintain as open space in perpetuity. On

Shelter Island, thanks to the Nature Conservancy and the Peconic Land Trust, fully a third of the island's 8,000 acres had been set aside by the start of the twenty-first century. Another island in the Peconic Bay estuary was also well on its way to preserving open space.

## Robins Island

The preservation of Robins Island was the doing of financier Louis Bacon, who purchased this very special piece of real estate in Peconic Bay in the waning years of the twentieth century. Bacon had his first look at the island from a fishing boat out of Montauk more than a decade before. He was a young deckhand at the time and longed to see the island up close and personal but, alas, that wouldn't happen for a while. Bacon had to make his fortune on Wall Street first and then he had to beat out other prospective buyers of the alluring land mass, which straddles the bay between the North Fork and the Hamptons. In certain respects, Bacon's infatuation with the largely pristine island was similar to that of a previous owner, James W. Lane. Lane took notice of the island, which had been a private hunting club in the late 1800s, when his firm was conducting torpedo testing in the Peconic Bay estuary in the early 1900s. He decided that he simply had to have the place; the rest, as they say, is history— but in Lane's case, a very sad history.

While his dream house overlooking the bay was being erected, Lane's wife died and he abandoned the project. The exterior, complete with two huge chimneys, was finished; but except for a number of stone fireplaces and partitions to mark the rooms, the interior still needed a lot of work. All construction ceased abruptly, in fact so quickly that workers' tools and clothing were left behind. The island subsequently passed through several hands, becoming a sportsmen's preserve once again. In the mid-twentieth century Long Islander John W. Mackay, whose wealth could be traced to a Nevada silver fortune and the Western Union Telegraph Company, bought the island, complete with the unfinished mansion and a caretaker's cottage, which had been transformed by various owners into a very ample residence. In 1979 Mackay sold the island to the Southold Development Corporation.

Despite its local name, the company was a German-Swiss real estate syndicate that planned to build twenty-eight luxury homes on the island. This did not exactly thrill Suffolk County nor New York State, which immediately began scrambling for federal funds to purchase the island. The $2 million sought from Washington was included in an application to have Peconic Bay declared a National Estuarine Sanctuary. Interestingly, some of the East End towns opposed this idea, fearing federal oversight might interfere with commercial fishing and in other ways diminish home rule. Dr. Lee Koppelman, Long Island regional planning director and director of the Suffolk County Planning Department, wanted to forge ahead, however. When the developers dismissed the idea of selling the island, Koppelman reminded them that their prized acquisition could be condemned. Pointing to a major downside of development, Koppelman told the *New York Times* that it "would put an end to maintaining the high quality of the waterways."[59] The paper contrasted the status of Robins Island with that of the 2,000-acre Mashomack Preserve on Shelter Island, which had recently been acquired by the Nature Conservancy. "The preserve, which encompasses almost a third of Shelter Island, resembles Robins Island in that both are important breeding grounds for waterfowl and shellfish," said the *Times*.[60]

In recognition of the ecological value of the island, one of the biggest undeveloped islands in the state, concerned citizens launched a petition campaign to persuade the Southold Town Board to get behind an attempt to raise public and private money to purchase the island. Nearly a decade later the Robins Island Preservation Fund sued the European owners of the island on the grounds that Parker Wickham, the ancestor of those who established the fund, had been wrongfully divested of the island following the American Revolution. New York State grabbed the island because of Parker's allegedly pro-British sympathies, something his descendants denied. The modern-day Wickhams hoped to get the island back and preserve it as a sanctuary. In the newsletter published by Friends of the Wickham

Claim, Dwight Holbrook, author of a definitive book on the claim, spoke about the attempt to preserve a place "that is a living window into Long Island's antiquity."[61] Describing what was at stake, Holbrook said that Robins Island was "part of an ecosystem that is at once fragile and interconnected," yet the island's future "and its potential impact on the bay—is in the hands of one man."[62] The fact that the man was not an American was interpreted by Holbrook as a sign that the United States was no longer determining its own destiny.

As the Wickham case proceeded, Suffolk County was batting zero in its attempt to buy the island. The developers, who paid $1.3 million for the place, turned down a county offer of $7.5 million. They had hoped to sell to a California developer for $15 million and change, but that prospective buyer backed out and sued the European owners because of the title issue dating back to the Revolution. The owners were also sued by North Fork Bank for arrears in mortgage payments. When the bank instituted foreclosure proceedings and announced it would auction the island, the Europeans finally accepted an offer from the county for $9.2 million.

What seemed to be a done deal unraveled, however, when the European owners neglected to attend the closing and soon thereafter filed for bankruptcy. At that point both the would-be California buyer and Suffolk County sued, each claiming a valid agreement to purchase the island. A federal district court ultimately ruled, in December 1989, that the contract with the California purchaser had expired. A court also ruled against the Wickhams, who appealed, but in March 1992 a federal appeals court in Manhattan upheld the lower court. The judge decided that two centuries was simply too long to wait to make a claim.

Within months the California developer was back in the picture and the county was talking about acquiring development rights to part of the island while permitting limited residential development. Assemblyman Steven C. Englebright was horrified by the prospect. A scientist at SUNY Stony Brook before running for public office, Englebright had been part of a research team doing an on-site investigation of the island. He concluded that "the beach and salt marsh habitats and coastal environment" of the island were one of the finest in the state and "essentially pristine."[63] Englebright characterized Robins Island as "Long Island's Yosemite," and insisted that "you wouldn't build houses on the dome."[64] He also called the island "a masterpiece" and asked: "What's the Mona Lisa worth if you cut the smile out of the painting?"[65]

Englebright's opposition to the development of the island notwithstanding, the future of Robins Island would indeed include limited development, but very limited, following Louis Moore Bacon's purchase of the entire 445-acre island for $11 million in 1993. The deal, which required the approval of a federal bankruptcy court, marked the beginning of a new chapter in the history of this very special place. Louis Bacon began formulating plans for a large vacation home and recreation building for his family but he also consented to a conservation easement, which is a legal encumbrance between a landowner and a government agency to restrict certain uses of the property. In the case of Robins Island this was done to preserve much of the island in its natural state. In 2001 Bacon made a donation to the Peconic Land Trust of a conservation easement on 540 acres of land on the South Fork. The property, known as Cow Neck, was acquired by Bacon in 1998. It is but a short hop across the bay from Robins Island. Once a dairy farm and then a shooting preserve and private estate, this is the biggest piece of land in private hands in all of Southampton. Bacon also donated a conservation easement on a thirty-acre parcel fronting on Sebonac Creek in the same vicinity.

## Going to Town

Preserving large parcels such as Cow Neck contributes mightily to the ecological well-being of the Peconic Bay estuary, but without orderly, planned development throughout the bay area this very special place will remain under siege. A survey of articles dealing with the forks in general, and the different municipalities on the East End in particular, indicates that for nearly half a century a lot of people have been talking about the changes sweeping over the region while wondering whether anything was being done to preserve the character of the area. Writing in *Newsweek* magazine in 1972 Shana Alexander described the East End as "a thin ribbon on which are strung some of the loveliest old farms, villages and hamlets in America, all loosely linked by time, ponds, people, potatoes, dunes, highways and wind."[66] Describing the nascent planning movement emerging in the region, the eloquent Ms. Alexander noted that the populace of the East End had suddenly found "themselves neck-deep in the new American reality: our spacious skies and amber waves of grain are not free, not limitless, and not even endlessly recyclable."[67] Newspapers had picked up on this theme nearly a decade earlier. In 1968 the *New York Times* ran a piece headlined "Potato-Farm Country Set for Change."[68] To the relief of bay area residents, the causal agent for the impending transformation, the cross-Sound bridge between Oyster Bay and Rye, proposed by Robert Moses, the planner responsible for Long Island's system of parks and parkways, never materialized but other agents of change did, as evidenced by an article in *Real Estate Illustrated* in 1984.

The page-one story on the condominiumization of the North Fork featured an appealing illustration by noted photographer Judy Ahrens, whose book *The North Fork: Photographs from Fifteen Years at the Suffolk Times* captures the spirit of the area. Through the lens of her camera Ahrens framed a family of four seated at an umbrella table on the deck of their waterfront condominium at Cleaves Point in East Marion. The scene was idyllic, yet multiplied by the number of condos projected for the North Fork it was anything but. Mike Rossler, author of the *Real Estate Illustrated* article, pointed out that condos on the North Fork had indeed arrived and "they're multiplying like mushrooms."[69] Actually an unknown person or persons attempted to make Cleaves Point go away by burning it down. Recounting the shaky early history of the project, Rossler said: "It was built in 1981, but was firebombed and had to be re-started from scratch. No one was ever apprehended for the firebombing."[70]

Attempts to block the Seacroft condo project in the hamlet of Cutchogue in the mid-1980s were more subtle, completely legal, and in the end successful. Concerned about the impact of 160 units upon the water supply and quality of life, opponents formed Southold Opposed to Seacroft (SOS) to sink the project; the town planning board eventually saw things their way and denied site plan approval for the project. Local opposition also doomed another eighties project, the Bay Club condos, which would have risen on the waterfront in the picturesque hamlet of New Suffolk. When it comes to nautical heritage and flavor, this little place is one of the saltiest spots on the East End. It is also one of the quietest and the locals want to keep it that way, which is why residents left no stone unturned between 2008 and 2010 to raise $2.6 million to reimburse the Peconic Land Trust, which had bought the New Suffolk Shipyard to prevent it from being developed. Once the purchase price for the 3.5-acre parcel was deposited in the trust's revolving land fund, the New Suffolk Waterfront Fund would manage the property.

Farther east on the North Fork, residents of Orient were doing battle with the Suffolk County Water Authority, which planned to extend water mains to the area. Fearing that the availability of public water would mean more development, which would compromise the rural ambience of the region, residents publicly denounced the plan, causing the Water Authority to back down.

While Orient strived to preserve the status quo, the bustling Village of Greenport a few miles to the west embraced change, whether new excursion boat service to Block Island in the summer of 2010; a passenger ferry linking Greenport with Sag Harbor in 2012; a municipal marina that attracted boaters whose home ports lay far beyond the Peconic Bay area; or mega-yachts such as the 222-foot *Archimedes*, built in the Netherlands and launched in 2008, the same year it paid a visit to Greenport. Named one of the eleven prettiest towns and villages in the United States by *Forbes* magazine in 2011, Greenport was chosen as a principal stop on a June 2012 tour of the North Fork, "Long Island's best kept secret," sponsored by the National Trust for Historic Preservation.[71] At times, Greenport sacrifices peace and quiet in order to rake in tourist dollars and not just during the popular two-day Maritime Festival held each September. From spring through late fall, day trippers flock to the village, including leather-clad motorcycle enthusiasts, B&B guests, and those who frequent the chic Greenporter Hotel and Spa or the equally upscale Harborfront Inn (which, thanks to its modular construction, went up in record time during the winter and spring of 2004). All these visitors create Hamptons-style gridlock at times. For those who remember the not-so-distant past when the little village by the sea was down at the heels, this may not be such a bad thing.

David Kapell, mayor of Greenport from 1994 to 2007, is widely credited with the resurgence of the village. Kapell can point with pride to such accomplishments as the new harborfront Mitchell Park, complete with a carousel donated to the village by Northrop Grumman Corporation after Greenport beat out several other Long Island communities eager to get the merry-go-round, which had once graced the lawn at Grumman's Calverton facility. Kapell obtained $3.1 million from New York State for the Mitchell Park project and additional funding for a marina and ice rink. Not one to shy away from controversy, Kapell knew what he wanted and went after it, whether it was a new park or the famous heron sculpture, which at the turn of the twenty-first century became Greenport harbor's equivalent of the Statue of Liberty.

The forty-foot-high two-ton steel heron was banished from a private bay beach in Southold after a judge ruled that the big bird was a structure and hence required a building permit. In 2001 the heron took up residence at the end of a dock in Greenport, where it evoked admiring looks from boaters and pedestrians alike. The bird returned to Southold in November 2001 after its owner secured a building permit. A year later, the Southold Zoning Board of Appeals reclassified the sculpture as a monument but ruled that it could stay put. Unhappy neighbors, whose opposition had led to the bird's earlier flight to Greenport, resorted to legal action. This resulted in a judicial directive to the board to reconsider its approval because the sculpture exceeded the town's eighteen-foot height limit for accessory structures. Meanwhile, a few miles to the east, Greenport undertook a successful campaign to obtain a replacement piece: a twenty-foot osprey on a piling of the same size. The osprey overlooked the harbor from 2002 until 2011 when it was relocated to an inland park in Southold. For a time, however, both sculptures were symbolic of Greenport's increasingly artsy ambience, as evidenced by the establishment of charming galleries in the 1990s. "Way to go!" some would say, considering that at the start of that decade the *New York Times*, citing the decline of fishing and tourism in the village, ran an article headlined "Greenport Faces Mounting Problems."[72] Compare that with an upbeat article headlined "Greenport on the Rise" published in *Newsday* in 2000.[73] A little more than a dozen years later, Greenport experienced the largest increase in tourism of any North Fork community, in part because vacationers who had previously flocked to the Jersey Shore sought new destinations in the wake of the devastation New Jersey experienced during Superstorm Sandy in the fall of 2012.

The period that saw the resurgence of Greenport was also a time of unprecedented development in Riverhead. New homes sprouted like weeds in the town's hamlets of Aquebogue and Jamesport. Critics decried the fact that the historic county seat had rolled out the welcome mat for developers. But, short of throwing themselves in front of bulldozers that were churning up some of the best farmland in North America to accommodate suburban-style housing, there wasn't much opponents of poorly planned growth could do, at least until they became organized. Besides the ubiquitous subdivisions, commercial development also occurred during the rah-rah 1990s. "If you build it, they will come," is probably what Steven Tanger was thinking when he acquired nearly fifty acres in a newly created factory overlay zone at the end of the Long Island Expressway. In 1994 the first phase of the Tanger Factory Outlet Center opened. The rest, as they say, is history. Who would have thought as the decade of the nineties dawned that more than ten million people would descend upon Riverhead annually to shop for bargains in upscale discount stores? But that's exactly what they were doing. In response to the thumbs up it received from shoppers, Tanger expanded, more than doubling its original size while continually adjusting the mix of stores to reflect shoppers' preferences and changing economic circumstances.

To the east of Tanger, along Route 58, new shopping centers featuring such big box stores as The Home Depot and Target added to Riverhead's allure as a retail mecca. By the second decade of the twenty-first century, Route 58 was lined with Lowe's Home Improvement Center, Costco, and a new 170,000-square-foot Walmart built to replace the chain's original Riverhead store. A Hilton Garden Inn, a Holiday Inn Express, and the prospect of a Marriott Residence Inn reflected the development fever that had made Route 58 a commercial hot spot. While Route 58 blossomed into a mega-retail hub, historic downtown Riverhead languished. Summer music festivals along the Peconic River and the weekend-long Polish Festival, held in August in Polish Town, not far from the heart of Riverhead's once-thriving Main Street, attracted crowds but revitalization efforts sputtered. "The town America seems to have left behind" is how a journalist for the *Guardian Weekly*, published in Sydney, Australia, characterized the county seat in the mid-1980s.[74] (See fig. 11.) In the nineties, as artists' lofts sprouted in the wonderful old brick commercial buildings on Main Street, there were those who envisioned Riverhead as "Soho East." Some imagined canvas-toting painters setting up their easels on the banks of the Peconic River in the linear park created as part of an earlier renewal effort. Would tourists disembarking from the paddle wheel excursion boats, which plied the Peconic River for a few years in the nineties, take time to have their portraits done? Would families emerging from the wildly successful Atlantis Marine World Aquarium, which opened in the late nineties, or the Hyatt Place hotel and exhibition center, which opened in 2011 next door to the Atlantis (now known as the Long Island Aquarium), pose for a group portrait?

It could happen if the recommendations made by a team of students from SUNY's College of Environmental Science and Forestry in 2011 are embraced. The group was accompanied on site visits by an enthusiastic professor, who observed that Riverhead's Main Street was virtually unchanged from a half-century earlier. In his view, other Long Island communities were attempting to recapture what Riverhead already possessed. To take advantage of Riverhead's assets, the study team suggested adding sculpture, a waterfall, greenhouses, and

11. West Main Street, looking east, Riverhead, 1936. Courtesy of Suffolk County Historical Society, Riverhead, N.Y.

other enhancements to the downtown business district. This time the long-awaited rebirth seemed poised for takeoff. In the spring of 2012 *Dan's Papers* proclaimed, "Riverhead Main Street Rising for Real!"[75]

In addition to the Long Island Aquarium and a Hyatt hotel, Suffolk Community College's culinary arts program helped anchor Main Street, a portion of which was placed on the National Register of Historic Places in 2013. In 2014 an indoor farmers' market opened in the former Swezey's Department Store building. The reopening the previous year of the renovated Suffolk Theater, built in 1933 and closed since 1987, was another positive sign; and so was the transformation of the building that for decades housed the Woolworth's variety store, which was turned into a mixed-use complex of stores, a gym, and workforce housing. Another workforce housing complex, Summerwind Square, opened downtown in 2013. Plans for luxury condominiums with views of the Peconic River were unveiled the same year. The historic heart of the county seat had awakened from a lengthy slumber, silencing naysayers who doubted that downtown would ever be revitalized. Yet, stranger things have happened, such as the reconstruction, in a hangar at the former Grumman facility in Calverton, of the TWA jetliner that plummeted to the bottom of the Atlantic Ocean off Suffolk County in 1996.

In 2001 Riverhead, which had been ceded the Calverton property by the U.S. Navy, sold 500 acres to a developer for an industrial park. That same year another development group presented a proposal for an entertainment complex that would include a movie studio, hotels, a theme park, and fairgrounds. Over the years, developers came and went, including a European company that missed an extended deadline in 2010 to close on the purchase of land on which it intended to erect a megaresort larger than Disneyland. Three years later, in an effort to jump-start development at EPCAL (Enterprise Park at Calverton), the New York State legislature passed a bill creating the EPCAL Reuse and Revitalization Area for which Riverhead would devise a generic environmental impact study. Once this was in place, developers presenting fully fleshed-out proposals would be assured of approval within ninety days. In the spring of 2014, a proposal by a group that included scientists and physicians to establish a drug addiction research facility at EPCAL received zoning approval, as did a proposed indoor skydiving facility consisting of a four-story building and a vertical wind tunnel.

Intensified development at EPCAL, combined with Riverhead's expanding retail base along Route 58 and the revitalization of its historic downtown, were cause for optimism. Some visionaries, while not minimizing the significance of economic expansion in the inland area of Calverton and the Route 58 corridor, remained mindful of Riverhead's ties to the sea. They could envision the stretch of the Peconic River flowing through downtown Riverhead, where New York State eased development restrictions in 2010 by reclassifying a stretch of the waterway from recreational to community, becoming the county seat's version of San Antonio's River Walk. Whether or not that occurs, the revitalization and nascent gentrification of down-town Riverhead is likely to result in the underemployed, unemployed, and otherwise poor becoming less visible. Yet, like the struggling Polish immigrants of the nineteenth and early twentieth centuries, who toiled away in the potato fields, the African American migrant workers of the mid-twentieth century and today's Hispanics, employed in agriculture, tourism, and various service occupations, they will probably not become totally invisible.

That the poor are always with us, even prerecession and in the Hamptons at that, may have come as a surprise to some people who were shocked to learn that a group of homeless people had taken up residence under a Long Island Rail Road trestle in Hampton Bays in the summer of 2001. Now and then, during the previous year, an occasional homeless person had sought shelter in this spot, but the creation of a real community under the trestle in 2001 alarmed home-owners in the area. Elsewhere on the South Fork, as real estate prices soared skyward, individuals and families with incomes that would have been considered adequate in most parts of America were finding it impossible to buy or rent homes. As long as the stock market remained buoyant, affluent buyers lined up to bid on a little or not so little piece of paradise on the East End. In the late nineties, multiple offers on houses were common and it was not at all unusual for properties to go for more than the asking price, all of which meant that local tradespeople and civil servants were hard-pressed to keep a roof over their heads unless they moved west, beyond the bay area.

Peter Wolf, a seasonal resident who had watched East Hampton evolve over more than three decades, came up with a solution to this vexing problem. In his book *Hot Towns: The Future of the Fastest Growing Communities in America*, published in 1999, Wolf recommended the creation of accessory apartments in existing houses (something Southampton was considering in 2004) and mandatory apartments in all new commercial buildings. Sounds good, especially since local workers residing within walking distance of their jobs would mean fewer vehicles snaking their way along Montauk Highway during the ever-lengthening morning and evening rush hours!

Reversible lanes and other improvements on the Southampton stretch of Montauk Highway were helping to ease congestion by the end of the first decade of the new century, and further road widening to accommodate an additional lane was planned. On the other side of the bay, the addition of a fifth lane and a reconfiguring of the traffic circle on Route 58 in Riverhead addressed a similar problem on the North Fork. There are those who say more needs to be done. Yet, many residents on both sides of the bay differ, arguing that, if you build it, they will come (with "they" referring to more vacationers, day-trippers, and second-home seekers).

On the North Fork, where Orient to New London ferry traffic increased dramatically following the opening of gambling casinos in Connecticut in the nineties, many local residents applauded a 2004 decision by the Southold and Shelter Island town boards to file a federal suit aimed at overturning East Hampton legislation banning ferry terminals in that municipality. With an estimated 30 to 35 percent of the New London ferry traffic heading to the South Fork, an East Hampton terminal was viewed as a way of alleviating some of the congestion on the North Fork and on the Shelter Island ferries used to reach the Hamptons. Even if a federal judge had not dismissed the suit, gamblers and others coming from the west would still clog the roads of the North Fork.

It's no wonder, then, that local residents were loath to remove bumper stickers featuring a turtle nattily attired in a baseball cap bearing the message "Local Motion" and proclaiming, in big red letters, "I Don't Care If You're Late for the Ferry!" That's telling them, all right, but one can't help but wonder if local residents themselves would be speeding along the North Road, heading west via the coastal evacuation route, if a major hurricane were about to bear down on the area. Were this to occur, there would probably be some people bemoaning the fact that the Long Island Expressway ends at Riverhead instead of extending east through the middle of the North Fork, as originally planned. In the aftermath of September 11, the realization that storms aren't the only thing necessitating evacuation began to sink in. Still, it's a terrifying thought many East Enders wish they could dismiss in light of the seemingly insurmountable problems associated with emptying out an area with only a handful of east-west roads.

## Storm Clouds

In addition to the ongoing war against terrorism, hurricanes and other powerful storms, including northeasters, which can wreak havoc, will continue to pose a threat to the bay area. Records going back to 1782 indicate that the East End was on the fringe of a colossal storm in September of that year. In 1815 the region was hit with a storm known as the "great September gale" but, as historian Osborn Shaw pointed out, concerning this and other big storms: "In none of these events, is there any mention of any loss of life, except by the swamping of vessels. This is because the people of a few generations ago did not live on the beaches except perhaps for a very few, who probably resided there only during the fishing or whaling seasons."[76] How different it is today! Given the ubiquitous waterfront development of recent decades, a direct hit by a Category 4 hurricane would cause enormous damage to trophy homes and unassuming cottages alike. But the possibility—nay, the probability—of such a disaster seems unlikely to discourage people from building their dream homes on the beach.

Hurricanes aside, lesser storms can wreak havoc. Gale-force winds in mid- and late October 1846 impeded shipping. Merciless winds battered the area again in 1851, 1859, and 1860. In 1869 the entire East Coast was affected by an October hurricane that had been preceded by a major storm a month earlier. Thereafter, until 1938, Long Island was brushed by a number of hurricanes but did not take a direct hit. Thus, when the big storm arrived on September 21 of that year, people were caught off-guard. The story of this legendary hurricane is recounted in a number of books, among them Everett S. Allen's *A Wind to Shake the World*, Ernest S. Clowes's *The Hurricane of 1938 on Eastern Long Island*, Roger Brickner's *The Long Island Express: Tracking the Hurricane of 1938*, and Richard G. Hendrickson's *Winds of the Fish's Tail*. Describing the aftermath of the storm, Clowes detailed the destruction along the oceanfront and the downed trees and damage to buildings elsewhere on the South Fork. To him the greatest loss occurred in Sag Harbor. "Of all the material losses on Long Island that day the most spectacular was that of the great steeple of the Presbyterian Church at Sag Harbor which had stood for nearly one hundred years," lamented Clowes.[77] He also said that damage was not limited to the South Fork. In Greenport "the shipyards were practically wrecked, the theatre was ruined, the Eastern Long Island Hospital lost part of the roof."[78] Farther east the causeway between East Marion and Orient was swamped; homes and boats were wrecked and there were downed trees everywhere.

In Orient Anne MacKay, who was a child in 1938, was "packing up to leave for school in the city" when the storm hit.[79] "As the wind and rain started to get strong, we realized that we were going to have what was called 'a blow,'" she said, adding:

> Soon the bits of leaves covered every window and screen in the Big House; you couldn't look out at all. The house started to shake. I was up in my room on the third floor, and when I think that if a super-gust had hit us, I could have been flying away; it makes you thankful. Being on the North shore of Long Island, we didn't have the terrible ocean waves and flooding which destroyed so much of the South shore and Rhode Island. But even protected, the waves threw up boats over the Orient barrier beach to the highway. . . . In the village all the horse-chestnut trees had shed their chestnuts, they were everywhere. Down by the dock, boats had been thrown up and around, and the bay had come way up Village Lane. Later we heard about some people . . . who had left their young children in their house by the bay with a nursemaid. Someone had to come by in a rowboat to get them out of a second story window.[80]

A less notorious but very devastating hurricane battered the region in 1944. In his article "The Hurricane of 1938 in Historical Perspective," David Ludlum states, "The Great Atlantic Hurricane of September 14–15, 1944 must be placed in the first category of the region's hurricanes. . . . The center cut across the eastern end of Long Island, probably between Westhampton and Southampton and over Peconic Bay."[81] The fifties was also an active decade, meteo-rologically speaking. Hurricanes Carol, Edna, Hazel, Connie, and Diane swept through the area. In 1960 Hurricane Donna produced 100-mile-per-hour winds at Montauk Point. The sixties and seven-ties were fairly quiet, with hurricanes skirting the island or morph-ing into tropical storms that dumped considerable rainfall. In 1985 Hurricane Gloria impacted the western part of the island more than the East End. Superstorm Sandy in October 2012 wreaked havoc on the New York area and, although the East End was spared the kind of destruction that occurred farther west on the island, as well as in New York City, the lower Hudson Valley, and New Jersey, homes and businesses on both sides of Peconic Bay were damaged and there was considerable coastal erosion. In the aftermath of Sandy, flood zone remapping and the prospect of higher premiums for flood insurance threatened to make homes on or near the water unaffordable except for the wealthy.

Although hurricanes have packed the most wallop historically, unnamed storms such as two deluges that caused unprecedented flooding on both sides of the bay in March 2010 have done consider-able damage. Winter storms have also wreaked havoc. Describing the Christmas storm of 1811 Henry Packer Dering reported that a sloop in Sag Harbor had its bowsprit go into a shop window. He also said that "a number of vessels" had come ashore at Oysterponds and Shel-ter Island.[82] Another bad December storm, in 1857, severed contact with New York City, causing the Sag Harbor *Corrector* to apologize to its readers for the reduced size of the newspaper. With Long Island Rail Road service curtailed, the *Corrector* could not obtain paper from its supplier in the city. Snow and winds associated with winter storms posed challenges but so, too, did the extreme cold that occasionally gripped the area. During the winter of 1853 ice boats and sleighs were used to transport passengers and cargo between Southold, Shel-ter Island and Sag Harbor. In 1856–1857, "Peconic Bay was frozen all winter, with regular ice boat service for passengers and freight between Greenport and Sag Harbor," according to James Deale, a Greenport resident.[83] In February 1905 the bay was again frozen over.

It was a similar situation during the winter of 1917–1918. The cold weather arrived early, causing lakes to freeze before Christmas. Some East Enders welcomed the opportunity to go ice skating, but the loss of late-season crops and the difficulty of getting anything to market during a heavy snowfall in December lessened whatever enthusiasm existed for cold weather. Before the month ended, parts of the Peconic Bay estuary were sufficiently frozen to permit pedestrian and carriage traffic. Mail was transported from Shelter Island to Greenport by eight men, who took along a rowboat and oars just in case the ice gave way, but the group made it across, on foot, without incident. Writing in the *Long Island Forum,* Shelter Islander Edith H. Shepherd observed: "All of Peconic Bay was frozen."[84] It must have been frozen quite solidly because "one man walked across the bay from Good Ground (Hampton Bays) to New Suffolk."[85] During the forty-six-day cold snap, lots of people took to the frozen bay, mostly without falling in. One notable exception was the keeper of the Long Beach Lighthouse off Orient. When he tried to walk ashore, the ice began breaking up; but he was spotted and a rescue boat was dispatched to pluck him from an ice floe.

The frigid winters the bay area has periodically endured have tested the mettle of East Enders but, for the most part, the hardy residents of the area have taken whatever Mother Nature dishes out in stride. When an occasional tornado struck the region, however, it was a different story. The suddenness and destructiveness of funnel clouds touching down on or near the bay have terrified eyewitnesses as well as victims. About noontime of an August Friday in 1909, actually Friday the 13th, a waterspout formed over Long Island Sound and galloped toward Shelter Island, where it made an abrupt U-turn and headed for Southold across the bay. No one was injured by this awesome meteorological phenomenon but boats at the Southold town dock, bathhouses, roofs, and trees in various parts of town were damaged. Six years later the North Fork was again visited by a tornado, which touched down in Orient. In August 1999, when the north side of the Peconic Bay estuary was pummeled by a tornado, Orient escaped but Mattituck, where a house had been torn apart by an

August 1981 tornado, as well as the Nassau Point area of Cutchogue and New Suffolk, were on the receiving end of Mother Nature's fury. The funnel formed over Deep Hole Creek by Peconic Bay in Mattituck and almost immediately demolished the roof on a nearby house. Then it roared toward Kimogenor Point in New Suffolk, inflicting severe damage on a historic windmill and tearing the roof off a house. Boats were tossed about in New Suffolk. On Nassau Point the tornado unleashed its fury against houses, boats, cars, and trees. Bad as it was, residents took comfort in the fact that no one, including boaters out on the bay, was killed; but they were hardly as jubilant as the children of New Suffolk back in 1911, when a tornado toppled the chimney of the local schoolhouse, giving the kids a welcome vacation!

**Forward Watch**

Legendary meteorological occurrences, especially tornadoes and hurricanes, have become part of the local lore of the East End. Yet, in the scheme of things, these rare events, which constitute high drama, are overshadowed by day-to-day life on the Twin Forks and the waterways lapping their shores. Ensuring the ecological health of these waters has necessarily become a top priority in recent years. For Peconic Bay the involved process of being designated an "Estuary of National Significance" was an important step in assuring the well-being of the waterway for the future. Back in the eighties, inclusion of the bay in the Environmental Protection Agency's National Estuary Program was viewed as a way of obtaining badly needed federal dollars to study the brown tide and undertake remediation efforts. Some municipalities bordering the estuary, however, as mentioned previously, had reservations. Fearing that they would have to forfeit local control of their waters, Shelter Island, Southampton, and Riverhead initially resisted passing resolutions supporting the inclusion of the bay in the federal program.

Riverhead was also wary about a proposal to designate the Peconic River as a scenic river under New York State's Wild, Scenic and Recreational Rivers (WSRR) Act. Once again, the issue was loss of local control of a natural resource, the very thing that spawned the movement to split the East End off from Suffolk County and create Peconic County. In 1996 voters approved a nonbinding referendum to establish a new county; but a judge ruled, in 2000, that the organization known as Peconic County Now, which had sued in an attempt to force the New York State legislature to provide a mechanism for the creation of new counties, had no legal standing. The self-determination goal held dear by proponents of Peconic County was very evident in Riverhead's opposition to the wild, scenic and recreational designation for the Peconic River. Viewing development along the riverbank as a key element in the revitalization of its downtown, Riverhead vehemently opposed the designation because it would have limited development within a half-mile of the river. In addition to impacting the town center, this would have affected an area near the end of the Long Island Expressway that had been zoned for industrial development. In an effort to maintain control over these important sites, Riverhead sought an injunction against the New York State Department of Environmental Conservation to prevent the state from regulating development near the river. Riverhead's request was denied in 1990, the same year that the Peconic was included in the Wild, Scenic and Recreational Rivers program. In 1993, however, New York State unveiled revised regulations permitting some development near rivers covered by what was generally referred to as the WSRR Act.

A year earlier, the Peconic Bay system had become part of the federal estuary program, which, by 2014, would include twenty waterways. In 1993 the Peconic was designated an "Estuary of National Significance" by the U.S. Environmental Protection Agency. At that time, Peconic Bay was the eighteenth and smallest estuary to receive this important designation. Peconic Bay was accepted by the federal government thanks to a five-year effort mounted by "a citizens' group seeking to find ways to fight the problem of the mysterious brown tide algae," but there were other issues motivating East Enders to press for inclusion of the Peconics in the federal program.[86] Enumerating some of them for *Newsday*, Jeanne Marriner, founder of the Save the Bays Coalition, observed: "There was lots of interest; tourism was off, the baymen were hurting and so we had all the chambers of commerce working with us."[87] The paper then went on to say: "The coalition—a group of 50 associations—spearheaded the campaign, which included lobbying in Washington by singer Billy Joel."[88]

The dedicated people who had fought so hard to get Peconic Bay into the federal program did not rest on their laurels once the bay was designated a national estuary. Forming an alliance known as the Peconic Estuary Program (PEP), consisting of all levels of government, business and industry, citizen and environmental groups, as well as colleges and universities, they provided input for a management plan for the bay. Just before Labor Day in 1999 the *Draft Comprehensive Conservation and Management Plan for the Peconic Bay Estuary* was released and in December 2001 it received formal approval from the U.S. Environmental Protection Agency. The plan's seventy-five concrete recommendations for enhancing water quality covered such issues as fertilizers and pesticides, no-discharge zones, and rethinking land-use planning. Throughout the month of October public hearings on the plan were held on both forks and then it was back to the drawing board to fine-tune the plan. The final draft contained 200-plus recommendations. The cost of implementing the plan was estimated to be $330 million, with funding coming from local, county, state, and federal governments. Vito Menei, director of the Suffolk County Health Department's Division of Environmental Quality, which developed the final plan, was quick to point out that the plan would be implemented over the course of "many years."[89] That being said, there was still remarkable progress in the first decade of PEP's existence. Among the achievements was the designation of the estuary as a no-discharge zone for vessel waste, an eelgrass monitoring program, the removal of invasive species from the Peconic River, and Suffolk County legislation aimed at lessening nitrogen pollution by reducing the use of fertilizer. The program also brought together scientists for a State of the Bays conference and conducted a unique virtual field trip of the estuary for students from all over the United States. In its second decade PEP continued its educational outreach program by holding public watershed meetings, inventorying and digitizing maps of the shoreline and submerged aquatic vegetation, and enlisting volunteers to hand-pull an invasive nonnative aquatic species from the Peconic River.

With more funding for the twenty-eight estuaries in the National Estuary Program, PEP will attain additional goals. When Senator Hillary Rodham Clinton of New York visited Sag Harbor in July 2001 she vowed to fight for funding for the National Estuary Program. Federal dollars earmarked for cleaning up the waterways amount to money well spent because projects that enhance the health of estuaries and surrounding land masses are vitally important for the economy. A study released in 1999 indicated that Peconic Bay produced nearly $500 million in annual revenue for East End businesses. However, the bay's value far exceeds the direct contribution it makes to the coffers of East End businesses, for, after all, can you put a price tag on an enjoyable day at the beach, a boat ride on the bay, or a fishing trip with the family?

In the aftermath of September 11, Americans began to quantify things differently. Having it all, in terms of material possessions, seemed less important than spending not only quality time but a greater quantity of it with loved ones. Family, patriotism, and peace became the overriding concerns of a nation at war. In the Peconic Bay area, people had been wondering for decades whether humans can live in peace and harmony with the natural environment, but after September 11 East Enders questioned whether we would ever be at peace with our fellow human beings on a global level. Let's hope that this is an attainable goal because, in the final analysis, it may be world rather than regional events that will determine whether this area, which in 2007 was included in *1,000 Places to See in the U.S.A. and Canada before You Die*, remains a very special place. In June 2012, when the twentieth anniversary of the Peconic Bay Estuary's federally recognized status as an estuary of national significance was celebrated, residents of the Hamptons and the North Fork took note of the fact that the Nature Conservancy had termed the estuary "one of the last great places in the Western Hemisphere."[90] One can only hope that this will still be the case on the eve of the twenty-second century, when the centennial of the special designation is celebrated.

*Notes*

*Bibliographic Note*

*Bibliography*

*Index*

# Notes

## 1. At Home

1. Joseph Barbaro and Lisa Weinerman, eds., *Heart of the Land: Essays on the Last Great Places* (New York: Pantheon, 1994), xii.

2. *Southampton Press*, September 4, 2003, 1.

3. *East Hampton Star*, December 17, 2009, A14.

4. *East Hampton Star*, June 17, 2010, 1.

5. Ibid., A12.

6. *East Hampton Star*, October 7, 2010, A14.

7. *East Hampton Star*, November 6, 2008, B6.

8. *East Hampton Star*, November 27, 2008, 1.

9. Marion Carter, "Ancient Indian Tribe Dwells Near Princely Estates of Money Kings of Long Island," September 4, 1934, clipping, courtesy of the East Hampton Library, Long Island Collection.

10. Ibid.

11. Ibid.

12. David McClure, *Diary of David McClure Doctor of Divinity, 1748–1820* (New York: Knickerbocker, 1899), 137.

13. Ibid.

14. Richard Farwell, "Intimate Sketches of Eastern Long Island, 1872–1882," *Bridgehampton News*, 1935, clipping, courtesy of the East Hampton Library, Long Island Collection.

15. Edith H. Shepherd, "The Funeral of a Pharaoh," *Long Island Forum* (February 1981): 38–41.

16. Ibid.

17. Ibid.

18. John A. Strong, "Who Says the Montauk Tribe Is Extinct? Judge Abel Blackmar's Decision in Wyandank v. Benson (1909)," *Long Island Historical Journal* 10, no. 1 (1997): 39–55.

19. John A. Strong, "*We Are Still Here!*"—*The Algonquian Peoples of Long Island* (Interlaken: Heart of the Lakes, 1998), 21.

20. *Annual Report of the Montauk Tribe of Indians for the Year 1916*, vertical files, Collection of the Suffolk County Historical Society, Riverhead.

21. Roger Wunderlich, "Lion Gardiner, Long Island's Founding Father," *Long Island Historical Journal* 10, no. 2 (1998): 172–85.

22. Ibid.

23. Gaynell Stone, "Long Island as America: A New Look at the First Inhabitants," *Long Island Historical Journal* 1, no. 2 (1989): 159–69.

24. Ibid.

25. *Southampton Press*, September 2, 1999, B8:1.

26. Ibid.

27. *Newsday*, August 14, 1999, A5:4.

28. Henry Hazelton, *Boroughs of Brooklyn and Queens, Counties of Nassau and Suffolk* (Salem, Mass.: Higginson, 1925), 3, 733.

29. *New York Times*, May 31, 1998, LI 11:1.

30. Henry P. Hedges, *Memories of a Long Life* (East Hampton, N.Y.: Boughton, 1909), 46.

31. Richard Bayles, *Historical and Descriptive Sketches of Suffolk County* (Port Jefferson: 1874), advertising inset.

32. Joshua Bradley, *Accounts of Religious Revivals in Many Parts of the U.S. from 1815 to 1818* (Albany, N.Y.: O. J. Loomis, 1819), 245.

33. Amy Osborn Bassford, "East End Colloquialisms—II," *Long Island Forum* (October 1962): 213–14.

34. *An Address to the Friends of Temperance from the Annual Meeting of Suffolk County Temperance Society, Held at Orient, October 14, 1851* (New York: J. P. Pratt, 1851), 4.

35. "The Temperance Work in Orient and Its Results," *New York Daily Witness*, February 22, 1876, Oysterponds Historical Society Scrapbook Number 1.

36. Ibid.

37. Ibid.

38. Augustus Griffin, *Griffin's Journal* (Orient, N.Y.: Augustus Griffin, 1859), 177.

39. Ibid., 179.

40. Ibid.

41. Daniel Hildreth, *Diary*, August 14, 1872, Long Island Collection of the Hampton Library, Bridgehampton.

42. Caroline Terry, *Diary*, December 31, 1830, Oysterponds Historical Society.

43. Prentice Mulford, "Our Old Home: Sag Harbor and Its People: January 19, 1872," courtesy of the East Hampton Library, Long Island Collection.

44. Ibid.

45. *The Watchman* (Greenport), July 28, 1927, clipping, courtesy of the East Hampton Library, Long Island Collection.

46. W. D. Snodgrass, "Whitman's Selfsong," *Southern Review* (Summer 1996): 572–94.

47. Katherine Molinoff, *Walt Whitman at Southold*, No. 4 in a Series of Monographs on Unpublished Walt Whitman Material, 1966, 5.

48. *Corrector* (Sag Harbor), April 18, 1835, 4:2.

49. Ibid.

50. Ibid.

51. *Corrector* (Sag Harbor), December 5, 1838, 4:4.

52. Ibid.

53. *Corrector* (Sag Harbor), April 18, 1835, 3:5.

54. *Suffolk Times* (Southold), August 27, 1998, 2:3.

55. *Corrector* (Sag Harbor), April 19, 1828, 3:4.

56. Ibid., May 28, 1831, 3:5.

57. Ibid.

58. Ernest S. Clowes, *Wayfarings* (Bridgehampton: Bridgehampton News, 1953), 176.

59. Ibid.

60. Edith H. Shepherd, "A World-Citizen Visits Shelter Island: Francisco de Miranda Venezuelan Patriot on Tour in 1784," *Long Island Forum* 53 (Summer 1990): 73–80.

61. Fitch Reed, "Old Days on Long Island," *Brooklyn Daily Eagle*, January 15, 1893, courtesy of the East Hampton Library, Long Island Collection.

62. Ibid.

63. Edward R. Merrall, Letter to His Mother, October 1, 1843, courtesy of the East Hampton Library, Long Island Collection.

64. Annie Burnham Cooper, *Annie Burnham Cooper: Her Diary. Sag Harbor, New York 1881–1894* (New York: Ballantine, 1986), 150.

65. Ibid., 160.

66. Ibid., 173.

67. Ibid.

68. Ibid., 82.

69. Cuyler Beebe Tuthill, *The Life and Work of Cuyler B. Tuthill* (Brooklyn: Pratt Institute School of Architecture, 1896), 1.

70. Malcolm M. Willey, "James A. Herne's Sag Harbor," *Long Island Forum* 61 (Fall 1998): 4–12.

71. *Brooklyn Daily Eagle*, November 5, 1904, 1:3.

72. Ella B. Hallock, *Cabin Paradise* (Southold, N.Y.: Privately printed, 1928), 1–2.

73. Ibid., 63.

74. Peconic Bay Real Estate Booklet, vertical file, courtesy of the John Jermain Memorial Library, Sag Harbor.

75. Ibid.

76. Ibid.

77. *New York Times*, April 30, 1916, I, 18:4.

78. *New York Times*, May 6, 1916, 6:2.

79. Ibid.

80. Ibid.

81. Ibid.

82. Ibid.

83. *New York Times*, May 7, 1916, 14:2.

84. Ibid.

85. *New York Times*, May 6, 1916, 6:3.

86. *New York Times*, May 11, 1916, 10:5.

87. "Wreckers Raze Shelter Island Mansion of Late Borax King," *Brooklyn Eagle*, February 13, 1939, clipping, courtesy of the East Hampton Library, Long Island Collection.

88. *Suffolk Times*, July 22, 1937, clipping, Office of the Southold Town Historian.

89. Ibid.

90. *Complete in Happiness* (Cutchogue, N.Y.: Chamber of Commerce, 1941), brochure, courtesy of the East Hampton Library, Long Island Collection.

91. Ken Robbins and Bill Strachan, *Springs: A Celebration* (Springs, N.Y.: Springs Improvement Society, 1984), 16.

92. *New York Times*, August 15, 1954, II, 15:7.

93. Ibid.

94. *Suffolk Times* (Mattituck), June 14, 2001, 18:4.

## 2. At Work

1. *New York Herald*, June 5, 1854, clippings, Scrapbook 22, Oysterponds Historical Society.

2. Ibid.

3. Ibid.

4. Ibid.

5. Ibid.

6. *New York Herald*, October 26, 1854, clipping, Scrapbook 22, Oysterponds Historical Society.

7. Ibid.

8. H. R. Talmage, "Potato Growing on Long Island," *New York State Agricultural Bulletin* 13 (September 1920): 133–37.

9. "Orient's 1925 Crop of Potatoes Will Break All Records," clipping, Scrapbook No. 24, local news items 1877–1925, Oysterponds Historical Society.

10. *New York Times*, February 10, 1944, 12:5.

11. Ibid.

12. Ibid.

13. Ibid., 12:6

14. Roy Latham to Dan Youngs, September 21, 1958, ms. letter, Oysterponds Historical Society.

15. Roy Latham to Dan Youngs, June 14, 1959, ms. letter, Oysterponds Historical Society.

16. *Southampton Press*, October 12, 2000, 1:2.

17. *Suffolk Times*, 1859, clipping, Oysterponds Historical Society.

18. Ibid.

19. Daniel Hildreth, "Diary," August 17, 1871, Long Island Collection of the Hampton Library, Bridgehampton.

20. *New York Times*, October 24, 1999, 38:2.

21. B. Roueche, "Fine Day for Ducks: Biggest Duck Farm in the World Raises Pekins," *New Yorker*, September 22, 1945, 58.

22. *New York Times*, September 25, 1994, 8:1.

23. Ibid., 8:2.

24. Edna Howell Yeager, *Peconic River Mills and Industries* (Riverhead, N.Y.: Suffolk County Historical Society, 1965), 222.

25. *Long Island Traveler* (Southold), August 21, 1858, clipping, vertical files, Cutchogue–New Suffolk Library Local History Collection.

26. Ibid.

27. George A. Finckenor Sr., "The Salt Works of John Mitchell at North Haven," *Long Island Forum* 46 (October 1983): 190–91.

28. Clarence Ashton Wood, "Southold's Great Western Mill," *Long Island Forum* 18 (January 1955), 3.

29. Ibid.

30. Yeager, *Peconic River Mills*, 187.

31. Clarence Ashton Wood, "Riverhead's Famous Carriages," *Long Island Forum* 8 (May 1945): 87.

32. Ibid.

33. *Sag Harbor Express*, October 23, 1879, clipping, Courtesy of the East Hampton Library, Long Island Collection.

34. Ibid.

35. Ibid.

36. H. D. Sleight, "Once Sag Harbor Tried to Operate Cotton Mills," clipping, Courtesy of the East Hampton Library, Long Island Collection.

37. Clipping, November 6, 1880, Courtesy of the John Jermain Memorial Library.

38. *American Eagle*, May 22, 1819, transcription of clipping, Courtesy of the John Jermain Memorial Library.

39. Elisabeth S. Lapham, "Echoes from the Past: The Riverhead Waterfront, Circa 1900: Part I," *Community Journal*, November 19, 1980.

40. Ibid.

41. Ibid.

42. *Suffolk Times*, August 12, 1858, clipping, Oysterponds Historical Society.

43. *The Launching of the Barkentine "Wandering Jew," at Greenport April 28, 1880, at the Shipyard of Messrs. Smith & Terry* (Orient, N.Y.: Oysterponds Historical Society), 3.

44. William B. Minuse, "Shipbuilding in Suffolk County" (Riverhead, N.Y.: Suffolk County Tercentenary Commission, 1983), 7.

45. *Corrector* (Sag Harbor), November 30, 1833, 3:5.

46. *Corrector* (Sag Harbor), December 7, 1872, 2:5.

47. *Republican Watchman*, December 11, 1869, clipping, Courtesy of the East Hampton Library, Long Island Collection.

48. G. Brown Goode, *A History of the Menhaden* (New York: Orange Judd Company, 1880), 42.

49. George Brown Goode, *The Fisheries and Fishery Industries of the United States*, Section V (Washington, D.C.: U.S. Government Printing Office, 1887), 1:409.

50. *Brooklyn Daily Eagle*, July 28, 1899, 11:4.

51. Ibid.

52. *New York Times*, July 12, 1879, 4:2.

53. Clarence Ashton Wood, "Bunkers and Other Fish," *Long Island Forum* 17 (May 1954): 89–90.

54. Clipping, Oysterponds Historical Society.

55. Ibid.

56. Ibid.

57. Ibid.

58. *East Hampton Star*, April 4, 1924, 1:6.

59. Ibid.

60. Ibid.

61. Ibid.

62. Arnold Leo to Arthur N. Field, April 17, 1989, East Hampton Baymen's Association Collection, Box 4, Folder 283, Courtesy of the East Hampton Library, Long Island Collection.

63. Ibid.

64. Ibid.

65. Ibid.

66. Testimony Prepared by Arnold Leo for Public Hearing, February 23, 1980, East Hampton Baymen's Association Collection, Box 12, Folder 268, Courtesy of the East Hampton Library, Long Island Collection.

67. Arnold Leo, Statement, December 21, 1986, East Hampton Baymen's Association Collection, Box 13, Folder 279, Courtesy of the East Hampton Library, Long Island Collection.

68. Ibid.

69. *New York Times*, April 27, 1997, 33:1.

70. Ibid.

71. *New York Times*, May 28, 2000, LI 3:3.

72. Ibid.

73. *The Board of Trustees of the Freeholders and Commonality of the Town of Southampton* (Southampton, N.Y.: n.p., 1968), 21.

74. Ibid.

75. George Brown Goode, *The Fisheries and Fishery Industries of the United States*, Section II (Washington, D.C.: U.S. Government Printing Office, 1887), 360.

76. Ibid., 356.

77. Ibid.

78. Ibid.

79. Charles R. Street, *Opinion Concerning the Title to Lands under Water in the Town of Southold, Together with the Trustee Law* (Southold, N.Y.: Town of Southold, 1893), 29.

80. Ibid., 31.

81. Ibid., 36.

82. Ibid.

83. H. D. Sleight, "Southold and Shelter Island Once Part of Connecticut, Hence Boundary Dispute That Lasted over 250 Years," *Brooklyn Daily Eagle*, August 12, 1924, clipping, Courtesy of the East Hampton Library, Long Island Collection.

84. Ibid.

85. Newspaper clipping, 1900, Courtesy of the John Jermain Memorial Library.

86. *Brooklyn Daily Eagle*, November 5, 1904, 1:3.

87. *Riverhead News*, October 17, 1913, transcription, vertical file, Suffolk County Historical Society.

88. Mattituck Oral History Project, 5, 709. Courtesy of Mattituck-Laurel Library.

89. Stuart Vorpahl Jr., Memorandum of Law, November 19, 2001, 2. Docket #SH-01991384.

90. Ibid., 22.

91. *New York Times,* July 7, 2007, 1.

92. Long Island Heritage Project, Tape 1258, 21–22, Hallockville Museum Farm.

## 3. At Play

1. *Sun,* September 24, 1911, clipping, Courtesy of the East Hampton Library, Long Island Collection.

2. Ronald G. Pisano, *Henry and Edith Mitchill Prellwitz and the Peconic Art Colony* (Stony Brook, N.Y.: Museums at Stony Brook, 1995), 9.

3. Ibid., 11–12.

4. Ibid., 7.

5. Ibid., 8.

6. John H. Morice, *First Out-of-Door Art School in the U.S.* (N.p.: Privately Printed, 1945).

7. Ibid.

8. "Thomas Moran: A Search for the Scenic," Catalogue, Guild Hall Exhibition (November 1980–January 1981).

9. Connie Koppelman, "Back to Nature: The Tile Club in the Country," *Long Island Historical Journal* 3, no. 1 (1990): 75–86.

10. *Corrector* (Sag Harbor), December 5, 1838, 4:4.

11. Ibid.

12. *Corrector* (Sag Harbor), August 20, 1851, 3:2.

13. Ibid., 3:5.

14. *Corrector* (Sag Harbor), June 21, 1879, 4:2.

15. *Corrector* (Sag Harbor), July 9, 1831, 4:3.

16. Ibid.

17. *Corrector* (Sag Harbor), July 19, 1837, 3:4.

18. *Corrector* (Sag Harbor), August 25, 1838, 4:4

19. *Corrector* (Sag Harbor), September 14, 1853, 4:1.

20. *Corrector* (Sag Harbor), May 11, 1860, 3:3.

21. Advertisements, Hunting Scrapbook, F72, Whitaker Collection, Southold Free Library.

22. "Montauk Steamboat Company: 1898" (Montauk Steamboat Company 1898), 4–5, Emory Collection, SUNY Stony Brook Library.

23. Ibid., 6–7.

24. Ibid., 7.

25. Ibid., 2–3

26. Ibid., 3.

27. Ibid.

28. Ibid.

29. *Corrector* (Sag Harbor), August 25, 1838, 4:4.

30. *Riverhead News*, September 23, 1893. Ackerly Scrapbook, Courtesy of the East Hampton Library, Long Island Collection.

31. Ibid.

32. Ibid.

33. *Corrector* (Sag Harbor), September 3, 1870, 2:5.

34. Ibid.

35. Ibid.

36. Ibid.

37. Ruth Marsland Demarest, "Early Days of the Camp Grounds," *Jamesport: A Scrapbook of Memories*, ed. Nancy Widmer, 1, Suffolk County Historical Society.

38. Ibid., 8.

39. Ibid., 9.

40. Rev. Henry Medd, "Jamesport Camp Meeting Colony," *Southampton Magazine* 1, no. 2 (1912): 38–42.

41. Ibid.

42. *Corrector* (Sag Harbor), August 17, 1878, 2:2.

43. *Shelter Island Grove Association News*, May 1, 1875, 1, Smithtown Library.

44. "A Trip to Shelter Island and What We Saw There," *Our Neighborhood* (July 1878): 1–2.

45. *New York Times*, July 8, 1873, 8:3.

46. Ibid.

47. Ibid.

48. Ibid.

49. "Prospect House: 1898," 4, Shelter Island Historical Society.

50. Ibid., 5.

51. Ibid., 12.

52. Ibid., 9.

53. Ibid.

54. Ibid.

55. Undated Prospect House Brochure, Courtesy of the East Hampton Library, Long Island Collection.

56. "Manhanset House Brochure: 1891 Season," Courtesy of the East Hampton Library, Long Island Collection.

57. Ibid.

58. "Manhanset House Brochure: 1896," 5, Courtesy of the East Hampton Library, Long Island Collection.

59. Ibid.

60. *New York Times*, August 14, 1896, 3:1.

61. Ibid.

62. Ibid.

63. H. W. Larson Coleman to Mrs. J. S. Wood, July 5, 1900, Shelter Island Historical Society.

64. Evans K. Griffing, "Shelter Island As I Have Known It, Past and Present," Address, Shelter Island Historical Society, June 7, 1974, 7.

65. *Brooklyn Daily Eagle*, July 23, 1899, 32:3.

66. Hand Bills for Miamogue Hotel, South Jamesport, Suffolk County Historical Society.

67. Ibid.

68. *Out on Long Island* (Long Island Rail Road: 1893), 60–61.

69. *The Beauties of Long Island* (Traffic Department, Long Island Rail Road, 1897), 72.

70. G. P. Lathrop, *Peconic Park: An Exploration of Long Island, N.Y.* (N.p.: Printed for Private Circulation, 1883), 7.

71. Ibid., 36.

72. Ibid., 37.

73. Ibid., 36.

74. Letter to the Editor, *Long Island Forum* (October 1956): 192.

75. Broadside, Courtesy of the East Hampton Library, Long Island Collection.

76. Undated Advertisement, Oysterponds Historical Society.

77. *By Sea and Land: An Account of a Steamboat Excursion by a Party of Ladies and Gentlemen from Worcester, Massachusetts in the Summer of 1868* (Worcester, Mass.: Chas. Hammill, 1868), 33.

78. Ibid.

79. Brochure: Bay House and Cottages, Oysterponds Historical Society

80. Ibid.

81. *Corrector* (Sag Harbor), September 3, 1860, 3:1.

82. A. A. Hayes, "A New England Colony in New York," *Harper's New Monthly Magazine* (August 1885): 350–58.

83. Ibid.

84. *New York Times*, July 15, 1929, V, 4.

85. *Prospectus of the Noyac Cottage Association on Peconic Bay, Town of Southampton, Long Island, N.Y.* (New York: n.p., 1888), 4.

86. Ibid., 3.

87. Ibid., 9.

88. Ibid., 4.

89. Ibid., 9.

90. *Long Island 1888* (Long Island Rail Road: 1888), 52.

91. Ibid.

92. *Corrector* (Sag Harbor), February 2, 1848, 3:4.

93. Ibid.

94. Ibid.

95. Ibid.

96. *Corrector* (Sag Harbor), January 16, 1830, 4:3.

97. *New York Times*, May 27, 1893, 9:1.

98. "Appaquogue: East Hampton, Long Island," *Brooklyn Advance* (1879), clipping, Courtesy of the East Hampton Library, Long Island Collection.

99. Ibid.

100. *Corrector* (Sag Harbor), July 18, 1874, 2:4.

101. *New York Times Illustrated Magazine*, October 30, 1898, clipping, Courtesy of the East Hampton Library, Long Island Collection.

102. Ibid.

103. Ibid.

104. Ibid.

105. Abigail Halsey, *An East Hampton Childhood* (East Hampton, N.Y.: Star Press, 1938), 29.

106. *New York Herald Tribune*, May 11, 1947, clipping, Courtesy of the East Hampton Library, Long Island Collection.

107. Advertisement, August 30, 1858, Hunting Scrapbook, F72, Whitaker Collection/Southold Free Library.

108. Ibid.

109. Ibid.

110. *East Hampton Star*, May 26, 1960, 1:7.

111. *Salt Water Fishing around Long Island* (The Long Island Rail Road: 1934), 2.

112. Ibid., 8.

113. *Here's the Outing of a Lifetime!* (The Long Island Rail Road: 1931), 1.

114. *Salt Water Fishing around Long Island* (The Long Island Rail Road: 1934), 8.

115. *Here's the Outing*, 1.

116. *Seagulls Will Tell You* (The Long Island Rail Road: 1937), 6.

117. Ibid.

118. Fishing Brochure (Long Island Rail Road: 1937), 1.

119. *New York Times*, September 1, 1895, 12:1.

120. *Daily Eagle*, July 23, 1899, 3:2.

121. Rosalind Case Newell, *Rose of the Nineties* (Southold, N.Y.: Long Island Traveler, 1962), 109.

122. Ibid., 108.

123. *Corrector* (Sag Harbor), August 4, 1860, 2:4.

124. *New York Times*, August 4, 1895, 12:1.

125. Ibid.

126. Ibid.

127. *New York Times*, July 23, 1893, 15:1.

128. Ibid.

129. Ibid.

130. Ibid.

131. *New York Times*, August 6, 1893, 15:1.

132. *Long Island 1901* (Long Island Rail Road: 1901), 69.

133. *Southampton Magazine* (August 1963): 227.

134. Oral History Interview with Anne MacKay, March 3, 1992, Oysterponds Historical Society.

135. Ibid.

136. Oral History Interview with Mildred Younie Cobb, March 3, 1992, Oysterponds Historical Society.

137. *New York Times*, August 11, 1895, 12:1.

138. *Cyclists' Paradise* (Long Island Rail Road: 1897), 3.

139. Ibid., 8.

140. *New York Times*, July 26, 1896, 10:5.

141. "The National Golf Club," *Southampton Magazine* 3 (Autumn 1912): 3–18.

142. Ibid.

143. Ibid.

144. *Corrector* (Sag Harbor), September 28, 1867, 2:3.

145. *New York Times*, September 2, 1894, 12:1.

146. Ibid.

147. *New York Times*, August 6, 1893, 15:1.

148. *New York Times*, July 30, 1893, 13:1.

149. Ibid.

150. State of New York, Bill Introduced by Assemblyman Downs (February 11, 1929), 1, Oysterponds Historical Society.

151. Oral History Interview with A. D. Duke, June 19, 1998, 4. The History Project: Rogers Memorial Library, Southampton, Long Island Collection.

152. *Long Island Real Estate Review* 1, no. 2 (1906), Bridgehampton Historical Society.

153. *On Land and Yet at Sea* (Brooklyn: Shinnecock Hills and Peconic Bay Realty Company, 1907), 3.

154. Ibid., 11.

155. *New York Times*, September 28, 1997, LI: 42.

156. *Washington Post*, March 15, 1998, W4.

157. *New York Times*, September 29, 2013, TR: 11.

## 4. At War

1. *Corrector* (Sag Harbor), July 29, 1899, 3:2
2. Ibid.
3. Ibid.
4. Ibid.
5. Ibid.
6. Ibid.
7. Richard F. Welch, "John P. Holland and the Creation of the American Submarine Fleet," *Long Island Historical Journal* 9, no. 2 (1997): 209–22.
8. Ibid.
9. *Brooklyn Daily Eagle*, July 27, 1899, 4:3.
10. *Long Island Traveler*, October 20, 1899, Holland Submarine file, Cutchogue/New Suffolk Library Local History Collection.
11. *Long Island Traveler*, November 10, 1899, Holland Submarine file, Cutchogue/New Suffolk Library Local History Collection.
12. *Long Island Traveler*, December 13, 1901, clipping file, Suffolk County Historical Society.
13. Ibid.
14. *New York Herald*, November 14, 1895, Ackerly Scrapbook, 4, Courtesy of the East Hampton Library, Long Island Collection.
15. Henry Onderdonck Jr., *Revolutionary Incidents of Suffolk and Kings Counties* (Port Washington, N.Y.: Kennikat Press, 1970), 81. Reprint of 1849 edition.
16. Ibid., 106.
17. Wayland Jefferson, *Southold and Its People in Revolutionary Days* (Southold, N.Y.: Long Island Traveler, 1932), 21.
18. Onderdonck, *Revolutionary Incidents*, 102.
19. Ibid.
20. Helen Otis Lamont, *The Story of Shelter Island in the Revolution* (Shelter Island, N.Y.: Shelter Island Historical Society, 1975), 39.
21. Onderdonck, *Revolutionary Incidents*, 102.
22. Ibid.
23. Ibid., 103.
24. Ibid.
25. Ibid., 100.
26. Edna Howell Yeager, *Around the Forks* (Interlaken, N.Y.: I-T Publishing, 1980), 27.

27. Ibid.

28. Ilse O'Sullivan, *East Hampton and the American Revolution* (East Hampton, N.Y.: East Hampton Town Bicentennial Committee, 1976), 67.

29. Ibid., 36–37.

30. Silas Wood, *A Sketch of the First Settlement of the Several Towns of Long Island with Their Political Condition to the End of the American Revolution* (Port Washington, N.Y.: Ira J. Friedman, 1968), 121–22.

31. Jefferson, *Southold and Its People in Revolutionary Days*, 10.

32. Frederic Gregory Mather, *The Refugees of 1776 from Long Island to Connecticut* (Albany: J. B. Lyon, 1913), 193.

33. Morton Pennypacker, "Boy Bound to Gardiner in 1787 Became Famous Joshua Penny in 1815," clipping, Courtesy of the East Hampton Library, Long Island Collection.

34. Morton Pennypacker, "Man or Monkey, Penny Found a Captain Williams to Ship Him to Southold," clipping, Courtesy of the East Hampton Library, Long Island Collection.

35. Morton Pennypacker, "Penny Tells How Torpedo Warfare in War of 1812 Started on Long Island," clipping, Courtesy of the East Hampton Library, Long Island Collection.

36. Ibid.

37. *The Life and Adventures of Joshua Penny* (Brooklyn: Alden Spooner, 1815), 48.

38. Barbara Marhofer, *Witches, Whales, Petticoats and Sails* (Port Washington, N.Y.: Kennikat Press, 1971), 131.

39. Henry Finckenor, "The Old Fort at Sag Harbor," *Long Island Forum* 49 (June 1984): 119–21.

40. William Donaldson Halsey, *Sketches from Local History* (Bridgehampton, N.Y.: H. Lee, 1935), 84.

41. Melita Hofmann, "The British at Orient in 1812," *Long Island Forum* 23 (October 1960): 221.

42. Ibid.

43. Ibid.

44. Henry Hazelton, *Boroughs of Brooklyn and Queens, Counties of Nassau and Suffolk* (Salem, Mass.: Higginson, 1997), 776.

45. Ibid.

46. Court-martial Transcription, January 5, 1815, Courtesy of the John Jermain Memorial Library.

47. Ibid.

48. *Long Island Almanac* (Brooklyn Daily Eagle, 1921), 65–66.

49. Emily Warren Roebling to John Augustus Roebling II, October 25, 1898, Rutgers University Archives.

50. *Brooklyn Daily Eagle* (Brooklyn), January 10, 1916, clipping, Courtesy of the John Jermain Memorial Library.

51. Ibid.

52. Ibid.

53. 1902 Clipping, Courtesy of the John Jermain Memorial Library.

54. Ibid.

55. Ibid.

56. *Suffolk Times* (Mattituck), July 29, 1982, 1:2.

57. Ibid., 1:4.

58. Ibid.

59. *New York Times*, September 18, 1977, LI, 15:1.

60. Ibid., 15:2

61. Unidentified newspaper clipping, October 10, 1923, Gildersleeve Scrapbook, III, 3. Courtesy of Mattituck-Laurel Library.

62. Clipping, December 27, 1933, vertical files, Cutchogue/New Suffolk Library.

63. Ibid.

64. Ibid.

65. Ibid.

66. Priscilla Dunhill, *The People of Sachem's Neck*, 72. Shelter Island Historical Society.

67. *East Hampton Star*, January 25, 1962, 1:6

68. Jeanette Edwards Rattray, *Montauk: Three Centuries of Romance, Sport and Adventure* (East Hampton, N.Y.: East Hampton Star Press, 1938), 21.

69. *Sag Harbor Express*, April 19, 1923, 1:1.

70. Manuscript, "A Chat With Einstein," Oysterponds Historical Society.

71. Ibid.

72. Ibid.

73. Ibid.

74. Ibid.

75. Ibid.

76. *Newsday*, July 28, 1989, Part II, vertical files, Cutchogue/New Suffolk Library.

77. Ibid.

78. Albert Einstein to Franklin D. Roosevelt, August 2, 1939, Franklin D. Roosevelt Library.

79. Ibid.

80. Ibid.

81. *Newsday*, July 28, 1989, Part II, vertical files, Cutchogue/New Suffolk Library.

82. "The Einstein Only a Few Persons Know," clipping, vertical files, Cutchogue/New Suffolk Library.

83. *Bowline* (Greenport), May 6, 1943, 1. Courtesy of Floyd Memorial Library.

84. Ibid., 3.

85. *Bowline*, July 3, 1942, 1. Courtesy of Floyd Memorial Library.

86. Ibid., 3.

87. Peter Moon and Stewart Swerdlow, *Montauk: The Alien Connection* (Westbury: Sky Books, 1998), 217.

88. Ibid.

89. Ibid.

90. Ibid., 219.

91. *Suffolk Times* (Mattituck), August 8, 1991, 1:4.

92. Ibid.

93. *Suffolk Times* (Mattituck), July 29, 1982, 1:3.

94. Ibid.

95. Ibid.

96. Ibid.

97. Ibid., 16:4.

98. *New York Times*, September 29, 1985, XXI, 19:1.

99. Ibid.

## 5. At Peace

1. *Suffolk Times*, November 18, 1999, 34:4.

2. *New York Times*, September 22, 1999, B6:1.

3. Ibid., B6:4.

4. *Suffolk Times*, November 25, 1999, 8:1.

5. *Newsday*, July 5, 1998, B7:1.

6. Ibid., B7:2.

7. *Southampton Press*, March 4, 1999, 1:3.

8. Ibid.

9. Ibid.

10. *East Hampton Star*, August 26, 1999, I, 11:5.

11. *Traveler Watchman*, November 4, 1999, 12:1.

12. *Southampton Press*, August 10, 2000, A13:5.

13. Ibid.

14. Julian Burroughs, "Porpoises and Escallops," *Forest and Stream* (March 11, 1911): 368–70.

15. *New York Times*, January 4, 1954, 17:8.

16. *New York Times*, December 26, 1982, LI3.

17. Ibid.

18. *New York Times*, September 14, 1985, I, l:1.

19. Ibid., I, 1:2.

20. Ibid., I, 1:3.

21. Ibid.

22. Ibid., I, 28:1.

23. Susan Pollack, "Algal Invasion Deals L.I. Scallopers a Crushing Blow," *National Fisherman* (December 1985): 2–4.

24. *New York Times*, October 13, 1986, B, I:1.

25. *New York Times*, October 16, 1988, XXII, 1:3.

26. Ibid., 10:1.

27. Ibid., 10:1.

28. *New York Times*, May 31, 1989, I, l:1.

29. Ibid.

30. Ibid., B4:3.

31. Ibid.

32. *Newsday*, October 13, 1994, A:3.

33. *News-Review* (Riverhead), February 3, 2000, 1:2.

34. Ibid., March 9, 2000, 6:1.

35. *Southampton Press*, April 13, 2000, 5:1.

36. *Southampton Press*, December 7, 2000, A4:1.

37. *Newsday*, August 18, 2000, A30:1.

38. Bill Smith to East Hampton Baymen's Association, March 25, 1996, Box 2, Folder 46, Courtesy of the East Hampton Library, Long Island Collection.

39. Ibid.

40. Ibid.

41. *Suffolk Times* (Mattituck), August 2, 2001, 2:2.

42. *News-Review* (Riverhead), February 18, 2010, 20.

43. *Baywatch 2011: The State of Long Island's Bays* (Quogue, N.Y.: Peconic Baykeeper, 2011), 5.

44. *New York Times*, June 16, 1974, 97:4

45. *Newsday*, May 7, 1985, Grace Estate Folder, East Hampton Baymen's Association Records, Box 5, Folder 110, Courtesy of the East Hampton Library, Long Island Collection.

46. Ibid.

47. Carolyn A. Zenk, "History in the Making: Hampton Hills and Land Preservation in Suffolk County," *Long Island Historical Journal* 4, no. 1 (1991): 79–91.

48. *New York Times*, February 25, 1990, XII, 1:3.

49. *A Report by the 1991 US/UK Countryside Stewardship Exchange Team to the People of the Town of Southold, North Fork, Long Island—Executive Summary* (November 1991), 1.

50. Ibid.

51. Ibid.

52. *Report by the 1991 US/UK Countryside Stewardship Exchange Team*, 2.

53. *Suffolk Times* (Mattituck), June 19, 1997, 3:1.

54. *Group Action* (Southold, N.Y.: Group for the East End, 2012), 9.

55. *News-Review* (Riverhead), October 16, 1997, 1:1.

56. *Suffolk Times* (Mattituck), February 18, 1999, 16:4.

57. *Suffolk Times* (Mattituck), May 24, 2001, 4:3.

58. *Newsday*, July 26, 2001, A26:1.

59. *New York Times*, February 10, 1980, XXI, 6:6.

60. Ibid.

61. *Friends of the Wickham Claim Newsletter*, December 4, 1988, 2:1.

62. Ibid.

63. *Our Town USA*, September 18, 1992, 4:3.

64. *New York Times*, April 8, 1993, B5:7.

65. Ibid., B5:8.

66. *Newsweek*, August 7, 1972, 67:1.

67. Ibid.

68. *New York Times*, June 9, 1968, VIII, 1:4.

69. Mike Rossler, "The Condominiumization of the N. Fork," *Real Estate Illustrated*, Supplement to *The Suffolk Times* and *The News–Review*, August 23, 1984, 1.

70. Ibid.

71. *News-Review*, February 2, 2012, 23.

72. *New York Times*, June 24, 1990, B23:1.

73. *Newsday*, December 15, 2000, C6.

74. *Guardian Weekly* (Sydney, Australia), January 15, 1984, vertical file, Riverhead History, Riverhead Free Library.

75. *Dan's Papers*, April 20, 2012, 20.

76. Osborn Shaw, "Historic Storms and Gales—Part III," *Long Island Forum* (April 1960): 85–91.

77. Ernest S. Clowes, *The Hurricane of 1938 on Eastern Long Island* (Bridgehampton, N.Y.: Hampton Press, 1939), 16.

78. Ibid., 31.

79. Anne MacKay, *Excerpts from "Just Lucky, I Guess"* (Orient, N.Y.: Oysterponds Historical Society, 1995), 42.

80. Ibid., 43.

81. David Ludlum, "The Hurricane of 1938 in Historical Perspective," in Roger Brickner, *The L.I. Express: Tracking the Hurricane of 1938* (Batavia, N.Y.: Hodgins Print, 1988), 14.

82. Henry Packer Dering to Frances Mary Dering, December 28, 1811, Courtesy of the East Hampton Library, Long Island Collection.

83. Edith H. Shepherd, "The Cruel Winter," *Long Island Forum* 46 (March 1983): 56–58.

84. Ibid.

85. Ibid.

86. *Newsday*, September 10, 1992, 5:3.

87. Ibid.

88. Ibid.

89. *Southampton Press*, February 1, 2001, 1:3

90. Group for the East End, *Group Action* (Summer 2012), 8.

# Bibliographic Note

Historical societies and libraries on the North and South Forks have impressive collections on the history of Long Island's East End. Beginning in Riverhead and continuing east on the North Fork and then moving over to the South Fork, following the same west to east pattern, we begin with the Riverhead Free Library, which has a good collection of secondary sources on Long Island history; an oral history collection; and vertical files containing historical and contemporary material, including data on the Peconic Bay estuary. Environmental impact statements on aquaculture leasing are also available.

Located across the street from the library is the Suffolk County Historical Society, a major repository of material dealing with the East End. The society's large climate-controlled library on the main floor of its headquarters is a state-of-the-art facility. Excellent finding aids exist for the documentary treasures stored in acid-free folders, and the knowledgeable staff retrieves material quickly. Of particular interest for the study of the Peconic Bay area are newspaper articles and pictorial material on nineteenth-century resorts, maritime history, and agriculture. The collection also includes Dr. John Strong's research notes on the Shinnecock.

Heading east from downtown Riverhead one comes to the Hallockville Museum Farm, a collection of historic buildings where the agrarian way of life of a century ago is interpreted for modern-day visitors. Hallockville's extensive library, which includes a sizable collection of works on Long Island history, is located in the Hudson-Sydlowski House. Occupying several rooms on the second floor of this historic building, the library is the repository of scrapbooks compiled by Riverhead Town Historian Virginia Wines, who authored a number of works on Riverhead history. The scrapbooks contain numerous photographs plus letters, maps, and newspaper clippings. Especially helpful for the study of the Peconic Bay area are the John T.

Downs notes on farming and fishing. Also of interest is the Hallock Family Collection containing Hallock Family Association material and newspaper clippings. This material was accessed with the assistance of Hallockville's knowledgeable director and a helpful library staff member.

Moving east from Hallockville to the Mattituck-Laurel Library, one finds a readily accessible reference collection of secondary sources on Long Island history. The library also houses primary sources in its fine Local History Room. Of particular interest for the study of the bay area are the Gildersleeve Scrapbooks, a twenty-two- volume collection containing newspaper clippings covering the period from World War I through the 1980s. Extensive vertical files contain relevant information on Native Peoples, the environment, and the local economy. The library also has digitized versions of the *Long Island Traveler* newspaper, published in Southold; the *Corrector*, published in Sag Harbor in the nineteenth century; the *Suffolk Times* on microfilm from 1876 through 1999 (with the exception of a few missing years); the *Long Island Traveler*; and the *Mattituck Watchman* on microfilm from 1872 to 1898 and 1948 to 1968.

The Mattituck-Laurel Historical Society, a short distance east of the Mattituck-Laurel Library, maintains the renovated Jesse Tuthill farmhouse, which contains regional furnishings and other material cultural artifacts illustrative of the history of the area, as do the schoolhouses and other buildings on the property. The society's library, housed in the Tuthill farmhouse, has a collection that includes works on Long Island and local history, genealogy, primary sources relating to farming and maritime activities, and the Emily Tuthill Best Cramer collection of works on Long Island history and literature. To afford researchers greater access to its collections, the society is preparing a digital database.

Like the Mattituck-Laurel Historical Society and the Mattituck-Laurel Library, the Cutchogue-New Suffolk Library serves two communities as well as researchers who come from afar to access its splendid local history collection. A large space in the original part of the building houses a superb collection of secondary sources and genealogical material. This self-contained, climate-controlled area, where documents are stored under optimal conditions, contains a number of items that shed light on the history of the Peconic Bay area. There is a huge body of material on the Wickham Claim and the efforts to secure Robins Island for Suffolk County. The collection also includes the Joy Bear collection of architectural photographs; the

Richmond store account books; and the Louisa Hargrave Archives, donated by the cofounder of the North Fork's first vineyard. This comprehensive collection includes letters, newspaper articles, and ephemera relating to the Hargrave Vineyard. Vertical files on North Fork hamlets, Indians, lighthouses, the brown tide, the Holland Submarine Company, and whaling also contain useful items as does manuscript material on the Peconic Bay Oyster Company.

In addition to its own extensive holdings, the Cutchogue-New Suffolk Library's local history room houses the documentary collections of the Cutchogue-New Suffolk Historical Council, which preserves and interprets a number of historic buildings adjacent to the library. These structures, which contain material cultural artifacts, include the Old House, a superb example of a seventeenth-century English-style home; the eighteenth-century Wickham Farmhouse; and a barn, carriage house, and schoolhouse.

Farther east, the Southold Free Library's Whitaker Collection, housed in what had been the board room of the former bank building that forms the nucleus of the library, is a superb resource for the study of the Peconic Bay area. Files on agriculture, historic businesses, lighthouses, ferries, maritime history, Prohibition, temperance, World War II, and wineries shed light on the history of the Peconic Bay region. The Whitaker Collection also includes the Whitney Booth photographic collection. Like other repositories, it adheres to the highest standards of preservation and at the same time is user-friendly thanks to excellent finding aids and a knowledgeable and courteous staff.

The Southold Historical Society, just a short stroll from the Southold Free Library, is another excellent source of information about the Peconic Bay area. The historical society has an enormous collection of manuscripts, vertical files, photographs, and oral history interviews covering the town's history from its founding through the early twenty-first century. These items are housed in the society's archives located in the historic Prince Building. Although the archives are on the second floor, which is reached by a long staircase, there is a chair lift. Once inside the cavernous, well-lit space containing rows of shelves lined with acid-free boxes, researchers will find a fine collection of secondary sources, maps, oral histories, and pictorial material including the Charles Meredith and Frank K. Hartley photographic collections. Researchers interested in the bay area will find the following files of interest: maritime (including piracy, ships, and shipwrecks), North Fork

Environmental Council, Southold history, hotels, Revolutionary War, War of 1812, World War I, World War II, water supply, and waterways. All of this material is quickly produced by the society's knowledgeable and very helpful archivist.

In addition to the Southold Historical Society and the Southold Free Library, the Office of the Southold Town Historian is a well-maintained repository presided over by an extremely knowledgeable historian. In addition to photographs and postcards, the collections in the office of the Town Historian contain helpful documentary material on the economy of the town.

Another fine resource is the Southold Indian Museum's Stanton Mott Memorial Library, the repository of site reports, maps, and other material relating primarily to the Native Peoples of the East End, especially the North Fork. The collection includes the field notes of Roy Latham, Charles Goddard, and Nat Booth. Researchers can also access the holdings of the Long Island Archaeological Association Chapter of the New York State Archaeological Association here while benefiting from the expertise of the president of the Long Island chapter, who is on hand to assist researchers and is in the process of creating a digital database of the Southold Indian Museum's documentary collections.

Moving east to Greenport, the William Floyd Memorial Library has a fine local history collection, housed in its own climate-controlled room. For the study of the Peconic Bay area the *Bowline*, an in-house publication of the Greenport Basin and Construction Company from 1941 through 1945, when the company built 400 ships for the war effort, is important as are vertical files on the menhaden fishery and whaling. Also in Greenport, the Stirling Historical Society's Berger House Archive Center is amassing a growing collection of Greenport-specific material and items relating to the history of East Marion.

The easternmost repository on the North Fork, the Oysterponds Historical Society in Orient, has a large and impressive array of secondary and primary sources, including nineteenth-century diaries that shed light on the history of the bay area; a rare rumrunner's code book that was recovered, in a fisherman's net, from Peconic Bay; the account book of the Orient Wharf Company; the Brigham Shipyard ledgers; handbills and tickets from the Montauk Steamboat Company; and extensive material on fisheries and the temperance movement. The library features digitized finding aids and employs state-of-the-art preservation techniques. Amassed over the course of many years, its holdings were previously housed in the historic school building that is part of the society's multistructure complex located on both sides of picturesque Village Lane. Within the past decade, the library was moved to the society's Hallock Building. Here the visiting researcher can peruse documentary and pictorial treasures in climate-controlled comfort while enjoying the historical ambience and invaluable assistance of the society's knowledgeable archivist.

Moving over to the South Fork and proceeding from west to east, the first repository one encounters is the Hampton Bays Library, which has an accessible collection of secondary sources on Long Island history and local newspapers, including the *Hampton Chronicle*, the *Hampton Bays News*, the *Hampton Chronicle News*, and the *Hampton Bays Compass* on microfilm. Moving farther east, the Shinnecock Museum and Cultural Center in Southampton has a library/archive that contains extensive material on the Shinnecock Nation, as well as material on other Long Island tribes and North American tribes. The collection includes both primary and secondary sources, videos, and research material contributed by Dr. John A. Strong, who has written extensively on the Shinnecock.

Also in Southampton, the Rogers Memorial Library houses a large collection of secondary sources on Long Island history and the history of South Fork communities. The collection also includes genealogy, items relating to the whaling industry, the full run of the *Southampton Press*, primary and secondary source material on the Shinnecock Nation, agriculture, fishing, summer camps, art and artists, estates, sports and leisure, and other local topics. Vertical files containing material relevant to the study of the Peconic Bay area include the following: Group for the South Fork, Peconic Estuary Program, Peconic Land Trust, War of 1812, water pollution, wetlands, whaling, windmills, World War I, and World War II. There is also an impressive oral history collection. These items are housed in a large climate-controlled room containing a huge table where researchers can spread out. A knowledgeable librarian seated in the reference area, just outside the Local History Room, is available to answer questions and locate material.

The same can be said for the Southampton Museum and Rogers Mansion Research Center, which has a multiroom archive on the second floor of the historic Rogers mansion. One large room, where researchers examine materials retrieved by the society's very competent archivist, is lined with bookshelves containing works on general Long Island history, the history of individual communities, genealogy, and the Social Register. Another room contains vertical files. For the study of the Peconic Bay area the following files are helpful: agriculture, Bayberry Land, bay scallops, Conscience Point, Dongan Patent, Native Peoples, Revolutionary War, and Shinnecock Hills. The collection includes whaling logs, diaries, oral histories, and the Native Peoples and Montauk Peoples collection donated by Dr. John A. Strong, who has published extensively on the Montauketts as well as the Shinnecock.

Moving east the Hampton Library in Bridgehampton has a charming and spacious local history room, where one finds a large collection of works on Long Island history plus primary sources, including diaries that shed light on the Peconic Bay area. The collection's finding aids, superb preservation, and knowledgeable archivist ensure that the researcher has a positive experience. The same holds true for the Bridgehampton Historical Society. A knowledgeable archivist and new state-of-the-art climate-controlled quarters for the collections, housed in a restored barn less than a mile east of the society's historic Corwith House, facilitate access to a fine array of secondary sources on Long Island, the history of East End communities, and genealogy. Primary sources dealing with the economic history of the community plus diaries and photographs are helpful for the study of the Peconic Bay area. Of particular note are the Corwith family correspondence and assorted documents, including wills, deeds and receipts from the Rose and other local families. Regarding the rich agricultural heritage of the area, the Long Island Potato Exchange material, documents pertaining to the Suffolk County Agricultural Fairs held in Bridgehampton, and farm ledgers are worth noting. The historical society's archives also house considerable material on the automobile road races held in Bridgehampton in the early twentieth century until World War I and again from just after World War II until 1953, when racing on the public roads of New York State was outlawed. Other interesting items in the society's collections are documents relating to shipwrecks, whaling maps, and school district ledgers.

Moving north from Bridgehampton to Sag Harbor, there are two archival repositories of note. One is the Sag Harbor Historical Society, located in the historic Annie Cooper Boyd house. The society's holdings are well organized and made accessible to researchers by an extremely knowledgeable historian/archivist. Particularly helpful for the study of the Peconic Bay area are materials on Native Peoples as well as letters, insurance policies, and other items pertaining to whaling; and the Willey Collection, which includes boat-building records. Also helpful are vertical files on the following topics: Bulova Watch Case Factory, Native Americans, whaling, and Cedar Point Lighthouse. The second Sag Habor repository, the Sag Harbor History Room in the John Jermain Memorial Library, houses the research collection of William Wallace Tooker, an expert on the Algonquian culture and language, primary sources on whaling, genealogical material, and vertical files yielding considerable information on such topics as Fahys and the Bulova Watch Case Factory, pottery, lighthouses, North Haven, Noyac, rumrunning, Revolutionary War, and War of 1812. This material is well organized and quickly retrieved by a knowledgeable staff member.

Heading south and east from Sag Harbor, one finds the Long Island Collection at the East Hampton Library. With the enormous array of items amassed by historian Morton Pennypacker as its nucleus, the Long Island Collection, which is the most comprehensive source for local and regional history on the East End, features state-of-the-art preservation, climate and light control, excellent finding aids (some of them digitized), and a knowledgeable and helpful archivist. In addition to deeds, letters, diaries, newspaper clippings, and newspapers on microfilm, the collection contains photographs and a wealth of secondary sources dealing with Long Island and the East End. The East Hampton Baymen's Association Collection and the Thomas Moran Biographical Collection, as well as the East Hampton Historical Society's Collection, are also available to researchers.

In contrast with East Hampton's Long Island Collection, the Amagansett Library's local history collection is compact but it includes a large number of works on Long Island history and East End communities. The Carlton Kelsey Collection, covering the 1930s through 2005, includes material on Bonac, the unique dialect found in the Accabonac and Springs areas of East Hampton township, plus material on Northwest and the bunker fishery. The library also houses the Smith Collection containing documents, diaries, genealogical material, photographs, and family recollections from 1858 through the early twenty-first century. The Amagansett Village Improvement Society Collection contains documents and minutes from 1921 through the early twenty-first century. The researcher's experience when accessing these collections is enhanced by a knowledgeable archivist and the ambience of the historical setting. The nearby Amagansett Historical Association has a fine collection of material cultural artifacts reflecting the lifestyle interpreted in Miss Amelia's Cottage, a collection of local carriages and buggies, and the Carlton Kelsey Archive of historical photographs housed in the Phebe Edwards Mulford House.

To the east, the staff of the Montauk Library maintain, in the general reference area, not only a good collection of books on Long Island history and government documents, including environmental impact and planning studies pertaining to the local area, but vertical files as well. What makes these files truly outstanding is that each folder contains a complete list of contents. Each item is numbered, thereby providing quick access for researchers. Relevant for the study of the bay area are the following files: Indians, fishing, Gardiner's Island, and hurricanes. In addition to the local history material in the reference area, the Montauk Library has a Local History Room. The same climate control, preservation techniques, and high standards for creating finding aids that characterize the reference collection are evident here. An ongoing digitization project undertaken by the knowledgeable archivist will result in this fine collection's becoming better known. Of particular interest are the Carlton Kelsey Collection of Montauk material; the oral history collection, which contains descriptions of each interview and material on the hurricane of 1938; and the Perry Duryea Scrapbooks, containing letters and deeds dating from the eighteenth century.

Jumping from Montauk to Shelter Island, the Shelter Island Historical Society has an impressive local history collection that occupies a portion of the Havens House, the society's headquarters. A fine professional archivist and a group of dedicated volunteers adhere to the highest preservation standards. Rare documents are stored in a mammoth room-sized safe and the collection has excellent finding aids. For the study of the bay area, ledgers for the menhaden fishing industry, ships' logs, material relating to the Sylvester Manor archaeological project, and documents dealing with slavery are of interest. The collection also contains local newspapers, photographs, glass plate negatives, and postcards.

The author's experiences at libraries and historical societies where research was conducted confirmed that history is alive and well thanks to the efforts of dedicated archivists, librarians, volunteers, and those who fund restoration, preservation, and processing of archival collections. Without their ongoing commitment, precious items from bygone centuries would not be available. Thanks to their commitment, these historic gems will continue to shed light on the past and in the process enlighten future generations about the history of a very special place.

Whether now or in the future, anyone wishing to learn more about the North and South Forks might be interested in perusing Suffolk Historic Newspapers, a superb digitized collection of nineteenth- and twentieth-century papers available online through the Suffolk County Library system. For those embarking upon a research project, the secondary sources listed below are an excellent place to begin.

# Bibliography

## North Fork and Shelter Island

Anderson, Ceylon W., et al. *Riverhead Bicentennial Album*. Riverhead: Riverhead Town Bicentennial Committee, 1976.

Baker, Wesley L. *Southold, Long Island List of Inhabitants 1658 to 1616 & Other Information about Early Settlers from 1640 to 1686*. Douglaston, N.Y.: n.p., 1981.

Berger, Steve. *52 Weeks on the North Fork*. Jamesport, N.Y.: Steve Berger Photography, 2012.

Booth, Antonia. *Trawling My Town: Glimpses of Southold Past and Present*. Southold, N.Y.: Academy Printing, 2011.

Booth, Antonia, and Thomas Monsell. *Greenport*. Charleston, S.C.: Arcadia, 2003.

Bramson, Ruth Ann, Geoffrey Fleming, and Amy Folk. A World unto Itself: The Remarkable History of Plum Island. Southold, N.Y.: Southold Historical Society, 2014.

Brill, John Rothman. *My Father and Albert Einstein*. New York: Lincoln, 2008.

Brooks, Rachel G. *The Artistic Achievement of a Rural Community*. Southold, N.Y.: L.I. Traveler Print, 1930.

Budd, Lily Wright. *John Budd 1599–1670 and Some of His Descendants: A Historical Journey through Four Centuries to Fifteen Generations*. Parker, Col.: Parker Printing, 1892.

Corwin, David S., and Gail Horton. *Greenport*. Charleston: Arcadia, 2013.

Corwin, Elsie Knapp. *Greenport, Yesterday and Today, and the Diary of a Country Newspaper*. Greenport, N.Y.: Suffolk Times, 1972.

Dennehy, Gerald. *The Halyoake Farm in Orient*. Orient, N.Y.: Oysterponds Historical Society, 2008.

Doering, Elizabeth, ed. *The Orphan Path: Journals of Horace Hallock, 1819–1834*. Charlotte, N.C.: Delmar, 1988.

Doughty, David, et al. *History of Jamesport and South Jamesport*. N.p.: Suffolk County Historical Society, n.d.

Duvall, Ralph. *The History of Shelter Island, 1652–1932*. N.p.: Shelter Island Heights, 1932.

Fleming, Geoffrey K. *Gladys Lee Wiles: Rival of Her Father*. Southold, N.Y.: Southold Historical Society, 2007.

Fleming, Geoffrey K. *Lemuel Maynard Wiles: A Record of His Works, 1864–1904*. Southold, N.Y.: Southold Historical Society, 2009.

Fleming, Geoffrey K. *Southold*. Charleston, S.C.: Arcadia, 2004.

Fleming, Geoffrey K., and Amy Kasuga Folk. *Hotels and Inns of Long Island's North Fork*. Charleston: History Press, 2009.

Fleming, Geoffrey K., and Amy Kasuga Folk. *Munnawhatteaug: The Last Days of the Menhaden Industry on Eastern Long Island*. Southold, N.Y.: Southold Historical Society, 2011.

Fleming, Geoffrey K., and Amy K. Folk. *Murder on Long Island: A Nineteenth Century Tale of Tragedy and Revenge*. Charleston: History Press, 2013.

Fleming, Geoffrey K., Sara Evans, and Amei Wallach. *A Shared Aesthetic: Artists of the North Fork*. New York: Hudson Hills Press, 2008.

Golder, William C. *Long Island's First Inhabitants: Paleo, Archaic, Transitional, Woodland: A 9,000 Year History of Indian Occupation of Long Island*. Southold, N.Y.: Southold Indian Museum, 1989.

Green, Louise Tuthill. *Images of America: Shelter Island*. Dover, N.H.: Arcadia, 1997.

Griffin, Augustus. *The Diaries of Augustus Griffin*, ed. Frederica Wachsberger. Orient, N.Y.: Oysterponds Historical Society, 2009.

Griffin, Augustus. *Griffin's Journal*. Orient, N.Y.: A. Griffin, 1857.

Griswold, Mac K. *The Manor: Three Centuries at a Slave Plantation on Long Island, New York*. New York: Farrar, Straus & Giroux, 2013.

Hallock, Ella. *Cabin Paradise*. Brooklyn: Brady-Palmer Press, 1928.

Hallock, Joseph, and Geoffrey K. Fleming. *Southold Reminiscences: Rural America at the Turn of the Century*. Charleston: History Press, 2008.

Hargrave, Louisa. *The Vineyard: A Memoir*. New York: Penguin Books, 2004.

Hargrave, Louisa. *The Vineyard: The Pleasures and Perils of Creating an American Family Winery*. New York: Viking, 2003.

Hayes, Katherine Howlett. *Slavery before Race: Europeans, Africans and Indians at Long Island's Sylvester Manor Plantation, 1651–1884.* New York: New York University Press, 2013.

Healy, Clement. *North Fork Cemeteries.* Charleston: Arcadia, 2005.

Herman, Stewart. *The Smallest Village: The Story of Dering Harbor, Shelter Island, New York, 1874–1974.* Shelter Island, N.Y.: Shelter Island Historical Society, 1976.

*Historical Review: A Word and Picture Journey into Orient's Past.* Orient, N.Y.: Oysterponds Historical Society, 1959.

*Historic Orient Village: A Short History of Orient.* Orient, N.Y.: Oysterponds Historical Society, 1976.

*Houses of Southold: The First 350 Years.* Southold, N.Y.: Southold Town Landmark Preservation Commission, 1990.

Jacobson, Judy. *Southold Connections: Historical and Biographical Sketches of Northeast Long Island.* Baltimore: Genealogical Publishing, 1991.

Johnson, J. Stewart, James W. Kent, and Richard L. Venton, et al. *A Sense of Place: Vintage Photographs of Orient and East Marion on Long Island's North Fork.* Orient, N.Y.: Oysterponds Historical Society, 2006.

Koppelman, Lee. "Peconic County: The Myth and the Reality." *Long Island Historical Journal* 9 (1997): 152–67.

Lambert, Edward. *History of the Colony of New Haven.* Jordan, Utah: Stemmons, 1988.

Lamont, Helen D. *The Story of Shelter Island in the Revolution.* Shelter Island, N.Y.: Shelter Island Historical Society, 1975.

Lathrop, G. P. *Peconic Park: An Exploration of Long Island, N.Y.* N.p.: Privately printed, 1883.

Mackay, John W. *Robins Island.* N.p.: Privately printed, 1984.

Mayne, Katherine Newell. *The History of Nassau Point.* N.p.: Privately printed, 1998.

McKinley, Rosemary. *101 Glimpses of the North Fork and the Islands.* Charleston, S.C.: History Press, 2009.

Medd, Rev. Henry. "Jamesport Camp Meeting Colony." *Southampton Magazine* 1, no. 2 (1912): 38–42.

Meier, Evelyn R. *The Riverhead Story, 1792–1967.* Huntington, N.Y.: Long Islander, 1967.

Morris, Richard Knowles. *John P. Holland.* Annapolis, Md.: United States Naval Institute, 1966.

Newell, Rosalind Case. *Rose of the Nineties.* Southold, N.Y.: Long Island Traveler, Inc., 1962.

Newell, Rosalind Case. *Rose Remembers.* Southold, N.Y.: Academy Printing Services, 1976.

Parson, Maria. *Up-Lot Reveries: An Oral History of the North Fork.* Mattituck, N.Y.: Amereon House, 1984.

Pietromonaco, Maria Orlando. *Long Island's North Fork.* Charleston, S.C.: Arcadia, 2003.

*Riverhead and Its Vicinity.* New York: George W. Richardson, ca. 1918.

Ross, John. *The Food and Wine of the North Fork.* Huntington, N.Y.: Maple Hill Press, 2005.

Stark, Thomas M. *Riverhead: The Halcyon Years, 1861–1919.* Huntington, N.Y.: Maple Hill Press, ca. 2005.

Studenroth, Zachary N. *Cutchogue and New Suffolk.* Charleston: Arcadia, 2013.

Terry, Constance J., ed. *In the Wake of Whales: The Whaling Journals of Captain Edwin Peter Brown 1841–1847.* Orient, N.Y.: Old Orient Press, 1988.

Twomey, Thomas. *Seeking the Past: Writings from 1832–1905 Relating to the History of the Town of Riverhead, Suffolk County New York.* New York: Newmarket Press, 2004.

Wallace, Terry. *Caroline M. Bell and the Peconic Bay Impressionists.* East Hampton, N.Y.: M. T. Fine Arts, Inc./Wallace Gallery, 2006.

Welch, Richard F. "John P. Holland and the Creation of the American Submarine Fleet." *Long Island Historical Journal* 9, no. 2 (1997): 209–22.

Wells, Betty. *Robins Island. Reflections, 1639–2001.* Sevierville, Tenn.: Insight, 2001.

Wells, Justine. *A Brief History of Early Riverhead Town.* Riverhead, N.Y.: n.p., 1987.

Wells, Justine., ed. *Passing It On.* Riverhead, N.Y.: Riverhead Printing Co., 1993.

Wick, Steve. *Heaven and Earth: The Last Farmers of the North Fork.* New York: St. Martin's, 1996.

Wickham, Case J. *Heritage Books Archives: Records of the Town of Southold, Suffolk County, New York.* Vols. 1 and 2. Bowie, Md.: Heritage Books, 2003.

Wines, Virginia. *Pioneers of Riverhead Town*. Riverhead, N.Y.: Suffolk County Historical Society, 1987.

Wines, Virginia. *West From the Canoe Place*. Riverhead, N.Y.: Genealogy Section, Suffolk County Historical Society, 1975.

Womback, Norman, Jeffrey M. Walden, and Gerard M. Matoveik. *Mattituck and Laurel*. Charleston: Arcadia, 2013.

Yeager, Edna Howell. *Peconic River Mills and Industries*. Riverhead, N.Y.: Suffolk County Historical Society, 1965.

## South Fork

Adams, James Truslow. *History of the Town of Southampton*. Bridgehampton, N.Y.: Hampton Press, 1918.

Adams, James Truslow. *Memorial of Old Bridgehampton*. Bridgehampton, N.Y.: Privately printed, 1916.

Ayres, J. A. *The Legend of Montauk*. Hartford, Ct.: Edwin Hunt, 1849.

Barnes, Gean Finch. *Chronicles of the Colonial Village of Amagansett*. Amagansett: n.p., 1920.

Barons, Richard. *Sag Harbor: Classic Houses Great and Small*. Sag Harbor, N.Y.: The Gallery, 2007.

Bellows, Emma. *Memoirs of a Town and Country Doctor*. New York: Vantage Press, 1982.

Bellows, Emma. *When Hampton Bays Was Young*. N.p.: Privately printed, 1979.

Benson, Elaine. *Our Hampton Heritage*. Bridgehampton, N.Y.: Dan's Papers, 1983.

Boyd, Annie Cooper. *Anchor to Windward: The Paintings and Diaries of Annie Cooper Boyd*. Sag Harbor, N.Y.: Sag Harbor Historical Society and the Society for the Preservation of Long Island Antiquities, 2010.

Breen, T. H. *Imagining the Past: East Hampton Histories*. Athens: University of Georgia Press, 1996.

Clowes, Ernest S. *Wayfarings*. Bridgehampton, N.Y.: Bridgehampton News, 1953.

Cummings, Mary. *Hurricane in the Hamptons, 1938*. Charleston: Arcadia, 2006.

Cummings, Mary. *Southampton*. Charleston: Arcadia Publishing 1996.

Curts, Paul H., ed. *Bridgehampton's Three Hundred Years.* Bridgehampton, N.Y.: Hampton Press, 1956.

Dolgon, Corey. *The End of the Hamptons: Scenes from the Class Struggle in America's Playground.* New York: New York University Press, 2005.

Domatob, Jerry K. *African Americans on the East End.* Charleston: Arcadia, 2001.

Fleming, Geoffrey K. *Bridgehampton.* Charleston: Arcadia, 2003.

Fleming, Geoffrey K. *Hampton Bays.* Charleston: Arcadia, 2014.

Gaines, Steven. *Philistines at the Hedgerow: Passion and Property in the Hamptons.* Boston: Little, Brown, 1998.

Geus, Averill Dayton. *From Sea to Shining Sea: 350 Years of East Hampton History.* West Kennebunkport, Me.: Phoenix, 1999.

Goddard, David. *Colonizing Southampton: The Transformation of a Long Island Community, 1870–1900.* Albany: SUNY Press, 2011.

Halsey, Abigail F. *An East Hampton Childhood.* East Hampton, N.Y.: East Hampton Star Press, 1938.

Halsey, Abigail F. *In Old Southampton.* New York: Columbia University Press, 1940.

Halsey, William Donaldson. *Sketches from Local History.* Bridgehampton, N.Y.: 1935.

*The Hamptons Real Estate Horror Show.* New York: iUniverse, 2011.

Hand, Alice E. *Wainscott Dumplings.* Southampton, N.Y.: Yankee Pedler, 1977.

Healy, Clement. *South Fork Cemeteries.* Charleston: Arcadia, 2006.

Heatley, Rose. *History of North Haven.* Sag Harbor, N.Y.: William Ewers, 1976.

Hedges, Henry P. *A History of the Town of East Hampton.* Sag Harbor, N.Y.: J. H. Hunt, 1897.

Hedges, Henry P. *Memories of a Long Life.* East Hampton, N.Y.: E. S. Boughton, 1909.

Hedges, Henry P. *Tracing the Past: Writings of Henry P. Hedges 1817–1911 Relating to the History of the East End, Including East Hampton, Southampton, Sag Harbor, Bridgehampton, and Southold in Suffolk County, New York.* New York: Newmarket Press, 2000.

Kelsey, Carleton. *Amagansett: A Pictorial History.* Amagansett, N.Y.: Amagansett Historical Association, 1986.

Kelsey, Carleton, and Lucinda Mayo. *Images of Amagansett.* Dover, N.H.: Arcadia, 1997.

Kennedy, Nina, and Jacqueline Scerbinski. *Our Water Mill: Stories of Families, Friends, Farming, Fishing and Freedom.* Southampton, N.Y.: Sixsyllables, 2010.

Lauren, Ricky. *The Hamptons: Food, Family and History.* New York: Wiley, 2012.

Matthiessen, Peter. *Men's Lives: Surfmen and Baymen of the South Fork.* New York: Random House, 1986.

*Montauk Beach.* Montauk: Montauk Beach Development Corp., 1932.

Mulvill, William. *South Fork Place Names.* Sag Harbor, N.Y.: Bricklin Press, 1993.

"The National Golf Club." *Southampton Magazine* 1, no. 3 (1912): 3–18.

Osmers, Henry. *American Gibraltar: Montauk and the Wars of America.* Denver: Outskirts Press, 2011.

Osmers, Henry. *Living on the Edge: Life at the Montauk Point Lighthouse, 1930–1945.* Denver: Outskirts Press, 2009.

Osmers, Henry. *On Eagle's Beak: A History of the Montauk Point Lighthouse.* Denver: Outskirts Press, 2008.

O'Sullivan, Ilse. *East Hampton and the American Revolution.* East Hampton, N.Y.: East Hampton Town Bicentennial Committee, 1976.

Panchyk, Richard. *101 Glimpses of the South Fork.* Charleston: History Press, 2009.

Petrow, Steven, and Richard Barons. *The Lost Hamptons.* Charleston: Arcadia, 2004.

Powers, Joan. *Holding Back the Tide: The Thirty-Five Year Struggle to Save Montauk: A History of the Concerned Citizens of Montauk.* Sag Harbor, N.Y.: Harbor Electronic Publishing, 2005.

*Prospectus of the Noyac Cottage Association on Peconic Bay: Town of Southampton, Long Island, N.Y.* New York: 1888.

Rae, John W. *East Hampton.* Charleston: Arcadia, 2000.

Rajs, Jake, Jesse Browner, and Paul Goldberger. *Portraits of Long Island: The North Fork and the Hamptons.* New York: Monacelli Press, 2011.

Rattiner, Dan. *In the Hamptons: My Fifty Years with Farmers, Fishermen, Artists, Billionaires, and Celebrities.* New York: Harmony Books, 2008.

Rattiner, Dan. *In the Hamptons Too: Further Encounters with Farmers, Fishermen, Artists, Billionaires, and Celebrities.* Albany, N.Y.: SUNY Press, 2010.

Rattiner, Dan. *Still in the Hamptons: More Tales of the Rich, the Famous and the Rest of Us.* Albany, N.Y.: SUNY Press, 2012.

Rattray, Jeanette Edwards. *Discovering the Past: Writings of Jeanette Edwards Rattray, 1893–1974 Relating to the Town of East Hampton, Suffolk County, New York.* New York: Newmarket Press, 2001.

Rattray, Jeanette Edwards. *Montauk.* East Hampton, N.Y.: Star Press, 1938.

Safina, Carl. *The View from Lazy Point.* East Hampton, N.Y.: Picador, 2012.

Sandford, Ann. *Grandfather Lived Here: The Transformation of Bridgehampton, New York 1870–1970.* Bridgehampton, N.Y.: Poxabogue, 2006.

Siminoff, Faren Rhea. *Crossing the Sound: The Rise of Atlantic American Communities in Seventeenth-Century Eastern Long Island.* New York: New York University Press, 2004.

Sleight, Harry D. *Sag Harbor in Earlier Days.* Sag Harbor, N.Y.: Hampton Press, 1930.

Sleight, Harry D. *Sleights of Sag Harbor: A Biographical, Genealogical and Historical Record of 17th, 18th, and 19th Century Settlers of Eastern Long Island and the Hudson Valley in the State of New York.* Salem, Mass.: Higginson, 2007.

Stone, Gaynell. *The History and Archaeology of the Montauk.* Stony Brook, N.Y.: Suffolk County Archaeological Association, Nassau County Archaeological Committee, 1993.

Stone, Gaynell. *The Montauk Native Americans of Eastern Long Island.* East Hampton, N.Y.: Guild Hall, 1991.

Stone, Gaynell. *Native Forts of the Long Island Sound Area.* Stony Brook, N.Y.: Suffolk County Archaeological Association/Nassau County Archaeological Committee, 2006.

Stone, Gaynell. *The Shinnecock Indians: A Culture History.* Stony Brook, N.Y.: Suffolk County Archaeological Association, 1983.

Strong, John A. *The Algonquian Peoples of Long Island from Earliest Times to 1700.* Interlaken, N.Y.: Empire State Books, 1997.

Strong, John A. *The Montaukett Indians of Eastern Long Island.* Syracuse, N.Y.: Syracuse University Press, 2006.

Strong, John A. *We Are Still Here!: The Algonquian Peoples of Long Island Today.* Interlaken, N.Y.: Empire State Books, 1998.

Talmage, Ferris. *The Springs in the Old Days.* Southold, N.Y.: Steamboat Press, 1970.

Tobler, Nina, and E. L. Doctorow. *Voices of Sag Harbor: A Village Remembered.* Sag Harbor, N.Y.: Friends of the John Jermain Memorial Library, 2007.

Twomey, Tom. *Awakening the Past.* New York: Newmarket Press, 1999.

Twomey, Tom. *Exploring the Past: Writings from 1798–1896 Relating to the History of East Hampton.* New York: Newmarket Press, 2001.

Twomey, Tom. *Origins of the Past: The Story of Montauk and Gardiner's Island.* East Hampton, N.Y.: East End Press, 2013.

Wettereau, Helen M. *Good Ground Remembered.* Southold, N.Y.: Academy Printing Services, 1983.

Wettereau, Helen M. *Shinnecock Hills Long Ago.* Ed. Vincent Seyfried. East Patchogue, N.Y.: Searles Graphics, 1991.

Wiley, Nancy. *The Story of Sag Harbor.* Sag Harbor, N.Y.: Long Island Herald House, 1939.

Zaykowski, Dorothy, Joseph Zaykowski, and Ronald Lowe. *The Early History of North Haven, Long Island, New York.* Ronkonkoma, N.Y.: Ocean Printing, 2006.

Zaykowski, Dorothy. *Sag Harbor: The Story of An American Beauty.* Sag Harbor, N.Y.: Sag Harbor Historical Society, 1991.

# Index

agriculture: agritainment, 59, 73,
75, 76; agritourism, 64, 73, 75;
Bridgehampton, 66; cauliflower,
68; cranberries, 68–69; Long
Island Cauliflower Association, 68;
Mattituck Lions Club Strawberry
Festival, 69; murder mystery on
farm tour, 60–62; New York State
Department of Farms and Mar-
kets, 64; Orient, 64–67; potatoes,
60, 64, 66, 68, 70; Southampton,
64–65, 68; Southold, 64, 66;
strawberries, 69; Water Mill, 68
Alexander, Shana, 234
Andros, Sir Edmund, 108
Andros Patent, 109–10
Annan, Kofi, 202–3
Appleby, Jacob (Capt.), 98
aquaculture, 111, 219, 273
artists: Edward Bell, 117–18; William
Merritt Chase, 117–19; William
Steeple Davis, 118; Benjamin
Rutherford Fitz, 117; Thomas
Moran, 119; Edith Prellwitz,
116; Henry Prellwitz, 116; Irving
Ramsey Wiles, 117–18
Atlantic Mail Steamship Company,
125
Atlantic States Marine Fisheries Com-
mission, 113

Barton, Clara, 159–60
Bayberry Land: International Brother-
hood of Electrical Workers, 157;
Michael Pascucci, purchase by, 157;
Sebonack Golf Club, 157; Donald
Trump, interest in, 157
Bay Street Theater, 87
Behan, Nicholas, 61
Blackmar, Abel (Judge), 12
Bliss Torpedo Company, 159–60,
182
Blydenburgh, Charles, 83
Bonac, 115, 279
Bonackers, 104, 115
Borghese, Ann Marie, 71
Borghese, Marco (Prince), 71
Bottini, Mike, 215
Boyd, Annie Cooper, 278
Boys and Girls Harbor Camp, 155
Bradish, Joseph, 184, 189
breast cancer, 211
Brecknock Hall, 45
brickyards, 84
Bridgehampton, 26, 28, 33–35, 42,
66, 90, 123, 144, 170, 189, 209
Brinkley, Christie, 104, 208
Brookhaven National Laboratory
(BNL), 201, 210–11, 216
Brown, Martha, 94
Brown, Peter (Capt.), 93–94

brown tide: East Hampton Town Baymen's Association, 212–16; Northwest Harbor, 214; Orient harbor,
220; presence, 1980s, 212–14, 218;
presence, 1990s, 214–18; sewage
pollution, 215–16
Buell, Samuel (Rev.), 33
Bug Light, 51–53, 151
buses: Hampton Ambassador, 123;
Hampton Express, 123; Hampton
Jitney, 123; Hampton Luxury
Liner, 123; Sunrise Express, 123

Camp Hero, 155, 199–200
camp meetings: Greenport, 128;
Jamesport, 128–30; Shelter Island,
130–32; Southold, 128
Camp Wikoff, 178
Cavett, Dick, 28
Cedar Point Lighthouse, 51, 279
circuses, 41–42
Citizens for a Progressive Energy
Policy, 207
clams, 107, 111–12, 214, 219, 222
Clark, Joshua (Dr.), 33
Claudio's, 184
Clinton, Hillary Rodham (Sen.),
250
Clinton Academy, 33, 40, 44
Cobbett, William, 76–77
condominiums, 36, 55, 86, 234–35,
240
Corchaugs, 15
Cornell Cooperative Extension, 70,
220–21
Cornell University Cedar Beach
marine laboratory, 219
Corwin, Douglas, 71, 78
craft beer, 75, 190

Damianos, Herodotus (Dr.), 72
Davenport, James (Rev.), 34
Defend H$_2$O, 215
DeLuca, Bob, 225
Dering, Henry Packer, 90, 245
Dominy, Nathaniel, 81
Dongan, Thomas (Gov.), 78–79, 106
Dongan Patent, 79, 112–13
Downs, John, 83
Downs Creek, Cutchogue, 15
drug smuggling, 201–2
duck farms: Big Duck, 77; Crescent,
77; Flanders, 77; Hampton Bays,
77; Riverhead, 77; Water Mill, 77
Duke, Anthony Drexel, 155

East Hampton: Board of Health, 144;
East Hampton Farm Museum,
226; East Hampton Town Bay-
men's Association, xi, xiv, 102–4,
212, 216, 279; East Hampton
Town Shellfish Hatchery, 219;
Hollywood East, 3, 63
Edison, Thomas Alva, 181
Einstein, Albert, 191–96
Electric Boat Company, 160, 164
Enterprise Park at Calverton
(EPCAL), 216, 240
Estuary of National Significance,
247–48, 250
Everett, Edward, 125
E. W. Bliss Company, 179

Fahys, Joseph, 85–86
Fenians, 161
Fireplace Lodge Camp, 156
Floyd, David, 45
Floyd, William, 32, 45, 56, 276

Ford, John, 201
Fort Terry, 199
Fournier, Francis, 70
Fournier, John, 169

Gardiner, Howell, 130
Gardiner, Robert David Lion, 19, 183
Gardiner, Sarah Diodati, 19
Gardiner's Island, 16–19, 82, 139,
    156, 165, 170–71, 177, 183–85,
    199, 280
Garetano, Christopher P., 200
Gergela, Joseph, 228
Gibbs, George C., 125
Gobler, Christopher (Dr.), 220
Godfrey, Arthur, 148
Goelet, Alexandra Gardiner Creel, 19,
    183
golf clubs: Laurel Links, 2–3, 153;
    Long Island National, 153;
    National Golf Links, 152; North
    Fork Country Club, 153; Sebo-
    nack, 157; Shinnecock Hills, 3, 5,
    152
Grapes and Greens, 63
Great War (World War I), 179–82
Green, Seth, 101
Greenport: art galleries, 237; har-
    bor, 235; Maritime Festival, 235;
    Mitchell Park, 236; sculpture, 236
Grimson, Robert, 211
Group for the South Fork, 209,
    223–24, 277

Hamptons International Film Festival,
    63
Hargrave, Alex, 70
Hargrave, Louisa, 70

Harrison, Anna Symmes, 44
Hawkins, Edward, 98
Hawkins, Simeon, 98
Hedges, Henry P., 33
Hedges, Mary Hildreth, 33
Hildreth, Aurela, 38
Hildreth, Daniel, 38, 68, 70
Holland, Ellen, 61
Holland, John, 159–64
Holland, Michael, 161
Holland Company, 159–64
Horn, Floyd, 205
horses: Barker, 153; Conklin, 153;
    Entenmann, 153; Fleet's track,
    153; Riverhead fairgrounds, 153
hotels:
—Hampton Bays: Canoe Place, 143;
    Clifton, 143; Hampton Pines, 143;
    Union, 143
—Riverhead and North Fork: Bay
    House, 139; Bay Side, 136; Booth,
    138; Great Peconic Bay House,
    136; Clarke, 138; Eagle House,
    138; Fairyland, 137; Hallock
    House, 136; MacNish's, 138;
    Mattituck, 137; Miamogue, 136;
    Mount Pleasant, 138; Orient Point,
    138; Paumanok, 138; Peconic, 138;
    Pipe's Neck, 138; Riverside, 136;
    Shady Point, 137; Southold Hotel,
    138; Sterlington, 138; Sunnyside,
    136; Village, 138; Wyandank, 138
—Sag Harbor: American, 26, 143,
    154, 166, 180; Bay Side, 143;
    Mansion, 143; Nassau, 143; Ross,
    143; Sea Breeze, 143
—Shelter Island: Manhanset, 126,
    133–35, 150, 154; Prospect
    House, 131–33
Hudson, S. Terry, 82

Joel, Billy, 20, 89, 104–5, 109, 249
Jones, Steve, 227

Kaku, Michael (Dr.), 210
Kapell, David, 55, 236
Keller, Helen, 56
Kellis, Mary Rebecca, 9
Kidd, William, 58, 183
Koppelman, Lee (Dr.), 111, 227, 231

Landon, Samuel (Judge), 33
Latham, Roy, 66
Lauren, Ralph, 28, 139
Leavitt, Frank, 159, 180
Leo, Arnold, xi, 102, 104
Long Island Pine Barrens Society, 224
Long Island Rail Road, 5, 12, 83–84, 90–91, 122, 125–26, 136–37, 142, 146–47, 150, 178–79, 241, 245
Long Island University, 220–21
Long Wharf (Sag Harbor), 27, 85, 87, 90–91, 166, 179–81

Madoff, Bernard, 145
Magnuson-Stevens Act, 113
Maniscalco, Peter, 207
manufacturing: Aquebogue, 83; Mill Creek, 84; Riverhead, 82–83; Robins Island, 84; Sag Harbor, 84–86
Marriner, Jeanne, 248
Matthiessen, Peter, 102
McAllister, Kevin, 215, 220–21
McCauley, Jeremiah, 130
Menei, Vito (Dr.), 214, 249
menhaden (mossbunkers, bunkers): American Fisheries Company, 96; companies of farmers, 96; measuring of, 97; odors, 97, 89, 131, 144; processing plants, 97–98
Merrall, Edward R., 43
Mid–Atlantic Fishery Management Council, 113
mills, 80–82
Millstone Nuclear Power Facility, 1, 206–11
Miranda, Francisco de, 43
Mitchell, John, 80
Montauk: Arthur Benson, 12, 145; Camp Hero, 155, 199–200; Austin Corbin, 142, 146; Carl Fisher, 14, 145–46, 199; *Montauk Chronicles*, 200; Montauk Manor, 14, 145, 199; Montauk Project, 23, 199–200
Montauketts: acquisition of Montauk by Arthur Benson, 145; Freetown, 10–12; Fort Hill Cemetery, 15; intermarriage with African Americans, 10–13; land claims, 14; ruling of Judge Abel Blackmar, 12
Montauk Steamboat Company, 90, 125–27
Moon, Peter, 199–200
Morton National Wildlife Refuge, 97, 166, 223
Mrozowski, Stephen, 21
Mulford, Prentice, 39

Nassau Point, Cutchogue, 45, 137–38, 185–87, 191, 195–96, 247
Nature Conservancy, 1, 25, 223, 230–31, 250
Nelson, Ozzie, 156
New York State Wild, Scenic and Recreational Rivers Act, 247

Northeast Utilities, 207, 209–10
North Fork Environmental Council,
209, 221, 223
Northwest (port), 27, 51, 78, 90, 98,
102, 109, 187, 212, 214, 223
Noyac Bay, 133, 179, 181
Noyac Cottage Association, 141–42
Nuclear Regulatory Commission,
207–8

open space preservation: Barcelona
Neck, 223; Grace Estate, 223;
Group for the East End, 223,
225; North Fork Environmental
Council, 209, 221, 223; Peconic
Land Trust, 15, 223, 226, 230,
233, 235, 277; Riverhead Transfer
of Development Rights Program,
226; South Fork Land Foundation,
223; Suffolk County Farmland
Preservation Program, 66
Orient: cholera epidemic, 37; hotels,
138–39; Orient Yacht Club, 151;
temperance movement, 35–37
Ostby, Eben Fiske, 22
oysters, 107–8, 110–12, 219

parks: Camp Hero, 155; Cedar Point,
155; Hither Hills, 155; Meschutt
Beach, 155; Montauk Downs, 155;
Montauk Point State, 155; Orient
State, 155; Shinnecock East, 155;
Theodore Roosevelt County Park,
155
Parrish, Samuel L., 118, 142
Peconic Bay Estates, 47
Peconic Baykeeper, xi, 209, 215, 217,
220, 222

Peconic Bay Region Community
Preservation Fund, 225
Peconic County (proposed), 248
Peconic Estuary Program (PEP),
249
Peconic Park, 137
Penny, Joshua, 172–75
Perot, H. Ross, 89
Pharaoh, David, 11–12
Pharaoh, Stephen Talkhouse, 11–12
Pierson, Henry, 184
piracy, 182–85, 275
Plum Island, 1, 199, 205–6
Powell, Robert, 52
Prohibition: *Charlotte*, seizure
of, 185; Claudio's, 184; *Helen
G. McLean*, 188; Vinnie Hig-
gins, 186; *Madonna V*, 188–89;
Mashomack, 187; Shelter Island,
187; Southold, 190; Three Mile
Harbor, 188; W. W. Woods, 188

Revolutionary War: Canoe Place, 169;
Charles Cochrane, 169; Mrs. John
Corwin, 170; *Culloden*, 171; John
Davis, 170; Francis Fournier, 169;
John Fournier, 169; David Gar-
diner, 167–68; Nathaniel Gardiner,
170; Mrs. John Hurlburt, 169;
Elnathan Jennings, 166; Jessup's
Neck, 166; Ezra L'Hommedieu,
168; Mattituck, 170; "Return"
Johanthan Meigs, 165–66; Mon-
tauk, 169; William Nicoll, 167; Sag
Harbor, 166–67; Moses Sawyer,
167; Shelter Island, 168; South-
ampton, 169; Southold, 166–68;
Parker Wickham, 171–72; Thomas
Wickham, 171

Riverhead: Calverton, 8, 63, 68, 76, 197, 216, 218, 236, 240; downtown, 238–40; Hallockville Museum Farm, 71, 83, 273; manufacturing, 82–83; Miamogue Wharf & Ways Co., 91; Polish Festival, 238; separation from Southold, 108; Tanger Factory Outlet Center, 237

Robins Island: Louis Moore Bacon, 230, 233; Steven C. Englebright, 232; Dwight Holbrook, 232; James W. Lane, 230; John Mackay, 230–31; Robins Island Preservation Fund, 231; Southold Development Corporation, 231; Suffolk County's attempt to acquire, 231

Roebling, Emily, 179

Roosevelt, Robert, 101

Roosevelt, Theodore, 9, 162, 178

Rose's Grove, 47, 149

Rothman, David, 192–93, 195–96

Rubino, Ken, 221

rust tide, 222

Sabin, Mrs. Charles Hamilton, 156, 190

Sagaponack, 26, 55, 71, 184

Sage, Margaret Olivia Slocum, 44

Sag Harbor: customs, 89; Eastville, 53; hotels, 142–43; Long Wharf, 27, 85, 87, 90–91, 166, 179–81; manufacturing, 84–86

sailing vessels, 83, 87, 118, 121, 151

Saland, David, 3

salt works, 80

Sang Lee Farms, 64

Save the Bays Coalition, 248

scallops: labor of women and children, 108, 110; opening day of season, 213–14, 221–22; pollution, impact of, 212; yields, 107

Schumer, Charles (Sen.), 113

sea serpents, 100

seaweed, 78–79, 106

shark, 149

Shelter Island: archaeological excavation, 21–22; deer, 47–50; Dinah's Rock, 97, 154; Manhansetts, 19–20; murder on, 60; New York Yacht Club, 150; settlement of, 20; Frank Smith, 50

Shinnecock: federal recognition, 6–8; land infringement lawsuit, 6; Mashantucket Pequots, 7; pow–wow, 4; Southampton Town Board, 6

Shinnecock Hills, 70, 118–19, 142, 152–54

Shinnecock Hills and Peconic Bay Realty Company, 156

shipbuilding: Greenport, 88–89; Riverhead, 87–88; Sag Harbor, 87; Shelter Island, 89; Southampton, 89

Smith, Bill, 217

Smith, Chris (Dr.), 220–21

Smith, Kate, 197–98

Smith, Liz, 24

Southampton: Bowers-Rogers-Hunting House, 26; Conscience Point, 25; Halsey House, 26; rivalry with Southold, 22–23; Southampton Academy, 40; South Fork Groundwater Task Force, 209

Southold: John Booth, 30, 32; deer, 49–50; Fisher's Island, 30; Charity Floyd, 32; Founders Landing wharf, 23; Mary Catherine Havens, 33; Ezra L'Hommedieu, 96, 168; Mrs. Ezra L'Hommedieu, 32, 168; New Haven Colony, 30, 109; rivalry with Southampton, 22–23; settlement, 23; Southold Academy, 40

Southold Project in Aquaculture Training (SPAT), 219

Spanish-American War, 177–79

Springs, The, 27, 54, 104, 107, 120, 156

Squires Pond, Hampton Bays, 4

Standing for Truth About Radiation (STAR), 208

steamboats: *Argonaut*, 124; *Artisan*, 125; *Cataline*, 125; *Cleopatra*, 124; *Clifton*, 124; *Endeavor*, 126; *General Jackson*, 124; *Massachusetts*, 124; *Montauk*, 125–26; *Olive Branch*, 121; *Shelter Island*, 125; *Shinnecock*, 125–26; *Statesman*, 121; *Sunshine*, 125

Sterling, George, 42–43

Stewart, Martha, 12, 20, 41, 59, 63, 154

storms, 243–47

striped bass: ban on fishing for, 104; General Electric settlement, 103–6; PCB contamination, 103; reopening of fishery, 105; size limits, 105

Suffolk County Water Authority, 235

Sullivan, Anne, 56

SUNY Stony Brook Marine Sciences Research Center, 219

Sylvester, Brinley, 20

Sylvester, Mary Burroughs, 20

Sylvester, Nathaniel, 20

Sylvester Manor, 19–22

Temik, 211

temperance movement, 35–37

Terry, Caroline, 38

Terry, Jonathan B., 91

Tettelbach, Stephen (Dr.), 221

Thiele, Fred, Jr. (assemblyman), 209–10

Tollefsen, Skip, 215

Tooker, William Wallace, 15

Torres, Alfonso (Dr.), 205

Townsend, Solomon, 82

trapping, 115

Triton Oil and Fertilizer Company, 98

trustees, role of, 79, 106–8

turtles, 148–49

Tuthill, Cuyler B., 45

Tuthill, Frank (Capt.), 101

Tuthill, James, 36, 91

Tyler, Julia Gardiner, 44

UFOs, 200–201

Underhill, Helena, 32

Underhill, John (Capt.), 32

United Nations, 202

U.S. Army Chemical Corps, 205

U.S. Department of Agriculture Animal Disease Laboratory, 1, 205

U.S. Environmental Protection Agency, 247–49

U.S. Life Saving Service, 89

U.S. Open, 3

U.S./U.K. Countryside Stewardship, 224

Vail, Jasper, 83

Vail, Samuel, 84

Van de Wetering, Peter, 63

vineyards and wineries: Borghese, 71; Duck Walk, 72; Duck Walk North, 72; Empire State Cellars, 75; Hargrave, 70; La Reve, 72; Laurel Lake, 71; Lieb Cellars, 72; Martha Clara, 71; McCall, 72; NoFo Rock and Roll Festival, 74; Peconic Bay Winery, 74; Pindar, 72; Ternhaven, 70; traffic congestion, 73; Vineyard 48, 73–75

Vorpahl, Stewart, Jr., 103, 106, 112–13, 115

Walden, John, 180
Warner, Hollis, 77
War of 1812: Arshmomoque, 174; Eliphalet Beebe, 176; Gardiner's Island, 177; Sir Thomas Hardy, 172–74; *Jupiter*, 176; Jemima Terry Latham, 176; Abraham Mulford, 175; Orient, 176; Joshua Penny, 172–75; *Ramilies*, 172, 174; Ebenezer Sage, 175; Sambo, 175; *Superb*, 176; Noah Terry, 175

Water Mill, 26, 28, 68, 72, 77, 82, 118, 123
whaling: Chinese rescue, 93; Greenport, 93; Jamesport, 93; Japanese rescue, 93–94; Orient, 93; Sag Harbor, 92–93; whales in Peconic Bay, 94–95; women on whaleships, 94
Whitfield, George (Rev.), 34
Whitman, Walt, 39–40
Wickham, Frances Post, 61
Wickham, James, 61
Wilkins, Brady, 215
Winston, Stephen, 61
wood sloops, 78
World War I (Great War), 179–82
World War II: *Bowline*, 197; Camp Hero, 199; Greenport Basin and Construction Company, 197–98; Montauk Manor, 199; Picket Patrol, 198–99; Plum Island, 199; Lily Pons, 197; Kate Smith, 197–98
Wyandanch (Chief), 10, 13, 16–18

Youngs, John (Rev.), 20, 22, 31
Youngs, Selah (Capt.), 45